Why Elections Fail

Unfortunately too often elections around the globe are deeply flawed or even fail. What triggers these problems? In this second volume of her trilogy on electoral integrity, Pippa Norris compares structural, international, and institutional accounts as alternative perspectives to explain why elections fail to meet international standards. The book argues that rules preventing political actors from manipulating electoral governance are needed to secure integrity, although at the same time officials also need sufficient resources and capacities to manage elections effectively. Drawing on new evidence, the study determines the most effective types of strategies for strengthening the quality of electoral governance around the world. With a global perspective, this book provides fresh insights into these major issues at the heart of the study of elections and voting behavior, comparative politics, democracy and democratization, political culture, democratic governance, public policy making, development, international relations and conflict studies, and processes of regime change.

Pippa Norris is the McGuire Lecturer in Comparative Politics at the John F. Kennedy School of Government, Harvard University, and Laureate Fellow and Professor of Government and International Relations at Sydney University. She directs the Electoral Integrity Project (www.electoralintegrityproject.com). Her work compares democracy and democratization, elections and public opinion, gender politics, and political communications. Recent companion volumes by this award-winning author include *Driving Democracy* (2008), *Cosmopolitan Communications* (2009), *Democratic Deficit* (2011), *Making Democratic Governance Work* (2012), and *Why Electoral Integrity Matters* (2014). In 2011 she was awarded the Skytte Prize and the Kathleen Fitzpatrick Australian Laureate.

Why Elections Fail

PIPPA NORRIS

*Kennedy School of Government, Harvard University;
Department of Government and International Relations,
University of Sydney*

CAMBRIDGE
UNIVERSITY PRESS

CAMBRIDGE
UNIVERSITY PRESS

32 Avenue of the Americas, New York NY 10013-2473, USA

Cambridge University Press is part of the University of Cambridge.

It furthers the University's mission by disseminating knowledge in the pursuit of
education, learning and research at the highest international levels of excellence.

www.cambridge.org
Information on this title: www.cambridge.org/9781107679023

© Pippa Norris 2015

First published 2015

A catalogue record for this publication is available from the British Library

Library of Congress Cataloguing in Publication data
Norris, Pippa.
Why elections fail / Pippa Norris, Kennedy School of Government, Harvard University.
  pages   cm
Includes bibliographical references and index.
ISBN 978-1-107-05284-0 (hardback) – ISBN 978-1-107-67902-3 (pbk.)
1. Elections – Management.   2. Elections – Corrupt practices.   3. Election
monitoring.   4. Political corruption.   I. Title.
JF1001.N66   2015
324.6–dc23   2015005351

ISBN 978-1-107-67902-3 Paperback

Contents

Figures and Tables

Figures

Tables

Preface and Acknowledgments

This book is the second volume of a planned trilogy on the challenges of electoral integrity around the world, including why it matters, why electoral integrity fails, and what can be done to address these problems.

The study is part of the Electoral Integrity Project (EIP), a six-year research project. Research has been generously supported by the award of the Kathleen Fitzpatrick Australian Laureate from the Australian Research Council, as well as grants from International IDEA, Global Integrity, and at Harvard by the Weatherhead Center for International Affairs, the Roy and Lila Ash Center for Democratic Governance and Innovation, and the Australian Studies Committee. I am also most grateful to the World Values Survey Association for including the electoral integrity battery in the sixth wave survey.

The EIP is based at Harvard University's John F. Kennedy School of Government and the Department of Government and International Relations at the University of Sydney. I am indebted to Graeme Gill, Duncan Ivison, Michael Spence, and Simon Tormey for facilitating the arrangement in Sydney, as well as to all colleagues in the department. The book would not have been possible without the research team at Sydney, who have played an essential role in stimulating ideas, providing critical feedback and advice, generating related publications, and organizing events, especially developing the Perception of Electoral Integrity (PEI) dataset. I owe an immense debt to Richard W. Frank, Ferran Martinez i Coma, Max Grömping, and Andrea Abel van Es, as well as Fellows and interns visiting the project.

The intellectual foundations for this study build upon a series of earlier books for Cambridge University Press that have compared electoral institutions, voting behavior, political culture, and processes of democratization, particularly the first volume of the trilogy, *Why Electoral Integrity Matters* (Cambridge University Press 2014).

As always, this book also owes immense debts to many friends and colleagues. I also appreciate all colleagues and friends who provided encouraging comments about this project during its gestation, including Sarah Birch, David Carroll, Ivor Crewe, Larry Diamond, Jorge Dominguez, Jörgen Elklit, David Ellwood, Mark Franklin, Ben Goldsmith, Thad Hall, Carolien Van Ham, Susan Hyde, John Keane, Judith Kelley, Alex Keyssar, Larry LeDuc, Jane Mansbridge, Ian McAllister, Marc Plattner, Ben Reilly, Andy Reynolds, Sidney Verba, and Chad Vickery. The book has also been shaped by many students who have taken my Harvard classes over the years, where we discuss challenges of electoral integrity, theories of democratization, measures of the quality of democratic governance, and the most effective policy reforms to address these issues. Invaluable feedback has been received at several international workshops and meetings, including the Montreal pre-IPSA Workshop on Electoral Integrity in June 2014, the American Political Science Association annual meeting and EIP workshop in Washington, DC, in 2014, and faculty seminars at Harvard's Kennedy School and the Government Department.

I have also learned a tremendous amount from collaborating with many other international development agencies working with the EIP, including the United Nations Development Program, the Carter Center, the International Foundation for Electoral Systems, the International Institute for Democracy and Electoral Assistance, the Organization for Security and Cooperation in Europe, the Organization of American States, the Kofi Annan Commission, the Sunlight Foundation, the National Democratic Institute, USAID, the UK Electoral Commission, and many others.

Finally, as always, the support of Cambridge University Press has proved invaluable, particularly the patience, efficient assistance, and continuous enthusiasm of my editor, Lew Bateman, as well as the helpful comments of the reviewers.

PART I

INTRODUCTION

I

Introduction: Why Do Elections Fail?

Numerous types of flaws and failures undermine elections. In some, opponents are disqualified. District boundaries are gerrymandered. Campaigns provide a skewed playing field for parties. Independent media are muzzled. Citizens are ill-informed about choices. Balloting is disrupted by bloodshed. Ballot boxes are stuffed. Vote counts are fiddled. Opposition parties withdraw. Contenders refuse to accept the people's choice. Protests disrupt polling. Officials abuse state resources. Electoral registers are out of date. Candidates distribute largesse. Votes are bought. Airwaves favor incumbents. Campaigns are awash with hidden cash. Political finance rules are lax. Incompetent local officials run out of ballot papers. Incumbents are immune from effective challengers. Rallies trigger riots. Women candidates face discrimination. Ethnic minorities are persecuted. Voting machines jam. Lines lengthen. Ballot box seals break. Citizens cast more than one ballot. Laws suppress voting rights. Polling stations are inaccessible. Software crashes. "Secure" ink washes off fingers. Courts fail to resolve complaints impartially. Each of these problems can generate contentious elections characterized by lengthy court challenges, opposition boycotts, public protest, or, at worst, deadly violence.[1] In some, failures are intentional; elsewhere, they arise through happenstance, although it is tricky to nail down which is which.

Today all but a handful of countries around the world hold parliamentary elections, but contests can be marred by all these problems – and many more. Flaws corrode democratic governance. As the previous book in this trilogy demonstrated, lack of integrity has many serious consequences, with the capacity to undermine the legitimacy of elected authorities, to erode satisfaction with democracy, to reduce public confidence in political parties and parliaments, and to weaken electoral turnout.[2] Violent protests can destabilize states, especially in hybrid regimes lacking the coercive powers of absolute autocracies and the legitimacy of mature democracies.[3] In emerging economies such as Kenya and Thailand, disputed procedures have generated instability and undermined investor confidence. Competitive multiparty elections are the bedrock for democratic accountability, linking citizens and the state, empowering electors to "throw the rascals out" if dissatisfied by unpopular leaders. Where contentious elections are seriously flawed, or even failed, however, this mechanism is far from sufficient to rid the world of corrupt, venal, or incompetent rulers, prompting critical citizens to resort to the barricades rather than ballots. The vertical chain of electoral accountability linking citizens and authorities becomes corroded or broken.[4] Elections alone are not sufficient guarantees for democratic governance, where other horizontal channels of public accountability remain weak, but they remain the foundation.

To understand these issues, the first part of this chapter presents the conceptual framework and evidence used to compare electoral integrity around the world. The second part outlines the theoretical argument and the roadmap for the rest of the book.

I: The Concept of Electoral Integrity

The core notions of "flawed" or "failed" elections, which lie at the heart of this book, require clear standards and consistent benchmarks against which to judge the quality of any contest. To lay the groundwork, as conceptualized and defined by this trilogy, the overarching notion of *electoral integrity* refers to *contests respecting international standards and global norms governing the appropriate conduct of elections.*[5] These standards have been endorsed in a series of authoritative conventions, treaties, protocols, case laws, and guidelines by agencies of the international community.[6] Authority derives primarily from resolutions and treaties passed by the UN General Assembly, the UN Security Council, and UN human rights bodies, supplemented by agreement reaching within regional intergovernmental bodies such as the Organization for Security and Cooperation in Europe (OSCE), the Organization of American States (OAS), and the African Union (AU), and the European Union.[7]

The International Covenant on Civil and Political Rights provides the broadest guarantees of the rights to political participation, including the right to self-determination (Article 1) and the right for everyone to take part in the running of the public affairs of his/her country (Article 25), among others. The treaty has been in effect since 1976 and today 168 countries, out of 193 UN member states, are parties, including the Russian Federation, China, Syria, Belarus, and Zimbabwe. Following ratification, international standards apply universally to all endorsing countries throughout the electoral cycle, providing legal obligations for states, including during the preelectoral period, the campaign, on polling day, and in its aftermath. Treaties formalize agreement among sovereign states. As in any binding contract, upon endorsement states voluntarily limit their sovereignty by accepting international obligations. Of course, in many cases endorsement may simply exist on paper, and electoral rights continue to be repressed, if countries sign to avoid punishments for not going along with the international community, without experiencing any effective sanctions for non-compliance. Critics charge that many basic principles are widely flouted, and even some established democracies transgress, where the lofty language of human rights is coupled with weak enforcement mechanisms.[8] Many factors may influence how far states act in accordance with their treaty obligations, including international pressures and institutions, the prior values and preferences of particular governments, the capacity of the courts, and the strength of local human rights activists. One of the main reasons why ratification strengthens human rights is through domestic mechanisms; endorsement of international treaties empowers citizens to pressure government to meet their international obligations.[9] Where the world has agreed on the legitimacy of certain minimal standards of electoral rights, then activists can appeal to these principles when organizing to protest against domination and oppression. Survey evidence demonstrates that citizens' demands for democracy and human rights are universal today, although there is also widespread dissatisfaction about how far states observe these principles in practice, generating an expectation gap.[10] Transitions from autocracy, and the expansion of competitive elections around the world, have strengthened the public's capacity to mobilize when challenging power. The international community has also become increasingly active, by providing technical assistance and aid to reform movements seeking to strengthen democratic governance. Thus states face growing pressures at home and abroad to realize electoral rights and to respect international jurisprudence. How abstract principles are interpreted and translated into domestic laws and administrative procedures, however, is a complex process. Textual interpretations differ among countries and cultures, so that what one society regards as appropriate standards may be seen elsewhere to violate fundamental human rights – such as practices concerning whether polling should be voluntary or compulsory, whether registration should be an individual or state initiative, or whether voter identification should be required to be presented before casting a ballot.[11] The notion of "electoral integrity" founded on international human rights agreements is therefore far more powerful, comprehensive, and complex than the popular focus on electoral fraud, implying specific malpractices occurring on polling day such as illicit acts of ballot stuffing, vote-buying, or rigging the count.

What electoral rights are recognized in international treaties? International IDEA, working in conjunction with the Carter Center, has compiled the most comprehensive and systematic set of obligations derived from international jurisprudence, as listed in Table 1.1.[12] The foundation for these standards rests upon Article 21(3) in the Universal Declaration of Human Rights (UDHR 1948). This specifies that *"The will of the people shall be the basis of the authority of government; this will shall be expressed in periodic and genuine elections which shall be by universal and equal suffrage and shall be held by secret vote or by equivalent free voting procedures."* This statement has

TABLE I.I. *International standards for elections*

Principle	Interpretation
Rights and opportunities to participate in public affairs	The foundation respecting the rights and opportunities to participate through political parties, civil society organizations, and through voting processes for elected representatives.
Rights and equal opportunities to vote	Subject only to reasonable restrictions, such as a minimum age qualification.
Rights and opportunities to be elected	Free choice of candidates, with no unreasonable or discriminatory restrictions, such as political affiliation, education, or residency requirements.
Periodic elections	For example, by defining the length of elected terms and setting firm deadlines for steps in the electoral cycle.
Universal suffrage	The right to vote should be as inclusive as possible for every adult citizen.
Equal suffrage	One person, one vote should apply, affecting boundary delimitation and seat allocations.
Secret ballot	Prohibits connecting citizen identities with their ballot choices, to prevent coercion, corruption, or intimidation.
Freedom from discrimination and equality under the law	Prohibits discrimination based on race, color, sex, language, religion, political opinion, national origin, property, birth, or other status, essential to ensure that candidates, parties and voters can participate on an equal footing.
Equality between men and women	This includes ensuring that women have equal opportunities to participate in elections. CEDAW also recognizes the use of special temporary measures aimed as accelerating de facto equality between women and men, such as gender quota policies.
Freedom of association	This includes the right to form political parties and other civic associations, although the ICCPR recognizes restrictions necessary to secure national security, public order, or public safety.
Freedom of assembly	This includes the rights of candidates to organize election campaign meetings, although some restrictions are recognized by the ICCPR as reasonable in the interests of national security or public order.

Principle	Interpretation
Freedom of movement	Recognizes that contestants should be free to campaign without restrictions and persons entitled to vote should be free to exercise their rights.
Freedom of opinion and expression	These rights apply to the media, but also to parties and candidates.
Right to security of the person	This includes prohibition of injury, intimidation, arbitrary arrests, or detention, including candidates and activists, during campaigns.
Transparency and rights to information	Electoral authorities have an obligation to be transparent in their operations, as do stakeholders such as parties, candidates and civil society organizations.
Prevention of corruption	States are obliged to prevent corruption, including in the electoral process. UNCAC emphasizes that states should take measures to enhance transparency in the funding of candidates and political parties.
Rule of law	This includes equality before the law, and the independence and impartiality of the judiciary.
Rights to an effective remedy	This includes access to judicial review for election-related claims arising from voting and counting, to ensure public confidence in the process and results.
Right to a fair and public hearing	This right obliges states to provide timely or expeditious treatment by impartial and independent tribunals.
States must take necessary steps to give effect to rights	States are obliged to take necessary steps to give effect to the rights in the ICCPR, both by refraining from restricting these rights but also by protecting these rights.

Source: Domenico Tuccinardi, ed. 2014. *International Obligations for Elections: Guidelines for Legal Frameworks*. International IDEA: Stockholm. Chapter 4.

become the blueprint for subsequent standards. Agreement about the norms governing the conduct of elections was further specified in Article 25 of the UN International Covenant for Civil and Political Rights (ICCPR of 1966), which came into force a decade later. International standards continued to evolve, including through international conventions on the elimination of all forms of racial discrimination (ICERD 1966) and discrimination against women (CEDAW, 1979), the UN Convention against Corruption (UNCAC 2003), the Convention on the Rights of Persons with Disabilities (CRPD 2006), as well as agreements secured in the 1990 Copenhagen Document of the Conference on

Security and Cooperation in Europe (CSCE) and the 2002 Venice Commission's Code of Good Practice in Electoral Matters.[13]

This framework provides the legal mandate for electoral assistance by UN agencies and bureaus. Until the late 1980s, the role of the UN in elections was mainly to observe, supervise, and sometimes certify the results. After the end of the Cold War, however, the UN's role expanded in different contests, by providing more aid and technical assistance and also by directly organizing several elections in peacekeeping operations, such as Cambodia in 1993, Namibia in 1989, and the Democratic Republic of Congo in 2006. The Electoral Assistance Division (UNEAD) in the UN Department of Political Affairs coordinates electoral assistance within the United Nations and formulates policies and guidelines. The United Nations Development Programme (UNDP), in liaison with UNEAD, serves as the main UN agency that deploys technical assistance and aid when member states request help with the legal, operational, or logistical management of elections. The UNDP reports to its executive body and ultimately works within the broader mandate established by the UN General Assembly. Regional intergovernmental organizations have also expanded their roles in updating electoral standards and issuing practical guidelines, notably for observers to assess the quality of elections, as exemplified by the OSCE *Election Observation Handbook*.[14]

International standards are not static, however, as illustrated by the evolving language used in the UN General Assembly resolution 63/163 on "*Strengthening the role of the United Nations in enhancing periodic and genuine elections and the promotion of democratization*" passed every two years since 1988.[15] For example, the agreement on state responsibilities for organizing elections was strengthened in 1991, while the notion of an "electoral cycle" rather than event was added in 1993.[16] Norms continue to evolve at different stages of acceptance, like widening concentric circles rippling from a stone dropped in a pond.[17] The classic international conventions of human rights have been widely internalized today, regarded as appropriate guides to conduct elections around the world. For example, the principle of universal franchise for all citizens is now universally accepted, without restrictions of voting rights based on sex, class, caste, race, ethnicity, disability, or religion. Other standards continue to diffuse around the globe, as more and more countries adopt these norms, exemplified by the spread of gender quotas for elected office following CEDAW in 1979 and the 1990 Beijing Declaration adopting a target of 30 percent of seats for women.[18] Yet other canons are not yet entrenched in international jurisprudence, although principles are advocated by norm entrepreneurs, such as those governing political finance regulations proposed by Transparency International, the OAS, and the OSCE.[19]

Thus, in defining what is meant by elections that are free and fair, genuine, or democratic – some of the most commonly used terms in news headlines and observer reports in the international community – accounts typically emphasize a checklist reflecting the classic principles. The International IDEA guidelines identify the twenty international obligations, listed in Table 1.1, which are regarded as the key building blocks. Based on this understanding, states are obliged to protect the voting rights of all citizens, to safeguard opportunities for all candidates and parties to campaign freely, to hold contests at regular intervals, to protect candidates and citizens from threat of political violence or intimidation, to provide transparent processes of electoral administration, and to offer timely and expeditious judicial processes adjudicating complaints and disputes.[20] In practice, however, as mentioned earlier, how these abstract principles translate into national laws and detailed administrative procedures remains a complex process. For example, the concept of a "universal franchise" is widely agreed as a basic human right, yet states continue to differ in their legal definition of citizenship, minimal age requirements, qualifications to vote, and the exclusion of certain categories, such as prisoners or overseas populations.[21] Even greater controversy continues to surround several important issues where there is no global consensus. Normative values clash even among Western democracies, such as the appropriate standards guiding political finance regulations and thus the use of disclosure requirements, spending caps and donor limits, and public funding of political parties.[22] The obligations endorsed in international treaties therefore provide a *minimum* basis for electoral integrity and, while not absolutely relative, the abstract principles are open to differing legitimate interpretations when translated into national laws and practices.

To clarify the basic foundations, and avoid common misunderstandings, it is worth emphasizing at the outset how this conceptualization differs in several important respects from other common approaches.

Firstly, in this study normative authority is understood to derive from the body of human rights treaties and conventions in the international community; not directly from principles of democracy per se. Thus, while multiparty elections are essential for contestation and participation in liberal democracy, contrary to other scholars, democratic theories are not referenced as the authority for the origins of these ideas.[23] Instead, in line with the approach endorsed by such organizations as the Carter Center and International IDEA, the quality of elections is evaluated by principles and procedures derived from international jurisprudence.[24] As a result, one admitted limitation is that the core concept of electoral integrity used in this study is less coherent than tighter or minimalist scholarly notions, since electoral rights have not been codified in a consistent fashion. One major counterbalancing advantage, however, is that the universality of the concept applies to all independent nation states holding national elections. In practice this means that the empirical analysis measures the quality of national elections held around the world, including in one-party states such as Vietnam and Cuba, as well as in long-established democracies such as Sweden and Canada. Ultimately, the Universal Declaration of Human Rights can be traced back to underlying notions of democracy reflecting deeply held values among the Western great powers, following the end of the Second World

War. But the legitimacy of human rights treaties derives from endorsement by UN member states in the world community, not from political philosophy. Diplomatically, this powerful notion also means that human rights obligations are regarded as legally binding and applicable to autocratic states that have endorsed international treaties even if they reject liberal democratic principles.

Analytically, this also means that the book uses global comparisons and it does not focus on any particular regime type. This approach diverges from the conventional literature, which has evolved in two parallel streams during recent decades focused, respectively, upon electoral malpractices through the intentional repression of human rights in hybrid regimes such as Russia and through maladministration in established democracies such as the United States.

The turn of the century saw growing recognition among comparative and area scholars of the persistence of many hybrid regimes that are neither absolute autocracies nor consolidated democracies.[25] The end of the "transition paradigm" spurred renewed attention on how contests function to preserve the power of ruling elites in "electoral authoritarian" regimes in Latin America, Asia, and Central and Eastern Europe. From this perspective, studies assume that the key "puzzle" is to explain why and how ruling parties in these types of regimes intentionally manipulate the outcome to preserve their legitimacy and power within a façade of nominally competitive multiparty contests.[26] The main remedy, from this perspective, lies in how to restrict the abuse of power and fraudulent electoral acts by ruling parties, both domestically through strengthening transparency, accountability, and inclusive participation, as well as externally, from diplomatic pressures, including through the deployment of international observer missions.[27]

By coincidence, in the aftermath of the Florida debacle in the 2000 Gore versus Bush presidential election and the 2002 Help America Vote Act, another distinct stream of literature evolved simultaneously among scholars of American politics with a flood of contemporary studies analyzing the quality of electoral administration in the United States.[28] Drawing upon the disciplines of public sector management and electoral law, political scientists examined the technical problems of organizing and managing American elections, such as flaws in state-level electoral registration, provisional ballots, advance voting, and polling facilities. These problems are conventionally framed as largely managerial issues, where technocratic solutions – better performance indices, legal reforms, and procedural amendments – are typically proposed to improve the efficiency of the electoral process.

By contrast, rather than limiting the comparison to any particular type of regime, this study rejects the assumptions underlying these conventional approaches and adopts a global comparative framework. The book starts from the more agnostic position that electoral malpractices in any country around the globe can arise from limitations of *democratic governance*, that is to say, from either restrictions on fundamental human rights and violations committed by the regime or its opponents, and/or from lack of *state capacity* by electoral authorities to manage contests effectively. Democracy and governance should be understood as separate concepts.[29] It remains to be determined empirically whether problems are due to violations of basic human rights or failures of governance, or indeed, in many cases, to some combination of these problems. Established democracies such as the United States are not immune from partisan restrictions of electoral rights, just as many hybrid regimes have limited capacity to run flawless elections. Thus a skeptical approach to the precise reasons behind any electoral malpractices, open to the evidence, is more comprehensive and realistic than starting from the a priori assumption that any flaws must arise either from intentional manipulation or from administrative happenstance and incompetence.

There is another important reason to avoid using levels of democratization or regime types as possible explanations for the quality of elections; namely, this procedure raises serious risks of generating spurious correlations and tautological explanations, since the quality of elections is already baked into most conceptualizations, continuous measures of democratization, and typological classifications of democratic and autocratic regimes. As discussed more fully in the next chapter, the standard continuous concepts and measures of democracy and autocracy generated by Freedom House and Polity IV, as well as dichotomous classifications of democratic and dictatorial regimes, rely heavily upon the quality of elections. Therefore even though the Perception of Electoral Integrity Index is strongly correlated with standard measures of democracy, this book scrutinizes other types of explanations.

Sequential Stages in the Electoral Cycle

The overarching concept of *electoral integrity* remains highly abstract, so that in practice, to measure and monitor standards, it can be usefully broken down into its component parts. In an influential framework, Andreas Schedler has previously suggested that problems of democratic elections involve a "menu of manipulation" that ranges sequentially in a series of steps, from restrictions on the range of electoral offices through the formation and expression of preferences to the consequences of voting choices for office holders.[30] Conceived in this way, breaking any single link in the process is capable of undermining the legitimacy of elections. Almost a decade ago now, the international community also moved toward understanding that electoral assistance and monitoring should not be focused purely upon election day, or even on the short-term period of the official campaign. Instead, each election should be understood as a cyclical process involving a long series of sequential steps.[31] The idea of an electoral cycle has now become the "gold standard" for the international community seeking to strengthen the capacity of Election Management Bodies and to invest in long-term sustainable development.[32]

To operationalize the core notion, in this book the electoral cycle is deconstructed into a series of eleven sequential steps, illustrated schematically in

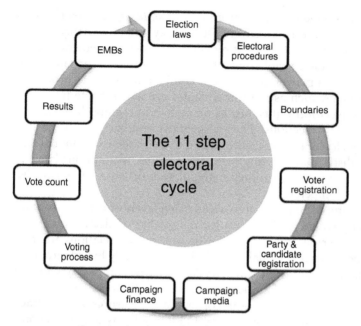

FIGURE I.I. Steps in the electoral cycle.

Figure I.I. This approach acknowledges that flaws can arise at any stage of the process. This includes from the design of electoral law, such as the use of overly restrictive or cumbersome nomination requirements for gaining ballot access or the adoption of excessively high vote thresholds. Electoral procedures can also be problematic, arising from the actions of partisan or incompetent local officials. Integrity is also undermined by partisan gerrymandering or by malapportionment favoring incumbents in the process of redistricting constituency boundaries. Voter registration processes may exclude many citizens, such as rural or illiterate populations, or specific minority groups, exemplified by inaccurate and incomplete electoral rolls or by intentional acts of voter suppression through onerous requirements. Party and candidate registration processes are also critical, with restrictions illustrated by courts banning specific political parties or by regimes imprisoning prominent opposition leaders. Campaign media can fail to provide a level playing field, such as patronage appointments eroding the independence of broadcasting regulatory bodies or uncritical coverage of government officials on state-controlled television channels. Political finance regulations pose another range of challenges, especially lack of equal access to state resources for government and opposition parties. Voting processes in polling places come under considerable scrutiny, including ballot irregularities, broken machines, or cases of fraudulent impersonation. Inaccurate counts or insecure ballot seals can undermine the vote tabulation process. The credibility of the results can suffer from undue delays in their announcement or by lack of transparency and audit processes in voting records. And finally, Election Management Bodies are vital to administering electoral processes and implementing the rules, and problems can commonly arise at any stage of the electoral cycle from authorities lacking capacity, resources, or impartiality.

II: Measuring Electoral Integrity

Given this conceptual framework, how do we know when elections are flawed – or even failing to meet international standards and global norms? What evidence is available? As discussed fully in the next chapter, previous studies have utilized several techniques and sources of data, each with certain strengths and weaknesses, including content analysis of observer reports, randomized controlled experiments, forensic autopsies of polling results, indices constructed for related proxy concepts, event analysis derived from news media reports, and analysis of public opinion polls.[33]

To supplement these sources, and to generate more reliable and authoritative evidence, the Electoral Integrity Project has established a new rolling survey gathering evaluations of electoral integrity from independent elections experts. Using a comprehensive instrument, the project seeks to assess whether contemporary national parliamentary and presidential contests meet international standards throughout the electoral cycle, including during the pre-election period, the campaign, polling day, and its aftermath. The questionnaire includes forty-nine items monitoring the quality of elections. The overall PEI Index is constructed by summing the separate items for each election and each country, with the results standardized to one hundred points. Similar standardized indices are constructed for each of the eleven components of the electoral cycle. In addition, the PEI Index is ranked and categorized by thirds into contests with high, moderate, and lower levels of electoral integrity.

This book presents the first results of the Electoral Integrity Project's expert survey of Perceptions of Electoral Integrity Index (PEI-2.8), providing evaluations for all national parliamentary or presidential elections held in independent nation states from mid-2012 to end 2014. PEI-2.8 facilitates comparison of a representative cross-section of 113 contemporary elections worldwide. The study covers ninety-seven of the globe's nations, from Afghanistan to Zimbabwe, with the exclusion of microstates (with a population less than 100,000) and those countries without any national contests during this period. In cases of simultaneous legislative and executive elections, the survey monitored the latter. In countries using second ballot (run-off) electoral systems, the survey assessed the final contest. Around forty domestic and international experts were consulted for each election, generating an overall response rate of 28% from in total 1,251 election experts. Data derived from the PEI expert survey is supplemented by information from many other sources, including from the sixth wave of the World Values Survey, providing public assessments of the quality of elections at microlevel in more than forty counties. Several aggregate datasets with cross-national time-series observations monitoring the quality of elections facilitate comparison of annual trends during the third wave era of democratization, since the early 1970s. The next chapter discusses the methodology and research design of PEI in more detail, along with robustness checks to see whether the PEI results are consistent with other independent sources of related measures.

To give an initial sense of what the book is trying to explain, Figure 1.2 provides a snapshot of the estimates derived from the overall PEI hundred-point index. The results are compared with a standardized measure of democratization derived from the combined Freedom House and Polity IV estimates.[34] Any measures can be questioned, as discussed fully in the next chapter, but if this initial cut of the data is treated for the moment as broadly correct, the key question that arises is: what best explains why some contemporary elections are seen by experts as far less successful than others in meeting global norms and international standards? The answers are not immediately obvious; for example, as shown in Figure 1.2, certain states, such as Mongolia, Georgia, and Lithuania are ranked substantially higher today, according to the PEI Index, than some other countries sharing a communist legacy, such as Armenia and Ukraine. Why? Similarly in sub-Saharan Africa, the election in Ghana is rated more positively according to the PEI experts than the contest in Angola, for reasons that are not immediately obvious. In Asia, why does Bhutan out-perform Pakistan and Cambodia? And among long-established democracies, why do expert evaluations place the quality of contests in Norway, Germany, and Iceland ahead of those in Italy, Japan, and the United States?

III: Theories Explaining Flawed and Failed Elections

Given that broader processes of democratization are closely linked with the spread of multiparty elections, intellectual frameworks derived from democratic theory can be ransacked as the steel girders and concrete foundations to construct plausible explanations and empirically testable propositions as to why elections may be flawed or failed. The fall of the Berlin Wall triggered exaggerated Western hopes for the triumph of democracy worldwide. The waves of democratization following the implosion of the USSR, the color revolutions, and then the Arab uprisings, appeared to many contemporary commentators to be an unstoppable tsunami capable of toppling autocratic regimes in diverse parts of the globe. These hopes subsequently faltered, and a more realistic perspective developed following the failure of several fledgling regime transitions, exemplified by military coups in Thailand and Egypt, instability in Afghanistan, Libya and Iraq, bloody civil war in Syria, state repression in Bahrain, a reassertion of autocracy, and nationalism in Putin's Russia, destabilizing Ukraine, and the forces of the Islamic State generating new turmoil in Iraq, Syria, and bordering states. The stubborn persistence of autocracy in several parts of the world, notably in China and throughout large swathes

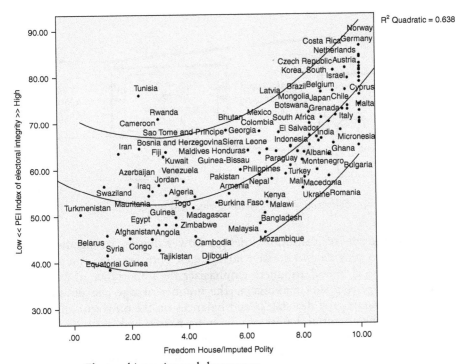

FIGURE 1.2. Electoral integrity and democracy.

Sources: Electoral Integrity Project. 2014. *The expert survey of Perceptions of Electoral Integrity*, Release 2.8 (PEI-2.8); *The Quality of Government Standard Cross-National Dataset* Teorell et al. 2013.

of Central Asia, Africa, and the Middle East, defied early over-optimistic predictions.[35] Today the contemporary political globe displays a checker-cloth of democratic, autocratic, and hybrid regimes scattered across Africa, South East Asia, and post-Communist Europe, exemplified by the sharp contrasts observed between the neighboring states of Poland and Belarus, Benin and Togo, or North and South Korea.[36]

The extensive body of research literature offers three alternative perspectives, which can throw light on processes of democratization and thus also, by implication, the phenomena of electoral integrity. This includes sociological theories (discussed in Chapter 3), emphasizing the importance of *processes of modernization* that can provide a more hostile or favorable terrain for organizing competitive elections in each society. Chapter 4 turns to accounts rooted in international relations that underscore the role of external *multilateral organizations and donor agencies* seeking to strengthen processes of democratization. Both of these are treated in this book largely as conditions that either constrain or provide important opportunities for domestic reformers seeking to strengthen electoral institutions. Chapter 5 focuses upon *power-sharing* theories,

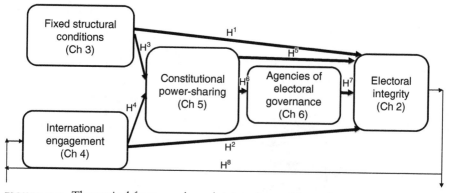

FIGURE 1.3. Theoretical framework explaining electoral integrity.

emphasizing the role of institutional design. Power-sharing arrangements are often thought to provide two decisive advantages, both negative and positive. Firstly, the classical liberal argument emphasizes the importance of executive constraints, suggesting that maximizing the number of veto players through institutional designs provides checks and balances on the power of any single actor, curbing the potential danger of governing parties and incumbents putting their thumb on the scales by manipulating the rules of the electoral game permanently in their favor. Secondly, the consociational argument emphasizes the need to build a reservoir of political trust and tolerance, suggesting that maximizing the number of parties and candidates gaining elected office broadens the number of stakeholders and thus engenders confidence in the rules of the game among elites and their supporters. Nevertheless, while preventing abuse, checks and balances also limit the capacity of governance agencies to get things done. Chapter 6 therefore deepens the institutional perspective by examining how far the performance of electoral authorities is shaped by their organizational structure, governance capacities, and bureaucratic ethos. Each rival perspective, supported by a wealth of research literature, generates a series of plausible propositions worth investigating through empirical analysis to establish the exact role of these determinants on the quality of elections, with certain important implications for public policy.

Rather than treating these alternative approaches as rival theories, in straw-men artificial debates, they are understood in this study more realistically as nested components operating within a comprehensive framework, as illustrated schematically in Figure 1.3. In the book's core theoretical framework, both structural conditions and international drivers are seen to exert a direct role on the broader conditions that are favorable or unfavorable to electoral integrity, serving as constraints on the effectiveness of constitutional arrangements and administrative agencies at the heart of electoral governance. Chapters seek to unpack these arguments in more detail, drawing upon what is known from the previous research literature comparing patterns of democratization and electoral integrity, before providing fresh empirical evidence analyzing these issues. The book seeks to determine the relative importance of structural conditions, international forces, and institutional designs on electoral integrity using both systematic cross-national evidence analyzed through rigorous and well-specified models, as well as selected national case studies illustrating changes over time within specific countries.

IV: Plan of the Book

To unpack the evidence in more detail, Chapter 2 starts by discussing the cross-national indicators from the PEI Index and its eleven subcomponents. These provide broad insights into the general patterns observed among contemporary elections in many parts of the world. The overall scorecard for electoral integrity through the PEI Index provides summary. The evidence can also be examined by scrutinizing any of the forty-nine disaggregated indices, which allow detailed comparison of specific issues within each component of the electoral cycle, such as pinpointing particular problems of district gerrymandering, weak campaign finance regulations, or inaccuracies in the voter register.

The PEI dataset provides more detailed and comprehensive evidence to compare all dimensions and components in the quality of contemporary elections than previous attempts to measure this phenomenon. Unfortunately, at the same time, data about the overall quality of elections observed at a single point of time, no matter how thorough and accurate, remain limited when it comes to identifying and determining causality. The problem can be illustrated by considering which societal conditions should properly be regarded as "fixed" conditions where complex interactive processes muddy the water. Therefore, the PEI dataset is supplemented in this book by drawing upon several selected national case studies that provide thicker and richer descriptions tracing the impact of structural conditions, international determinants, and power-sharing institutions on electoral integrity.

Modernization Theories: Structural and Cultural Constraints

Chapter 3 starts to analyze the evidence by drawing upon modernization theories which form the oldest tradition in the literature seeking to understand regime transitions from autocracy and the consolidation of democracy. This approach is rooted in theories of developmental political sociology and comparative politics that emerged in the mid-twentieth century, exemplified by the long tradition established by Seymour Martin Lipset.[37] Over the last six decades, an extensive literature has linked societal modernization with processes of democratization; simultaneous patterns of development, economic growth, industrialization, urbanization, the spread of communications, and wider access to education, are theorized from this perspective as the standard "usual suspects" to either drive democratization and cultural change, or else to sustain democratic regimes once societies reach a certain tipping-point of socio-economic development.[38] The long tradition of research has also expanded well beyond comparing simple and crude levels of a country's per capita GDP to embrace many other related structural and cultural macro-level factors loosely linked with the "modernization" paradigm,[39] including the role of class and income inequality,[40] the historical imprint of religious values,[41] the "curse" of natural resources,[42] the physical size and geography of states,[43] the role of cultural values,[44] and divisions across diverse ethnic communities.[45]

Structural constraints are treated in the mainstream tradition of political sociology and development studies as largely immutable social forces within each state and as path-dependent constraints for actors operating within the space of an election; thus many societies inherit colonial legacies, religious cultures, and national boundaries from historical events occurring many decades or even many centuries earlier. Similarly, the spatial relationships of each country's geography are treated as fixed antecedents, including national borders shared with neighboring states, mountainous terrains, or island shores. The physical distribution of natural resources such as oil, gas, gold, diamonds, and natural minerals, are not treated as amenable to short-term intervention.[46] The accumulated experience of living for decades under either autocracy or democracy, and the deep-rooted cultural values acquired from this experience, are also not possible to change by actors within the period of an election campaign. For all these reasons, fixed inhospitable conditions – exemplified by deep-rooted poverty and inequality, a legacy of inter-communal violence in deeply divided multicultural societies, or the curse of natural resources – can be expected to hamper well-meaning efforts by reformers to strengthen transitions from autocracy and the consolidation of democratic regimes. Thinking along similar lines, given the close links between democracy and elections, the logic of the classic "Lipset hypothesis" suggests that many observed problems of electoral integrity are probably best explained by the challenging socio-economic and cultural conditions under which many contemporary contests have been attempted in recent years, such as in Afghanistan or the Democratic Republic of Congo.[47]

Moreover, from a policy perspective, while constraining the effectiveness of positive interventions, path-dependent structural and cultural constraints in the most intractable cases are thought to remain largely outside the realm of *short-term* social engineering by either domestic or international actors. After all, social structures and values, which cultural accounts suggest provide the bedrock support for democratic institutions, evolved over decades or even centuries in Western Europe. From a policy perspective, explanations based on structural conditions carry conservative implications of social determinism, suggesting that stakeholders need to be highly strategic and realistic in their specific choice of interventions, as there is little which can be done in the short term to improve electoral standards in a contest held under inhospitable conditions, such as to counter pervasive corruption in

Afghanistan, the abuse of human rights following the military coup in Sisi's Egypt, or violence and instability in Libya. Therefore, it would be foolhardy to expect that war-torn countries and fragile states could transform societies and governance within the space of a few years in the run up to an election. To consider modernization theories in more detail, Chapter 3 examines the comparative and historical evidence and considers the most plausible interpretation of the results.

International Engagement

Chapter 4 turns to understanding the international community's attempts to uphold global norms and universal electoral standards. This provides an alternative argument seeking to explain why some elections succeed while others fail, and a perspective that has becoming increasingly popular in the research literature during the last decade. The most common strategies used by prodemocracy multilateral organizations and bilateral donors involve opening barriers to the diffusion of global norms through the free flow of information across national borders, targeting the provision of technical assistance and development aid invested in electoral processes and building the capacity of electoral management bodies, and supporting domestic and international teams of observers to monitor elections, combined with diplomatic pressures threatening or punishing regimes that violate standards.[48] These standard repertoires of "soft power" are designed to improve the quality of multiparty elections and thereby strengthen transitions from autocracy and consolidate processes of democratization in developing countries. Globalization through cosmopolitan communications, opening trade barriers and membership of regional organizations, can be understood as the most general long-term process, while the provision of development aid and assistance functions as a medium-term strategy over successive contests, and electoral observing is the most specific short-term activity in a particular contest. A wide range of multilateral organizations are engaged in strengthening democratic governance and elections through these strategies including the UNDP, the International Federation of Electoral Systems (IFES), OSCE, the European Union, the Commonwealth, the OAS, International IDEA, and the Carter Center, as well as bilateral donors such as USAID, DFID, and CIDA.[49]

Evaluation of selected cases suggests that development assistance can strengthen the quality of elections, not least through providing resources, transferring knowledge, and building technical capacity among electoral bodies.[50] At the same time there are several reasons why the overall impact of international engagement may prove limited. Heated debate continues over the general question of whether aid "works" by strengthening regime transitions and processes of democratization.[51] The most thorough research has explored whether the deployment of monitoring missions by regional organizations committed to global norms discourages ballot box fraud and count tampering in the observed polling place. Work suggests that this intervention generally has a modest impact on local polling places but this does not necessarily carry over to generating greater honesty elsewhere around the country; instead, displacement (whack-a-mole) effects have been spotted.[52] Moreover, monitoring organizations have proliferated in recent years, with some missions committed to upholding international standards while others prove indifferent to these values. As a result, governments can now pick and choose whom to invite to observe their contests, with authoritarian regimes likely to select monitoring organizations sharing their cultural ties and values.[53] The result has been to diminish the authority and impact of critical reports published by regional organizations such as the OSCE, OAS, and EU.

Even where international monitors report problems, however, this does not mean that states necessarily have the willpower, resources, or capacity to address them. At least in the past, efforts by the international community often focused most attention and aid upon the high drama of transitional elections, providing a short-term fix, such as spending on equipment, vehicles, temporary personnel, and consultants during the 2004 Afghanistan elections. The international community has not always had the commitment to invest in sustainable capacity building for election management bodies over successive contests and even decades.[54]

Less is known about the impact of technical assistance and development aid invested in programs designed to strengthen electoral processes. Due to competing foreign policy considerations, however, realists suggest that donor countries are likely to use electoral aid to further their foreign policy interests, such as trade and security, rather than pressuring governments to adopt democratic reforms and strengthen human rights and electoral integrity.[55] One of the clearest examples concerns the Obama administration's vacillating position toward Egypt following the military coup ousting an unpopular but freely elected President Morsi and the Muslim Brotherhood.[56] By continuing to give billions of dollars of military aid to Egypt, despite major human rights abuses by the Sisi regime, US foreign policy conveys an ambivalent signal, which may overwhelm any positive attempts to strengthen democratic governance through providing development assistance to countries such as Tunisia. Moreover, violating the "first do no harm" principle, studies have found that overall levels of development aid spending may have unintended consequences, by serving to prop up electoral support for entrenched incumbents, especially where governments divert funds to benefit their political supporters or punish those favoring the opposition.[57]

The international argument, therefore suggests that multilateral organizations and the donor community commonly use several types of "carrots and sticks," with some degree of modest success in strengthening electoral integrity, although the impact of observer activities and technical assistance remains highly constrained. Most previous research has focused upon determining the short-term effects of international electoral observers, such as whether the deployment of observers across different polling areas limits ballot box fraud within a country.[58] Far less is known with any certainty about the more complex medium-term or long-term impact of technical assistance and aid spending on institutional capacity-building initiatives over successive contests, such as the effectiveness of training workshops for electoral authorities or journalists covering the campaign. To consider the arguments in more depth, Chapter 4 examines the theoretical claims and analyzes new cross-national evidence to assess the impact of international forces on electoral integrity. The chapter focuses upon analyzing the effects of cosmopolitan communication flowing across national borders, technical assistance and development aid, and observer missions, understood to range from the most diffuse to the most specific types of international factors.

Power-Sharing Constitutional Checks and Balances

A growing body of research has examined the effects of structural conditions and international electoral observers on alternative indicators of the quality of elections. What has received far less systematic attention, however, concerns the institutions of electoral governance, including the overarching constitutional framework in any regime, and the more specific regulatory agencies that establish electoral governance in each state. On this basis, Chapter 5 seeks to understand the role of constitutional checks and balances in curbing the abuse of power and manipulation of the electoral rules and processes by any single actor, especially the governing party. The concept of "electoral governance" has been usefully defined by Hartlyn et al. as: "...*the interaction of constitutional, legal, and institutional rules and organizational practices that determine the basic rules for election procedures and electoral competition; organize campaigns, voter registration, and election-day tallies; and resolve disputes and certify results.*"[59] The notion therefore refers to two nested levels and it is valuable to maintain this analytical distinction. The higher-level *constitutional arrangements* in any state, which provide the broadest context for electoral integrity, are exemplified by the type of regime, the electoral and party systems, the role and powers of the legislature and executive, and the independence of the courts and judiciary. But electoral governance is also shaped by the role of the core administrative agencies exercising authority directly over the implementation of electoral laws and procedures, commonly known today as *electoral management bodies* (EMB), as well as a wide range of administrative agencies responsible for regulating specific dimensions, such as boundary delimitation, political finance, and campaign communications, all of which are embedded within the broader constitutional arrangements.[60] One of the key questions arising from this distinction is whether EMBs can be designed to be effective in strengthening the quality of elections, even in autocracies that have unfavorable constitutional conditions.

What institutional framework in any state is most likely to strengthen electoral integrity? One of the most important concerns electoral systems including, among other features, rules determining the electoral formulas, district magnitudes, constituency boundaries, and assembly size. These rules structure electoral competition over votes and seats. Competitive laws serve to provide procedural agreement about the rules of the game while also securing uncertainty about the electoral outcome. Strong and effective parliaments can be important as oversight agencies. In addition, the rule of law and the powers of the judiciary can also play a critical role in the electoral process, especially through deterring illegal acts, adjudicating complaints impartially, and resolving electoral disputes in a timely fashion. Civil society actors linking citizens and the state, notably the independent news media and watchdog organizations of domestic observers, can strengthen accountability and transparency among electoral authorities.

To understand the role of constitutional arrangements, drawing again upon the broader literature on democratization, insights can be derived from classical liberal theories that suggest that the more veto players are involved in electoral governance, the more safeguards exist against the potential abuse of power by any single actor, especially incumbents.[61] Through curbing Leviathan, it is thought that the electoral process becomes more trustworthy for losers as well as winners. This argument is supplemented by theories of "power-sharing" or "consensus" democracies. This general perspective has a long and distinguished intellectual pedigree, developed theoretically most fully in the ideas of Arend Lijphart.[62] Providing all parties with a stake in the process of electoral governance is thought to encourage buy-in from party elites, encouraging trust among rival communities. Building upon this foundation, Chapter 5 seeks to test the effects of several types of power-sharing constitutional designs on electoral integrity, including the propositions that electoral integrity is usually stronger in states with proportional representation electoral systems, an independent judiciary, effective legislatures, and freedom of the independent media. The chapter tests whether any institutional effects remain in properly specified models even after controlling for the external role of the international community (encouraging greater transparency and providing assistance designed to reform electoral malpractices), and the role of fixed and enduring social conditions such as levels of economic development (which serve as constraints on institutional effectiveness).

The Role of the Electoral Authorities

Finally the quality of a range of regulatory and administrative agencies responsible for implementing electoral laws and procedures is also expected to prove highly significant. Chapter 6 turns to compare the structure, functions, and culture of the administrative agencies involved in electoral governance.[63] Election Management Bodies (EMBs) are the central electoral authorities responsible for administering legal regulations and electoral procedures within the broader constitutional context. Electoral governance involves a complex set of constitutional provisions, legal statutes, and administrative procedures established to regulate many specific dimensions of competition throughout the electoral cycle, including the demarcation of constituency boundaries; the rules governing political finance and party funding; the legal status, funding, and registration of candidates and political parties; the regulation of the news media, political advertising, and campaign broadcasts; the provision of gender quotas and special arrangements for minority representation; and the process of dealing with election complaints and dispute adjudication.

In terms of the formal or de jure structural organization, two types of electoral governance can be distinguished, although in practice many countries have mixed arrangements rather than falling neatly into either category.

On the one hand, *governmental* types of arrangements exist where the senior officers heading the electoral authorities are typically permanent civil servants working in an elections unit within an official department of state, such as the Ministry of Interior, Ministry of Justice, or Home Office, reporting directly to a minister and cabinet, and indirectly accountable to parliament. Regulations are commonly implemented by staff working in local and regional agencies, including employees in state and local governments, with lower level agencies accountable to the central authorities. In terms of mandates, under this model the government department is usually responsible for many core tasks involved in regulating elections at national level, such as maintaining the electoral register, establishing guidelines for voting procedures, and standardizing local arrangements. Governmental departments may also fulfill multiple functions beyond the minimal role, including regulating candidate and party ballot access, monitoring political finance, determining boundary delimitation, allocating party political broadcasting, and dealing with dispute resolution. Alternatively, separate dedicated administrative and regulatory official bodies may be responsible for these matters, such as Boundary Commissions and Broadcasting Authorities.

As an ideal type, by contrast, the national electoral management body may be established legally as an autonomous administrative agency, although beyond the label, exactly what "autonomy" means in practice, and how de facto independence is determined, varies widely among countries. Independent administrative agencies typically have considerable control over the appointment of their own staff and control over their own budget, with security of tenure and lengthy fixed term appointments for senior commissioners so they do not need to fear dismissal by the party in government. Agencies may report directly to parliament rather than the executive. In composition, the chief commissioners are not permanent civil servants but they may instead be drawn from the judiciary, representatives nominated by political parties, or outside experts. To supplement the role of the national electoral agency, several electoral functions and roles may be dispersed among a variety of specialized administrative agencies so that broadcasting and telecommunication authorities are allocated primary responsibility for implementing a wide range of communication policies to serve the public interest, which may include regulating political advertising, party and candidate political broadcasts, campaign debates, the publication of opinion polls, and the partisan balance of campaign news coverage.[64] Party funding and political finance may also be regulated by the national electoral management body, or this function may also fall under the remit of a specialized agency established for this purpose, such as the Federal Election Commission in the United States.[65] Similarly the functions of dispute adjudication and legal electoral challenges may be delegated to civil and constitutional courts, not least to deal independently and justly with complaints directed against the electoral authorities.[66] Under decentralized arrangements, which are particularly common in federal countries, state and local agencies have considerable regulatory authority and administrative discretion to organize elections.

Given these distinctions, the core questions addressed by this study are whether the agency model of electoral governance is indeed associated with greater electoral integrity than the governmental model, as commonly assumed in the technical guidance issued by the international community, and also how far the actual performance of electoral authorities is influenced more by functional capacities and administrative cultures than by formal legal organizational structures. The answers have not yet been clearly established, in part because of the dearth of reliable evidence classifying the degree of *de facto* EMB independence. Indeed, some comparative research contradicts the claim that the autonomy of EMBs matters; Birch found that formal EMB independence (as classified by International IDEA) had no significant impact upon the degree of electoral malpractice.[67]

Further research is required because, despite a recent resurgence of interest, the study of electoral governance has largely been neglected, like an unfortunate uncle at a Christmas party.[68] The most comprehensive research has examined the organizational structure of EMBs in reports produced by international agencies, notably by IFES, International IDEA, and regional organizations.[69] The UNDP has also evaluated several cases using programmatic interventions and technical assistance designed to strengthen the capacity of EMBs.[70] The influence of electoral management bodies on violence has also been examined, with African case studies suggesting that more inclusive EMBs are important for reducing electoral conflict.[71] Researchers have also sought to understand the impact of the type of EMBs on public attitudes toward the electoral process.[72] Studies have also examined the proposition that the structural independence of EMBs has a consistently positive effect on processes of democratization, especially in sub-Saharan Africa.[73] Building upon the logic already developed, this chapter classifies types of electoral governance from data in the ACE project on http://aceproject .org/, the Electoral Knowledge Network, and then examines evidence to understand whether the structural organization, functional effectiveness, and predominant public administrative culture have strengthened electoral integrity (measured by PEI). Models control for the broader context of power-sharing constitutional arrangements, and whether any institutional effects remain even after controlling for the external role of the international community and the role of fixed and enduring social conditions.

Finally, the conclusion in Chapter 7 recapitulates the overall theoretical framework, summarizes the main findings, and considers their implications for theories of electoral integrity as well as for the policy-making community. Concern about electoral integrity is hardly novel, indeed it raises centuries-old problems. Nevertheless, the electoral revolution has renewed interest in the topic during the last decade. The rapidly growing literature remains somewhat scattered across many subfields, however, and often focused relatively narrowly upon ballot box fraud occurring in polling stations in electoral autocracies, and the role of international observer missions seeking to stamp out these practices, rather than on understanding these cases as part of a far wider range of problems, which happen throughout the electoral cycle in many types of regimes. This study seeks to present a richer and more comprehensive theory, demonstrated through systematic evidence and selected case studies.

Therefore, several main schools of thought have long dominated the literature seeking to explain electoral failures. This study seeks to deconstruct these arguments, and then reassemble them to generate a more comprehensive theory capable of accounting for the complex phenomenon of electoral integrity and malpractice. The book's conclusions summarize the overall lessons for understanding electoral integrity, as well as the insights useful for stakeholders and practitioners seeking to strengthen the quality of elections around the world. This volume therefore aims to lay the foundation for the final book in the trilogy, which addresses and evaluates policy interventions and "what can be done" most effectively to strengthen electoral integrity around the globe.

2

Evidence

Systematic and reliable evidence about the quality of elections is essential for scholars and practitioners. Within comparative politics, accurate data provide more precise regime classifications that can distinguish autocracies (with manipulated elections and façade competition) from democratic states (with contests characterized by regular alternation between governing and opposition parties and inclusive electoral procedures).[1] Classification and measurement are also critical for a comprehensive understanding of political attitudes and voting behavior, for institutional studies analyzing the effects of electoral systems and processes, and for research focused on the triggers of electoral violence. Accurate indicators are also equally valuable for aid agencies and electoral officials, especially for evidence-based evaluations seeking to determine what particular types of policy interventions are most effective to strengthen integrity in any society, such as programs designed to reduce vote corruption in Afghanistan, to restore trust in elections in Thailand, or to improve security in Nigerian contests.

Yet attempts at precise measurement are immediately confronted by the fact that the concept of electoral integrity is relatively abstract and multidimensional. In practice, evaluations of the actual quality of elections often prove highly contentious where contests end in a flurry of challenges concerning the legitimacy of the electoral authorities, the underlying procedural rules of the game, and the outcome.[2] News headlines amplify opposition cries of fraud and stolen elections. Sore losers have a natural incentive to contend that an election was rigged or stolen, both to excuse a poor performance (and thus deter leadership rivals) and to undermine the authority of the winners. Election disputes are fairly common; for example, one study suggests that during the last decade around 12 percent of elections worldwide saw opposition boycotts, 17 percent experienced post-election riots or protests, and 18 percent had electoral violence involving at least one civilian fatality.[3] These problems are particularly evident in hybrid states; for example, polling day ended with street protests about alleged ballot box fraud, corruption, and flawed voter registers in recent contests in Cambodia, Thailand, and Bangladesh. The most problematic cases, such as Kenya in 2007, generate bloodshed and growing instability in fragile states.[4] Disputes are also becoming increasingly common in long-established democracies; since the 2000 US presidential elections, for example, rival charges of voter fraud (by Republicans) and voter suppression (by Democrats) have become increasingly polarized in America.[5] Party supporters often appear to take their cues from the claims of their leaders.[6] A raft of new state laws regulating voter registration and identification requirements for American citizens has generated growing controversy in the courts.[7] In January 2014, a blue-ribbon bipartisan US Presidential Commission on Electoral Administration issued its report and recommendations.[8] North of the border, heated debates erupted over the proposed Fair Elections Act in Canada, with its elimination of "vouching" as a form of identification for transient populations lacking official forms of identification, and steps to curb the independence and powers of Elections Canada.[9] Debates about alleged electoral fraud and administrative irregularities have also intensified in recent years in the United Kingdom, surrounding the implementation of postal voting.[10]

When it is claimed that elections are flawed, or even fail, what standards are contests being held against? What comparative evidence is available to sort out genuine problems from sham complaints? To address this issue, Part I of this chapter briefly summarizes the core concept concerning international standards of electoral integrity. Part II considers the strengths and limits of alternative ways that cross-national evidence can be collected to operationalize and monitor these standards, including through analyzing observer and media reports, forensic scrutiny of poll results, public opinion polls, and randomized experiments. Part III describes the research design used by the Perceptions of Electoral Integrity (PEI) expert survey. As mentioned in the previous chapter, data from the 2.8 release of the data set (PEI-2.8) in this book, covering 97 countries and 113 elections worldwide, is the primary measure used to gauge whether contemporary elections succeed or fail. Part IV considers the criteria that any evidence needs to meet, and uses robustness tests to double-check the reliability of the data. Finally, Part V lays out the questions that need to be considered for a comprehensive understanding of the range of puzzles surrounding electoral integrity core phenomena, including identifying the "who" (key actors), "what" (types of malpractices), "where" (which types of countries and regimes), "when" (timing during the electoral cycle), and "why" (underlying conditions and proximate causes).

I: Conceptual Framework

To clarify the core concept, building upon the previous volume in this trilogy, the notion of electoral integrity is conceptualized broadly in this study in terms of international commitments and global norms surrounding elections, endorsed in a series of authoritative conventions, treaties, protocols, and guidelines. Conversely, the term electoral *malpractice* is used antithetically to refer to violations of international standards of electoral integrity. Universal standards apply to all countries worldwide throughout the electoral cycle, including during the preelectoral period, the campaign, on polling day, and its aftermath. The foundation for international standards is Article 21(3) of the Universal Declaration of Human Rights (1948). This specifies: "*The will of the people shall be the basis of the authority of government; this will shall be expressed in periodic and genuine elections which shall be by universal and equal suffrage and shall be held by secret vote or by equivalent free voting procedures.*" Agreement about the principles that should govern the conduct of elections was further specified in Article 25 of the UN International Covenant for Civil and Political Rights (ICCPR of 1966), namely the need for:

- Periodic elections at regular intervals;
- Universal suffrage, which includes all sectors of society;
- Equal suffrage, in the idea of one-person, one-vote;
- The right to stand for public office and contest elections;
- The rights of all eligible electors to vote;
- The use of a secret ballot process;
- Genuine elections; and that
- Elections should reflect the free expression of the will of the people.[11]

It is worth emphasizing that although several of the components are at the heart of notions of liberal democracy, nevertheless the claim that democracy is a universal right remains contentious, and the term is not explicitly featured in the Universal Declaration or the ICCPR. UN and regional treaties endorsed by member states are the most important sources of international law, but other documents interpreting and elaborating upon treaty obligations include official reports, working documents, guidelines, and court judgments. These documents establish the fundamental rights, codified in international law, that are often discussed when defining the quality of elections. Thus, the Carter Center maintains a comprehensive database of obligations for democratic elections in public international law, which is designed to aid monitors in assessing the quality of electoral processes.[12] The key topics are organized around traditional principles in the ICCPR, such as universal voting rights, access to information, and rule of law, as listed in Table 1.1. These principles of civil and political rights constitute the basic or minimum level acceptable by states that have endorsed these standards. But these are not static and frozen in the politics of earlier eras; instead, global norms continue to evolve and expand within the international community through a series of multilateral treaties, human rights conventions, legal instruments, and more detailed working guidelines.[13] Advocates continue to press for the adoption of additional standards to cover contemporary issues arising on the current policy agenda, exemplified by concern about the need to achieve gender equality in elected office, the deployment of new technological facilities for electronic voting, polling access for the physically disabled, as well as the regulation of political finance and the use of public subsidies for campaigns by political parties. In turn, as norms have diffused, human rights activists and local reformers who support these agreements have sought to implement them and codify normative standards through reforming domestic legislation and regulations.

II: Monitoring and Measuring Standard of Electoral Integrity

What evidence allows analysts to explore which contests meet international standards of electoral integrity – and which fail? Ideally, evidence needs to meet the standard requirements for scientific research, so that it is accurate, systematic, valid, reliable, and legitimate. A growing body of research has sought to measure the quality of elections, including studying problems of electoral fraud and malpractice,[14] the impact of international election monitors,[15] strategies used to manipulate contests in electoral autocracies,[16] and the consequences of malpractice for political legitimacy, electoral participation, and regime change.[17] The previous literature has deployed several common approaches to measuring the closely related bundle of concepts concerning electoral integrity.

Observer Reports

Reports published by international observer missions provide one widely respected source of many evaluations. These provide a systematic and authoritative assessment of the quality of elections, exemplified by publications issued by the Organization of American States, the Carter Center, IFES, the African Union, the European Union, and the Organization for Security and Cooperation in Europe.[18] *The Declaration of Principles for International Election Observation* – a statement seeking to establish agreed standards and norms for credible observation activities – was endorsed at the United Nations almost a decade ago.[19] Several widely used data sets developed by scholars, summarized in Table 2.1, have coded the contents of published observer reports to develop systematic indicators.[20]

Nevertheless, during the last decade the picture provided by these reports has become increasingly muddied by the proliferation of international election monitoring groups, producing divergent assessments of the same contest.[21] After observing the Azerbaijan presidential elections on October 9, 2013, for example, the OSCE/OFIHR mission reported numerous flaws, including ballot box stuffing, lack of transparency in the vote count, and candidate and voter intimidation.[22] By contrast, observers from the Parliamentary Assembly of the Council of Europe (PACE) concluded that there was "a free, fair and transparent electoral process."[23] Some scholars attempt to distinguish between "high quality" and "low quality" observer organizations.[24] In practice, however, given the lack of impartial accreditation of observer missions, the dividing line

TABLE 2.1. *Expert indices monitoring the quality of elections*

Project	PI	Period	N. nations	N. elections	Data sources	Core concept and measures
PEI Release 2.8	Norris, Frank and Martinez i Coma	Mid-2012 to End-2014	97	113	Expert survey	Evaluations of electoral integrity based on a rolling expert survey conducted after national parliamentary and presidential elections. The survey contains forty-nine substantive items divided into eleven stages in the electoral cycle. The overall PEI Index sums the forty-nine items to generate a standardized 100-point scale. www.electoralintegrityproject.com
Free and fair elections	Bishop and Hoeffler	1975–2011	169	1,114	News media archives, US Human Rights reports, and observer reports	The data set measures "free and fair" elections using ten variables, where "free" is defined in terms of the rules of the election and campaign, and "fair" refers to events on polling day. See http://www.csae.ox.ac.uk/data sets/free-fair-elections/default.html
National Elections across Democracy and Autocracy (NELDA)	Susan Hyde and Nikolay Marinov (Yale University)	1945–2010	162	2,948	Various including news media archives, election data handbooks, and online election guides.	The NELDA data set measures "electoral competition" in national constituent assembly, presidential, and legislative contests. The NELDA electoral integrity index was constructed by combining four items from the data set: Nelda11 "*Before elections, are there significant concerns that elections will not be free and fair?*", Nelda13 "*Were opposition leaders prevented from running?*", Nelda15 "*Is there evidence that the government harassed the opposition?*", and Nelda16 "*In the run-up to the election, were there allegations of media bias in favor of the incumbent?*" These items were summed for the aggregate index, and the combined scores were reversed and standardized. http://hyde.research.yale.edu/nelda/

Quality of Elections Data (QED)	Judith Kelley (Duke University)	1977–2004	172	1206	The QED data set codes multiple aspects of the "quality of elections." The QED electoral integrity index was constructed by using SA1 *Overall electoral quality* (coded (0) acceptable, (1) ambiguous, and (2) unacceptable), combined with SA2 *The extent of problems* (coded as (0) no problems, (1) minor problems only, (2) moderate problems, (3) major problems). These items were summed for the aggregate index and the combined scores were reversed and standardized. http://sites.duke.edu/kelley/data/
Index of Electoral Malpractice (IEM)	Sarah Birch (Essex University)	1995–2007	61	161	The IEM data set focuses upon measuring "electoral malpractice," defined by Birch as "the manipulation of electoral processes and outcomes so as to substitute personal or partisan benefit for the public interest". The data set codes: (i) the legal framework, (ii) campaign practices, and (iii) electoral administration. The IEM was constructed from fourteen items, each measured on a 5-point scale monitoring the legal framework, the independence of the electoral authorities, candidate contestation, voter registration, polling arrangements, voting processes, vote counting, the role of observers, balanced coverage by the media, regulation of campaign resources, vote buying, voter intimidation, and candidate intimidation. Missing data were replaced by mean substitution to avoid dropping cases. The overall score was then standardized. http://www.essex.ac.uk/government/electoralmalpractice/index.htm

(continued)

TABLE 2.1 (*continued*)

Project	PI	Period	N. nations	N. elections	Data sources	Core concept and measures
Liberal democracy	Freedom House	1973 to date	192		Freedom House	Freedom House classifies all countries worldwide based on their political rights and civil liberties. The Pakatan Rakyat (PR) scores include: 1) Is the head of government or other chief national authority elected through free and fair elections?; (2) Are the national legislative representatives elected through free and fair elections?; and (3) Are the electoral laws and framework fair? The scores are combined and standardized to 100 points to generate the Freedom House (FH) democracy index. www.freedomhouse .org
FH Electoral Processes	Freedom House	2005–2012	196		FH	The variable measures to what extent the national legislative representatives and the national chief authority are elected through free and fair elections. Countries are graded between 0 (worst) and 12 (best). www.freedomhouse.org

Notes: See the Technical Appendix for details.

is somewhat slippery; if the PACE report differs sharply from the OSCE, for example, which provides the more reliable source? In addition, it has not been clearly established whether observer reports are based on consistent standards over time, or whether expectations have altered with the expansion of international missions and developments in human rights thinking since the use of observers became more common in the mid-1980s.[25]

Media Reports and Events Data

Alternative assessments are available through events data gathered from news media reports of election campaigns. Secondary reference sources, such as Keesing's *Record of World Events, Facts on File, The New International Yearbook*, and *Factiva*, provide a record of events based on compiling journalistic reports published by multiple outlets around the globe. But do the news media sources, which form the basis for these standard reference works, provide reliable and consistent evidence of electoral quality? In any contest, journalists may ideally seek to provide objective reports, but communication studies recognize that in practice news coverage may be slanted to favor the government or opposition due to journalistic biases, newsroom cultures, party leadership cues, or each outlet's partisan leanings.[26] There is also a widely recognized systematic skew in the news media agenda whereby journalists report negative deviance rather than positive stories about elections, with headlines highlighting disputes, violence, and irregularities in the campaign and results. Deviant events that break social norms and laws are viewed as newsworthy and therefore deserving of prominent coverage, a tendency thereby exaggerating estimates of the actual occurrence of any electoral problems.[27] Like the dog that did not bark, few headline stories report when contests work well. It could be assumed that any problems not reported by the media did not happen, but equally in many parts of the world silence could more plausibly be attributed to lack of journalistic freedoms. In particular, reliable domestic coverage is limited in some of the most repressive regimes that muzzle critical coverage and independent reporting. Similarly, the courts and electoral authorities may be in the pocket of the ruling party. Overreliance on content and event count analysis derived from the English speaking international press and news agencies, such as Reuters News, BBC World Monitoring, Associated Press, and Agence France Presse, as well as use of the US State Department's Human Rights reports, also carries the danger of generating a systematic pro-Western foreign policy bias in the framing of the coverage and distortions in the center–periphery regional balance in event reporting.[28] Many studies have confirmed the claim that information flows from the richest and largest core states (notably the United States as well as Europe) to the periphery, so that world news coverage of many African and Asian societies is relatively limited.[29]

The traditional content analysis of texts is being supplemented by newer techniques based on Big Data analysis, designed to tap into the collective wisdom of crowds and social media, such as examining election comments posted on Facebook, Instagram, and Twitter. Content analysis of social media, as well as crowd-sourcing platforms such as Ushaidi, are a rapidly emerging source of data, which holds considerable promise for future research.[30] Yet it remains difficult to establish how far online postings reflect the general views of ordinary citizens, since partisan activists are probably far more likely to express political opinions online. Despite the rapid spread of mobile phones across the developing world, a substantial digital divide also remains in access and use of social media.

Public Opinion Surveys

By contrast, an alternative source of evidence is available from public opinion polls drawn from a representative cross-section of the adult population, making it easier to extrapolate from social surveys with confidence in the reliability of the data. Public attitudes toward electoral integrity have been monitored in several studies, including the sixth wave of the World Values Survey, Afro-barometers surveys, LAPOP surveys of Latin America, and the Gallup World Poll.[31] The body of cross-national survey evidence has been rapidly growing in recent years. Many surveys are limited to asking about only one or two types of electoral malpractices, however, such as experience of incidents of vote buying or electoral intimidation. Others use indirect measures, such as trust in electoral authorities, rather than monitoring all the multiple problems that can occur throughout the electoral cycle. Cross-national survey evidence from the sixth wave World Values Survey provides the most extensive battery of items that can be used to examine individual-level factors contributing toward perceived problems of electoral malpractice, and to supplement reliance upon expert evaluations.[32] The earlier volume compared public and expert evaluations of the quality of elections, based on identical questions in both surveys.[33] The correlation between mass and elite suggests that the general public is capable of making fairly rational and accurate assessments about electoral integrity in their own country. Public perceptions of electoral integrity are strongly colored by partisan cues and use of political communications, as well as by educational qualifications and thus cognitive skills. Nevertheless, in the most repressive autocratic regimes, where freedom of expression and media freedom are strictly controlled, there may be considerable divergence between public assessments and actual malpractice.

Proxy Indices

One other approach is to use indirect yardsticks; for example, it might be thought that because elections are central to liberal democracy, standard indices of democracy and autocracy provided by Polity IV, or the index of political rights and civil liberty by Freedom House, are reliable proxies for the quality of elections. As shown in Figure 1.2, levels of democratization (from Freedom House and Polity IV) and the PEI Index of Electoral Integrity are strongly correlated, but there are also important outliers. Even in long-standing democracies, recent years have witnessed major debates with electoral integrity, such as the "Robocall" scandal in Canadian provinces[34] and security flaws in the UK.[35] Although there is a general correlation, there is no simple one-to-one correlation between electoral integrity and democracy; the United States provides the clearest illustration of a long-standing democracy where a recent bipartisan Presidential Commission acknowledged a wide range of problems in electoral administration.[36]

Electoral Forensics

Another growing source of evidence comes from the techniques of electoral forensics; the autopsies conducted on the DNA of vote share and turnout rates in polling places. Thus statistical anomalies in certain districts arouse suspicion, for example concerning the government's share of the vote, patterns of electoral registration, or outliers in levels of voter participation. The study of electoral forensics is rapidly developing, with case studies scrutinizing voting results in countries such as Russia, Venezuela, and the United States. Nevertheless, there is no consensus about these methods with statisticians continuing to dispute the most reliable indicators.[37]

Court Prosecutions and Legal Records

Like corruption, many cases of illicit or fraudulent electoral acts come to light through scandals, prosecutions, or investigations. Direct evidence of court cases has been examined, for example to examine electoral fraud across districts in Costa Rica.[38] Incident reports by poll workers, and legal records of prosecutions and convictions, have also been used in the United States to monitor the frequency of criminal charges of voter impersonation (implying voting more than once).[39] These are a potentially useful data sources, although partisan polarization has generated numerous media stories with claims and counterclaims over the issue.[40] But even if agreement could be secured on the numbers, their interpretation remains open to debate. The number of prosecutions or convictions may indicate the zeal of the court and legal system when investigating electoral malpractice, and also the stringency of the laws on the books, more than the underlying frequency of malpractice. Indeed, there may be a converse relationship observed, if countries with the most stringent normative and legal standards against corruption are also the most likely to prosecute offenses. Moreover, several flaws that mean that an election falls short of international standards may be perfectly legal in several countries, such as the American practices of partisan gerrymandering of district boundaries.

Experiments

Experiments are also an increasingly common approach in political science, behavioral economics, and developmental policy studies – especially to make causal inferences about the effectiveness of alternative interventions, such as different ways of implementing programs on schooling, health, or poverty alleviation. Varied research designs, including laboratory, survey, field, and natural experiments, use randomization as the rigorous gold standard for making causal connections. A growing body of experiments has been conducted on elections, for example to determine the impact of international observer missions on ballot box fraud,[41] to assess the effect on voter turnout of using different technologies to cast a ballot,[42] as well as to test the influence of civic education, media exposure, or mobilization campaigns on citizen's attitudes and behavior.[43] Well-designed experiments constitute a valuable and precise tool to determine the direction of causality in any relationship, especially concerning short-term effects arising from specific policy interventions, and these techniques are therefore employed in the final volume of the trilogy. Social psychology and behavioral economics has made fruitful use of experimental methods to examine the microfoundations of individual-level behaviors. Nevertheless, this method is far more limited for cross-national research seeking to determine long-term consequences arising from macrolevel phenomena.[44] This book therefore uses conventional econometric statistical techniques to compare the conditions observed to be most closely associated with flawed and failed elections around the world, combined with several mini-case studies. No single perspective or technique provides a wholly convincing explanation, by any means, no matter how elegant and parsimonious, so a more comprehensive approach integrating alternative viewpoints, methods, and tools proves more satisfactory.

III: The Expert Survey of Perceptions of Electoral Integrity

This book draws primarily upon evaluations of whether elections meet international standards derived from the techniques of expert surveys. These techniques have been employed in several related fields, notably the annual worldwide survey conducted since 1995 by Transparency International to monitor perceptions of public-sector corruption.[45] Recent decades have also seen considerable advances in related standard-based expert measures of human rights and their increased use among NGOs, international organizations, and donor agencies.[46] Indicators have been used to monitor state compliance with various rights and to "name and shame" violations, to encourage human rights protections, and to mobilize diplomatic pressure. Cross-national and time-series measures of many dimensions of human rights based on expert judgments have also been widely utilized in the political and social sciences, notably Freedom House measures of political rights and civil liberties, the Polity IV measures of democracy–autocracy, the Cinganelli and Richards (CIRI) human rights data, and Reporters without Borders measures of press freedom.[47]

Expert surveys have become increasingly popular as a technique for evaluating many standards of democratic governance which are hard to observe directly through other means, such as perceived levels of corruption, rule of law, the quality of bureaucracy, and media freedom.[48] Widely used expert surveys in political science include Transparency International's expert survey of perceptions of corruption, the Varieties of Democracy project under development by the Institute for Good Government,[49] and several expert surveys of political party ideologies and policy positions.[50] More generally, expert judgments have also commonly been used for many decades in engineering, science, and commerce, for example to assess the risks arising from nuclear reactor accidents, investment decisions, or military conflict.[51] In the literature, expert judgments are also called "expert opinion," "expert forecasts," and "expert knowledge." The technique is often employed when many other standard approaches to measurement or direct observation are lacking. In general, expert judgments rely upon cognitive reasoning drawing upon information and skills acquired from specialized training, technical knowledge, and experience. Judgments reflect the contemporary elite consensus on any topic, although they need to be adjusted in the light of new information. Nevertheless, any expert judgments and perceptions are open to the charge of bias arising from many sources, such as the cultural values, normative assumptions, sources of evidence, and levels of knowledge of the experts. The external validity and accuracy of any estimates, therefore, need to be examined against independent evidence, wherever available.

The PEI data set used in this trilogy differs from previous approaches by drawing upon evaluations from a wider range of domestic and international experts, by facilitating disaggregated analysis at a finer level of granularity (including comparing forty-nine separate indices) than many summary indices, as well as by providing comprehensive coverage of all national parliamentary and presidential elections after the event in almost all countries in the world, not just those contests with international observer missions or news media reports.

To provide comprehensive evaluations of each stage of the electoral cycle, this study utilizes new data from the Electoral Integrity Project expert survey on Perceptions of Electoral Integrity (PEI-2.8), covering all national elections around the globe during a thirty month period from mid-2012 to end-2014, excluding microstates (with populations below 100,000). The study developed by Norris, Frank, and Martinez i Coma selects a cross-section of electoral experts to participate in the survey, including both domestic and international respondents. The survey asks around forty electoral experts from each country, generating a mean response rate of around 28 percent across the survey with replies from 1,251 experts. *Electoral experts* are defined in the PEI study as political scientists (or scholars in related social science disciplines, such as law, history, political economy, or political sociology) who are knowledgeable on one or more of the following topics: elections, electoral systems, electoral administration, voting behavior, public opinion, campaigns, political communications, mass media, democracy and democratization, political parties and party systems, human rights and national politics. All these topics touch on different dimensions of the underlying concept of electoral integrity. *Expertise* is defined by publication of scholarly articles, books, and conference papers, or teaching at university level on these topics, and/or by membership and participation in professional research groups, disciplinary networks, and organized sections on the above topics with organizations such as the International Political Science Association.

The instrument used for the expert survey was developed and conducted in conjunction with Andrew Reynolds and Jørgen Elklit.[52] The survey relies upon multiple questions, not simply an overall pass/fail summary judgment. Social psychological research suggests that breaking estimates into their components parts, or greater granularity, usually generates more accurate answers.[53] The forty-nine items about electoral integrity contained in the questionnaire are designed to capture expert judgments about whether specific national elections meet internationally recognized principles and standards of elections. Details are provided in Table 2.2. Respondents are not asked to report their own direct experience of elections, or to provide information about legal or factual technical matters in each country– such as the level of the vote threshold to qualify for parliamentary seats, or the proportion of the eligible electorate registered to vote – which can be gathered more accurately from alternative sources, including electoral laws and official statistics. Instead, expert respondents are asked to evaluate the quality of a wide range of electoral integrity and malpractice items in a specific national election within each country. The items are derived from a series of common and universally agreed global norms and values, reflecting the conceptual framework already discussed, such as the value of fairness, equality, inclusiveness, honesty, and efficiency in all the sequential steps in the electoral cycle.

One of the chief questions when trying to gauge electoral integrity is where to draw the boundaries when it comes to deciding which items are most relevant to electoral integrity? To reflect the conceptualization used in this book, it is important to go beyond polling day and the vote count, to include the broad determinants of electoral integrity throughout the electoral cycle. Hence many aspects of elections are monitored in PEI well before, or immediately after, polling day. Close attention is paid to each step in the electoral cycle. As with all survey work, experts are not cued by the questionnaire about the meaning of these items; instead they are asked to make their own judgments based on their own perceptions. One of the advantages of the PEI data set is that the disaggregated score is available for each of the items, allowing analysts to pinpoint the issues that are of most concern, for example whether the fairness of the EMB, the process of campaigning, or the aftermath of the results, as well as facilitating the process of aggregating the data flexibly so that analysts can fit alternative theoretical concepts.

To operationalize the core notion, the electoral cycle illustrated earlier in Figure 1.1 is employed where elections are understood as a sequential process broken down into eleven stages, ranging from the election laws, electoral procedures, and boundary delimitation to the voting process, vote count, to

TABLE 2.2. *Questions in the expert survey of PEI*

Period	Sections	Questions
Preelection	1. Electoral laws	1. Electoral laws were unfair to smaller parties
		2. Electoral laws favored the governing party or parties
		3. Election laws restricted citizens' rights
	2. Electoral procedures	4. Elections were well managed
		5. Information about voting procedures was widely available
		6. Election officials were fair
		7. Elections were conducted in accordance with the law
	3. District boundaries	8. Boundaries discriminated against some parties
		9. Boundaries favored incumbents
		10. Boundaries were impartial
	4. Voter registration	11. Some citizens were not listed in the register
		12. The electoral register was inaccurate
		13. Some ineligible electors were registered
	5. Registration process for parties and candidates to get on the ballot	14. Some opposition candidates were prevented from running
		15. Women had equal opportunities to run for office
		16. Ethnic and national minorities had equal opportunities to run for office
		17. Only top party leaders selected candidates
		18. Some parties/candidates were restricted from holding campaign rallies
Campaign	6. Media's coverage of these elections	19. Newspapers provided balanced election news
		20. TV news favored the governing party
		21. Parties/candidates had fair access to political broadcasts and advertising
		22. Journalists provided fair coverage of the elections
		23. Social media were used to expose electoral fraud
	7. Campaign finance	24. Parties/candidates had equitable access to public subsidies
		25. Parties/candidates had equitable access to political donations
		26. Parties/candidates publish transparent financial accounts
		27. Rich people buy elections
		28. Some states resources were improperly used for campaigning

(continued)

TABLE 2.2 (*continued*)

Period	Sections	Questions
Election day	8. When voting	29. Some voters were threatened with violence at the polls
		30. Some fraudulent votes were cast
		31. The process of voting was easy
		32. Voters were offered a genuine choice at the ballot box
		33. Postal ballots were available
		34. Special voting facilities were available for the disabled
		35. National citizens living abroad could vote
		36. Some form of internet voting was available
Post-election	9. After the polls closed	37. Ballot boxes were secure
		38. The results were announced without undue delay
		39. Votes were counted fairly
		40. International election monitors were restricted
		41. Domestic election monitors were restricted
	10. Official results announced	42. Parties/candidates challenged the results
		43. The election led to peaceful protests
		44. The election triggered violent protests
		45. Any disputes were resolved through legal channels
	11. Electoral authorities administering elections	46. The election authorities were impartial
		47. The authorities distributed information to citizens
		48. The authorities allowed public scrutiny of their performance
		49. The election authorities performed well

Source: Pippa Norris, Ferran Martinez i Coma, and Richard W. Frank. *The expert survey of Perceptions of Electoral Integrity*. 2.8 Release (PEI-2.8). Available at www.electoralintegrity project.com

declaration of results. Like complex links in a chain, violating international standards in any one of the sequential steps undermines principles of electoral integrity.[54] Thus, concern about electoral fraud often focuses on such acts as multiple voting, stuffing ballot boxes, or putting a thumb on the scales of the vote count, all of which clearly damage the people's choice. But the concept of electoral integrity emphasizes that many other problems can also undermine international standards, such as the use of electoral laws, ballot access requirements, and district electoral boundaries stacked to favor incumbents. Trumped up criminal charges can be used to disqualify opposition candidates well before the campaign starts. Harassment and intimidation of political activists is commonly threatened to discourage opponents. During the campaign, imbalanced access to media and money provides incumbents with major advantages.[55] Electors can find their names missing from outdated or inaccurate voter registers. Once the results are announced, lack of impartial and timely judicial processes for resolving electoral disputes can trigger protests and violence. Many of these sorts of problems are often suspected of arising from strategic manipulation by the regime, but, like any complex logistical operation, shortcomings may also arise from happenstance, lack of capacity, and sheer incompetence, as discussed further in Chapter 6. In Broward County, for instance, the notoriously confusing "butterfly ballot," leading Al Gore supporters to cast a mistaken ballot for Patrick Buchanan, was designed by Theresa LePore, a hapless Supervisor of Elections for Palm Beach, Florida, who was a registered Democrat, not a Republican.[56]

Another issue raised by this process is how to gauge the responses if respondents from different cultures, countries, or groups employ different standards, or if they understand the meaning of questions in divergent ways. Cultural biases are only to be expected; for example, experts living in long-established democracies may prove more critical of electoral fraud and inaccuracies in voter registers than those living in newer democracies. The data set was tested to see whether evaluations of electoral integrity varied systematically based on an expert's social and demographic background (age, education, and sex), country of birth, their length of time living in the country of the election, and their ideological views on a left–right scale. The analysis showed that the length of experience in living in the country of an election proved important; longer-time residents were more positive in their evaluations. Familiarity, it appears, may breed content. Equally importantly, however, nationality and citizenship were, perhaps surprisingly, not significant for electoral evaluations, suggesting that international and domestic experts shared largely similar assessments. Moreover, political ideology (across the left–right scale) was also unimportant, as were age and education.[57]

Individual items in the survey were recoded in a consistently positive direction and scored consistently on a 0 to 5 ordinal scale, with 0 representing the most negative evaluations and 5 the most positive. Individual scores were also averaged for the country as a whole. Where the standard deviation of the mean in any country proved higher than average, the individual scores were further examined. The items were then summed and standardized to 100 points to generate the PEI Index. Using similar procedures, for more accurate and detailed diagnosis, standardized 100-point indices were also generated for each of the eleven subdimensions in the electoral cycle.

The main advantages of the PEI data set, therefore, are that the evidence furnishes analysts with a multidimensional assessment of electoral integrity, reflecting the core concept developed in this book, which can be broken down into its component parts. The results show a considerable degree of external and internal validity. The annual survey will eventually provide comprehensive coverage of national elections held in all countries around the world. The PEI-2.8 data set used in this book covers half of all the independent nation

TABLE 2.3. *Characteristics of the countries in PEI-2.8*

Countries surveyed in PEI-2.8	FH/ imputed polity	GDP per capita, PPP (constant international USD)	Human development index	Land area (sq. km)	Population
Not included (N.97)	6.55	$12,738	.645	68,7508	29,908,474
Included (N.96)	6.79	$11,550	.665	66,5855	40,754,288
Total (N.193)	6.67	$12,100	.655	67,6511	35,416,557

Source: Electoral Integrity Project. 2014. *The expert survey of Perceptions of Electoral Integrity,* Release 2.8 (PEI-2.8).

states around the world (97 out of 193), selected based on those that held national presidential or parliamentary elections from mid-2012 to end-2014. This includes diverse types of societies and types of regimes, ranging from the United States, Japan, and the Netherlands, on the one hand, to Burkina Faso, Sierra Leone, and Belarus, on the other. Because of the rolling design of the survey, the data in PEI-2.8 provides a random cross-section of all contemporary elections in every country worldwide, with the exclusion of microstates. Table 2.3 compares the countries which are and are not included in this release of the survey against several standard indicators, showing no substantial differences except in mean population size. Thus, the generalizations emerging from the study can be extrapolated to elections elsewhere in the world with a fair degree of confidence. In subsequent chapters, the PEI Index and its subdimensions are compared with independent macrolevel measures of structural socioeconomic conditions and international development aid, derived from many indicators compiled in the Quality of Government cross-national data sets,[58] and classifications of types of power-sharing constitutions and electoral regulatory agencies from cross-national sources, including International IDEA and the ACE Project.[59]

IV: Evaluating PEI: Robustness and Reliability Tests

How do we know whether the data from PEI meet the standards required for scientific research, and whether the evidence can be relied upon by policymakers and electoral officials? As with similar measures of complex political phenomena such as human rights, democracy, or corruption, in scientific and applied research, evidence should meet acceptable standards for scholars and practitioners, striking a careful balance across several competing criteria.[60] Ideally, this includes the requirements of conceptual validity, lack of measurement error, comprehensive scope, precise measurement levels, reliable and robust measurement, and authoritative and legitimate sources. In practice, however, there are often trade-offs across these criteria: for example, the most comprehensive coverage over an extended period of time and around the world is likely to involve a loss of rich detail and disaggregated indices.

Any selected indicators should ideally be *conceptually valid*, meaning that the attributes relate logically and consistently to the overall concept of electoral integrity that is being operationalized. If extraneous attributes are included, this generates a muddy measure that is not properly delimited. For example, it would be inappropriate to use Polity IV index of democracy and autocracy as a proxy for electoral integrity, since this measure is constructed based on many features of executive office and institutional checks and balances well beyond elections per se. In addition, as observed with problems of electoral integrity in the United States, Britain, and Canada, democracy is no guarantee of well-run elections. The contrary danger is if certain core attributes are excluded from indicators, as this provides an incomplete and partial measure, for example, if electoral integrity is measured only by incidents of fraud on polling day, or by the legal opportunities for opposition candidates to gain ballot access.

When seeking to assess electoral integrity, other potential problems can arise from systematic sources of *measurement error*. Some of these can be attributed to the choice of data sources; for example, analysis of media reports of irregularities in campaign finance may reflect the independence of the press, the regulatory environment, and freedom of information laws in any society, more than actual incidents. Similarly, collecting data on legal prosecutions of voter fraud or vote buying will probably reflect the role of the courts and the influence of partisan politics, rather than the frequency of these problems. Other problems arise from secondary analysis of human rights reports issued from the US State Department, used by the Quality of Elections data set constructed by Judith Kelley, since these are likely to reflect American foreign policy interests and culturally bound interpretation of human rights, rather than international assessments. Other attempts to monitor the quality of elections, such as Sarah Birch's IEMs, have extracted data by coding information contained in international observer mission reports. Yet the countries included in the data set through this method may be systematically biased toward the worst cases, limiting generalizability; agencies use needs-assessment missions prior to deployment, and observers are not sent to elections seen as meeting international standards, generating a systematic bias toward more problematic contests. Measurement error can be reduced, although not wholly eliminated, by using multiple sources to extract data, for example by comparing observer reports issued by different organizations evaluating the same contests, although this can also complicate the analysis, for example if these reports disagree sharply in their assessments. Measurement errors can also be reduced by using cross-checks to confirm the external validity of measures.

The *comprehensive scope* of the coverage provided by any data set is important; the broader the range of countries and time periods included in data sets, the greater their generalizability. A broad scope allows measures to be used in diverse contexts, allowing comparisons across global regions, rather than being idiosyncratic and highly contextual. The capacity to generalize is strengthened by indicators that can be applied consistently to monitor elections held within and across diverse cultural regions, under different types of regimes, and during alternative time periods. On the other hand, several indicators are only available for one global region, such as Staffan Lindberg's evaluation of free and fair elections in sub-Saharan Africa.[61] Some subtle systematic biases can arise from seemingly innocuous decisions; for example, the NELDA data set follows the practices used by the Polity IV data set by excluding smaller countries (with a population less than 500,000). Since smaller countries tend to be more democratic than average,[62] the cross-national coverage of cases included in NELDA may over-estimate problems of electoral malpractice around the world.

Precise measurement levels, which can be at nominal, ordinal, or interval scales, need sufficient detail to allow analysts to identify the specific source and gravity of any violations of electoral integrity, and thus determine suitable remedies, rather than being so abstract and general that they prove too blunt for accurate diagnosis. For example, binary pass–fail judgments about the quality of elections (or even restricted ordinal categories) cannot identify the source of any flaws. At the same time, measures need to avoid spurious precision, which can arise from asking coders to make impossibly fine-grained distinctions between categories.

Any measures should be *reliable and robust*, so that independent studies are likely to arrive at similar interpretations of the evidence, meaning, in practice, that alternative indices constructed by different scholars are highly intercorrelated. To aid replication, methods used for gathering data and then constructing any summary indices should ideally be transparent, with detailed notes available about procedures, coding practices, and rules of aggregation, so that evidence can be subject to scrutiny and test by independent scholars, using standard techniques. For example, evaluations whether elections are free and fair, or judgments about whether the media provided a level playing field for contestants, require systematic procedural rules and tests of intercoder reliability.

Finally, to provide guidance for practitioners, indices of electoral integrity should also be *legitimate*, *credible*, and *intuitively understandable*, so that they come to be regarded as authoritative and usable by the international community and domestic stakeholders. What counts as legitimate, however, is difficult to determine with any certainty, since scientific and political legitimacy may not coincide. Measures that reflect global norms and official statistics, however, are more likely to prove widely acceptable and authoritative to the

TABLE 2.4. *Correlations of PEI with the expert indices of electoral quality*

		PEI Index of electoral integrity
Quality of electoral democracy standardized score 2000–2004 (QED Kelley)	Pearson correlation	.659**
	Sig. (2-tailed)	.000
	N	77
Electoral malpractice standardized scale 2000–2006, (Birch)	Pearson correlation	−.647**
	Sig. (2-tailed)	.000
	N	37
Free and Fair Score sum (Bishop Hoeffler)	Pearson correlation	.624**
	Sig. (2-tailed)	.000
	N	90
Electoral integrity standardized scale 2000–10 (NELDA Hyde and Marinov)	Pearson correlation	.574**
	Sig. (2-tailed)	.000
	N	85
Liberal democracy standardized scale 100 pts 2012 (FH)	Pearson correlation	.808**
	Sig. (2-tailed)	.000
	N	96
Electoral processes 2012 (FH)	Pearson correlation	.747**
	Sig. (2-tailed)	.000
	N	97
Democratic or autocratic regime, 2008 (Cheibub, Gandhi, and Vreeland)	Pearson correlation	.624**
	Sig. (2-tailed)	.000
	N	97

Note: For the expert indices, see Table 2.1 and the Technical Appendix for details about their construction and sources. The figures represent the simple Pearson correlations, the statistical significance, and the number of national cases for comparison, with each indicator matched by country. All Pearson correlation coefficients (R) are statistically significant (**) at the 0.01 level (2-tailed).

international community than specific indicators developed by think tanks or NGOs seeking to further their own agendas.

Each of the available expert indicators that could be used to monitor levels of electoral integrity therefore has different advantages and disadvantages. One way to examine the robustness of the expert indices produced by PEI is to compare the correlations across these estimates. Given their different construction, measurement, conceptualization, country coverage, and sources of information, it might be expected that the estimates would diverge sharply. If the measures are robust, however, then we would expect to observe significant inter-correlations. Table 2.4 shows the correlations of the PEI Index with several available independent measures of the quality of elections and of democratization.

Independent Measures of Electoral Quality

One major data set selected for the robustness tests is Susan Hyde and Nikolay Marinov's coding of *NELDA*.[63] This project has the advantage of providing the most comprehensive coverage that is currently available by monitoring the quality of 2,948 national legislative and presidential elections held from 1945 to 2010 in all independent nation states worldwide, excluding smaller nation states (with populations less than half a million). NELDA uses an extensive list of secondary sources, including academic election handbooks, online resources, news media, and official reports. The NELDA project codes multiple components of electoral integrity and it focuses upon measures of electoral competition. Their conceptual framework builds upon Alvarez, Cheibub, Limogi, and Przeworski (ACLP), who developed a dichotomous or binary classification of all regimes as either democracies or autocracies, based on competitive elections.[64] Hyde and Marinov suggest that the minimal conditions for competition are present in any contest if opposition is allowed, multiple parties are permitted, and more than one candidate appears on the ballot.

To create an index capturing several elements of electoral malpractice, for this study a standardized scale was constructed by combining four items contained in the NELDA data set which are most relevant to the idea of electoral integrity:

- *Before elections, are there significant concerns that elections will not be free and fair?* (Nelda11);
- *Were opposition leaders prevented from running?* (Nelda13);
- *Is there evidence that the government harassed the opposition?* (Nelda15); and
- *In the run-up to the election, were there allegations of media bias in favor of the incumbent?* (Nelda16).

These particular items do not provide a comprehensive measure of all dimensions of the broader concepts of electoral integrity and malpractice, by any means. Nevertheless, they do monitor several common problems, especially those observed in many electoral autocracies. The selected items were tested using principal component factor analysis with varimax rotation, and they were found to form a single dimensional (see Technical Appendix A for more details). Reliability checks further confirmed that the four items formed a consistent scale (Cronbach's Alpha 0.756). Accordingly the items were summed into a single NELDA index and the score was standardized, for ease of comparison.

In addition, as another robustness check, we can also compare PEI against an alternative data set developed by Bishop and Hoeffler based on their coding of free and fair elections. This data set covers 1,114 national parliamentary and presidential elections held in 169 nations from 1975 to 2011. Like NELDA, data are drawn from observer reports and standard sources, such as Keesing's Contemporary Archives and the US Department of State Human Rights Reports. The data set codes ten variables, where *free* elections are defined in terms of the rules of the election and campaign, while *fair* elections are defined by polling day and the aftermath. The data set codes ten stages in the electoral cycle, each by a simple binary 0/1 evaluation, ranging from the legal framework, EMBs, electoral rights and ballot access to the campaign process, media access, voting process, role of officials, and vote count.[65]

The results of the cross-national correlations presented in Table 2.4 confirm that the PEI Index is indeed strongly and significantly correlated with all indicators in the expected direction. Given important differences in the coverage, methods and techniques, and underlying concepts, a perfect correlation is not to be expected. Nevertheless the strength of the relationships is impressive, suggesting that the PEI data set has high levels of external reliability. The large-N comparison, therefore, is used to examine systematic patterns that hold across many instances, although this inevitably loses the depth derived from examining the process of elections through intensive case studies. Thus, qualitative case studies are also used in several chapters to trace the underlying forces at work.

Independent Measures of Democratization

PEI is also expected to be closely correlated with the most widely used measures of autocracy and democracy – and indeed this is what was observed earlier (see Figure 1.2). Nevertheless, any explanation of the quality of elections based on levels of democratization, or regime categories, risks proving tautological and spurious. Since elections are at the heart of notions of liberal democracy – although far from sufficient – the quality of these contests is also central to the standard measures that are widely used in the comparative literature to assess levels of democratization and to classify types of autocratic and democratic regimes.[66] For example, FH starts its expert assessment of political rights by rating whether countries hold free and fair elections for the chief executive and the national legislature, whether electoral laws are fair, and many of the other items in the FH index touch on elections.[67] Not surprisingly therefore, FH's assessment of political rights and of civil liberties (understood as proxy indicators of levels of democratization) are strongly correlated with the EIP index of electoral integrity (R = .808**, p = .000, N = 97). Similar observations can be made for the Polity IV autocracy–democracy index.[68]

To summarize the relationship, Table 2.5 compares the distribution of the categories of political integrity against the FH classification of regimes. The results show that all the states classified as having autocratic regimes have moderate or low quality elections, according to PEI. The hybrid category contains diverse regimes – including some states that are closer to the autocracies and others closer to the democratic category. The comparison shows that eight out of ten hybrid regimes were classified as having moderate levels of integrity, with the remainder having low integrity. Finally among democracies, there is a broad dispersion across the categories of electoral integrity, although most fall into either high or moderate types. The results confirm that electoral integrity is important for classifying types of regimes, since multiparty contests are at

TABLE 2.5. *Types of electoral integrity and types of regimes*

		Types of regime		
		Autocracies %	Hybrid regimes %	Democracies %
Type of electoral integrity	Low	48	15	20
	Moderate	52	85	37
	High	0	0	43
		100%	100%	100%

Notes: The regime classification is based on the annual FH classification of democracies (*free*), hybrid regimes (*semi-free*) and autocracies (*not free*) regimes matching the year of election. The PEI Index is categorized into thirds as low, moderate and high.
Sources: Electoral Integrity Project. 2014. *The expert survey of Perceptions of Electoral Integrity*, Release 2.8 (PEI-2.8); Freedom House. *Freedom around the World*. Various years 2012–2014.

the heart of competition and participation in liberal democracies. Nevertheless, elections alone are insufficient for the full panoply of democratic institutions and it would be a mistake to declare countries democratic based on their electoral record alone. And a glance at the comparison presented in Figure 2.2 quickly illustrates some of the outliers, including long-standing democracies such as the United States and India, which display moderate levels of electoral integrity, as well as cases such as Rwanda, Tunisia, and Botswana, which experts rate quite highly in the quality of their recent elections, despite the weakness of other democratic institutions.

Minimalist dichotomous regime classifications focus even more exclusively on elections; for example Cheibub, Gandhi, and Vreeland classify a regime as democratic if the executive and legislature are directly elected by a popular vote, there are multiple parties, and there has been no consolidation of incumbent advantage, for example by postponing subsequent elections.[69] Dictatorships are treated as the residual category. The categorization offered by Boix, Miller, and Rosatto also follows similar procedures, as democracies are defined as regimes that feature political leaders chosen through free and fair elections and that satisfy a threshold value of male suffrage.[70] In practice this means that three decision-rules are used: (i) the executive is directly or indirectly elected in popular elections and is responsible either directly to voters or to a legislature; (ii) the legislature (or the executive if elected directly) is chosen in free and fair elections; (iii) a majority of adult men have the right to vote. In turn, elections are defined as *free* if voters are given multiple options on the ballot and as *fair* if electoral fraud is absent and incumbents do not effectively eliminate the chance of opposition victory through peaceful contestation.

The standard dichotomous approaches to regime classification give lip-service to acknowledging the importance of free and fair elections in their conceptualization; however, in practice studies commonly lack any systematic evidence to gauge this with any precision. The measurement of malpractices is usually complex as it remains difficult to assess whether any fraud occurs and, if so, whether it tipped the balance in any election. For example, the United States is classified by Boix, Miller, and Rosatto as a continuous democracy since 1800 despite the long history of fraudulent practices including the suppression of votes (especially of African Americans), the inflation of ballots (where machine party politics bought votes through cash or favors), and the manipulation of the count.[71] In practice, while specific cases can be established, it is probably not possible to determine the overall extent of electoral fraud during previous centuries with any degree of confidence. Moreover, the core notion of electoral integrity in this book suggests that elections can and do fail at any of the multiple stages of the electoral cycle, without this necessarily being attributable to fraud or illicit activity. Similarly the thin notion of free elections used in the regime classifications, based on multiple options on the ballot, is inadequate to deal with the complexities of restrictions on electoral processes. Many factors may limit party competition – from gerrymandering and legal restrictions on ballot access to inequalities in access to campaign media and money – while still allowing more than one party or candidate to compete.

V: Key Puzzles in the Study of Electoral Integrity

Many questions are open to investigation using the PEI data set. To advance the measurement of electoral integrity, it is essential for studies to move beyond treating election events as a black box, evaluated by a simple pass–fail judgment of polling day and the results, by plunging into the details of how contests actually work – or fail to do so. The bigger question of why elections fail can be deconstructed into several more manageable diagnostic components, like any good story, using the classic "who, what, where, and when" format. A better grasp of all of these issues would help to illuminate more precisely the final key question: *why* are elections flawed or failed, at the heart of this book.

Who?

Who are the key actors? Previous studies have also often focused upon the role of governing elites and ruling parties in determining how the contest works. Rational actor models emphasize acts of intentional manipulation by autocratic leaders to secure power against challengers within and outside of ruling parties. This approach appeals to a deep vein of liberal suspicion and mistrust of state power. Yet governing elites may not be responsible for all problems that can arise from the complex interaction of multiple actors. Certainly governments control state resources, with the power to regulate and implement electoral procedures. Governments are accountable for ensuring a country's compliance with international norms. Ultimately, responsibility for any electoral failures rests with governing parties, especially in autocracies. It is straightforward to assume that rational vote-seeking politicians looking to retain power have a strong incentive to fiddle the outcome and thereby minimize electoral risks, guarantee victory, and deter rivals snapping at their heels. But state institutions are not unitary actors, even in electoral autocracies where power is concentrated at the apex. Malpractice can arise from many diverse agencies during the process of elections. Opposition challengers, party factions, and candidates may seek to undermine legitimate results. Local or national officials managing the contest may prove incompetent. Campaign broadcasting or political finance can be laxly regulated. The impartiality of the courts responsible for resolving electoral disputes can be questioned. Parliaments may have inadequate powers of oversight, legislation, and appointment over electoral authorities. Security forces may fail to manage peaceful protests, partisan gangs of thugs, or outbreaks of intercommunal conflict. Civil society may provide inadequate watchdogs from the independent media, election watch groups, and domestic observers. Finally, the international community may demonstrate lack of commitment by neglecting to monitor contests, apply diplomatic leverage, or provide adequate technical assistance and resources. While ultimate responsibility for elections lies with the state, multiple actors and agencies play a role in the process and their role and powers need to be determined.

The notion of an electoral cycle also draws attention to the role of different actors involved in the sequential stages of electoral governance. The initial step of setting the constitutional framework and legal arrangements, which determine many aspects of party competition and ballot access, is a process where the executive is predominant, although both the legislature and the courts can also play a critical role. Problems can arise from the actions of many players: opposition political parties can mobilize boycotts and protest riots delegitimizing the results, the news media can fail to provide informed and balanced coverage, and financial backers can make illicit donations undermining campaign finance regulations. Security forces, the electoral authorities, citizens, and the courts are key actors during the final stages of the process. The work of electoral authorities is also central to electoral integrity, including their autonomy, powers, and resources for managing electoral processes. Observers commonly report contests marred by technical irregularities in administrative procedures, typically concerning the inaccuracy of the electoral register, restricted processes of voter validation, or the insecurity of ballot papers, all of which are the primary responsibilities of electoral officials.

What?

What problems are most common, including under diverse types of regimes and contests, such as outbreaks of electoral conflict and violence, lack of a level playing field in terms of money and media, and irregularities arising from tampering with electoral registers and ballot tabulations? For example, Simpser measures electoral manipulation from published sources, including reference works, observer reports from selected regional observers and NGOs, and journalistic reports.[72] He codes reported incidents of voter or candidate intimidation, vote buying, tampering with voter registration lists, multiple voting, and problems of candidate or voter registration. These types of serious flaws are commonly monitored in published reports and therefore measurable with some degree of reliability from these sources.

Yet the overall conceptualization of electoral malpractice, and thus the checklist of items used in the Simpser study, remains too narrow by excluding some of the most common and important violations of international standards, for example through the strategic design of electoral laws or campaign money favoring incumbents.[73] An electoral process can be administratively efficient, orderly, and peaceful on polling day, when observers are watching, while party competition is unfairly restricted by high electoral thresholds, airwaves dominated by the government, or disputes where the courts consistently adjudicate in favor of ruling parties. The electoral chain can break at each stage of the cycle, casting doubts about the legitimacy of the outcome. The analogy of focusing only upon what goes wrong through petty malfeasance on polling day misses the bigger picture, rather like monitoring problems of illicit drugs by cracking down on petty dealers and heroin users on the streets rather than addressing the international drug cartels and opium producers far distant from the final transaction. Rather than over-simple pass–fail judgments, it is essential to disaggregate problems of elections into their heterogeneous component parts, not just to understand the issues but also to identify what policy interventions would be most effective to prevent them.

When?

When do problems typically arise, including during the long preelection phase, the official election campaign, on polling day, or during its aftermath? Popular accounts usually conceive of electoral fraud as crude attempts by incumbents to skew results on polling day, such as through stuffing ballot boxes, vote buying, or falsification of vote tabulations. Most media attention focuses on election day and the announcement of the results. In fact, however, this perspective is far too limited since problems can arise at every stage of the electoral cycle, including during the preelection period and the campaign, as well as on polling day and its aftermath. In addition, research needs to distinguish between short-term and cumulative effects. Figure 2.1 breaks down the PEI analysis by each of the eleven subcomponents. The results show that in many contests worldwide the campaign is often the most problematic stage, especially the role of political finance and campaign communications. These problems were seen as more common than many others, such as ballot box fraud. Any malpractice arising in a specific election may be a one-off event, for example a technical or administrative error, quickly rectified by swift remedial action. Or a series of contests can experience a succession of flaws which have a long-term impact, such as by damaging public confidence in the legitimacy of the process or by deterring challengers from entering subsequent contests.

Understanding the whole electoral process as a cycle allows analysts to identify problems with greater precision. Many previous studies have focused

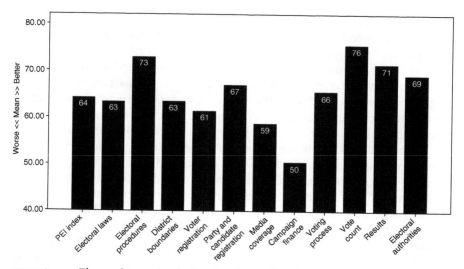

FIGURE 2.1. Electoral integrity during the electoral cycle.
Source: Pippa Norris, Ferran Martinez i Coma and Richard W. Frank. *The expert survey of Perceptions of Electoral Integrity*. (PEI-2.8).

upon intentional and illegal attempts to manipulate the results fraudulently through acts around polling day, exemplified by ballot stuffing, vote buying, voter intimidation, and inaccurate counts. The cyclical notion acknowledges that certainly some types of malpractice reflect these practices. A classic illustration is the West African oil-rich kleptocracy of Equatorial Guinea, ruled by President Teodora Obiang Nguema since a military coup in 1979, holding a series of sham contests boycotted by the opposition where he won a reported 96–98% of the vote. In the May 2013 general election, for example, the president's party, the Democratic Party of Equatorial Guinea, swept the board with 99 out of 100 seats in the Chamber of People's Representatives, and all but one seat in the Senate. The observer mission from the African Union, normally diplomatic and softly spoken in its reports, highlighted a series of irregularities facilitating potential abuses in this contest, including a lack of watchdogs monitoring polling, no voter identity checks, early closure of some polling stations, late and inadequate training of local officials, unsealed ballot boxes, and no opposition ballots available in some polling stations.[74] These practices were reinforced, Amnesty International reported, by major abuses of human rights, including disappearances, arbitrary arrests, and confinement of political opponents, prevalent throughout Equatorial Guinea.[75]

Yet focusing too narrowly on practices occurring at the end of the election, including illicit acts of voter fraud, overt ballot stuffing by ruling parties, or falsified vote tabulation, provides far too narrow a prism to account for the broader phenomenon of electoral malpractices. This common misconception is akin to focusing on the dealer shuffling the deck when the house has already stacked the game. In many cases, the early stages in the electoral cycle are arguably just as, or perhaps even more, important than later ones. Many technical and subtle forms of malpractice, through the strategic manipulation of the legal framework governing elections, occur months or even years in advance of polling day. The early stages of the cycle may also receive less scrutiny by short-term international monitoring missions, the news media, and citizen watchdog groups.[76] Figure 2.2 illustrates mean scores for each stage of the electoral cycle broken down by the type of regime, classified using FH's categories measured to match the year of the election. The results illustrate that there are consistent contrasts among democracies (with the best performance) and autocracies (with the worst), with hybrid regimes in the middle of the pack. But it is not the case that autocracies prove most repressive in the stage of the final stages of the cycle, such as the by manipulating the vote process, falsifying the vote count, and declaring fraudulent results. Instead, compared with other types of regimes, they score consistently poorly across all steps. And all types of regimes generally score worst in the campaign stage of money and media.

A vivid illustration of the most draconian restrictions occurring at an early stage of the cycle in an electoral autocracy comes from the June 2013 presidential elections in Iran, where all the registered candidates were screened by the Guardian Council of the Constitutions, a body appointed by Iran's Supreme Leader, Ayatollah Ali Khamenei. Out of 680 registered candidates, the Guardian Council selected only eight to run for election, and two would subsequently withdraw. The contests produced an unexpected outcome with the victory of a moderate presidential candidate, the cleric Hassan Rouhani, but nevertheless Iranian citizens faced only a strictly limited choice of vetted candidates at the ballot box.[77] One-party states provides the clearest example of limited competition; opposition parties and candidates are illegal in China, Viet Nam, and Cuba, while no political parties at all are allowed to stand for election in Kuwait and Swaziland. Registration requirements are loosened in such states as Belarus, but nevertheless in practice opposition candidates face limited ballot access. In many repressive states, prominent opposition leaders have been subject to enforced disappearances, arbitrary arrest, and confinement.

Not all restrictions on political party competition are as blatant, and more subtle techniques include malapportionment and gerrymandering in constructing boundaries for electoral districts. The 2013 parliamentary elections in Malaysia illustrate these issues, where the long-standing governing Barisan Nasional (BN) coalition continued its 56-rule by winning a majority of seats despite the opposition PR winning a bare majority of votes. One reason for this outcome arises from substantial malapportionment in the size of district electorates as these are designed to favor the rural districts (where ethnic Malays support the government), at the expense of the urban areas (containing ethnic Chinese).[78] In the 2013 elections, for example, the average constituency size for seats won by the governing BN (46,510) was 40 percent less than for Malay

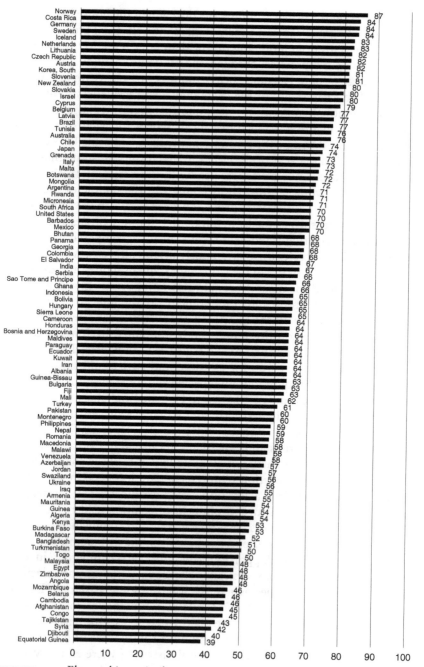

FIGURE 2.2. Electoral integrity by country.
Source: Pippa Norris, Ferran Martinez i Coma, and Richard W. Frank. *The expert survey of Perceptions of Electoral Integrity*. (PEI-2.8).

seats won by their PR opponents (77,655).[79] Even in established democracies such as Germany and Spain, certain types of political parties are banned by law, such as extremists associated with terrorist tactics. Elsewhere, minor parties face a thicket of hurdles in registering; for example, in the United States third parties are required to meet stringent ballot access laws at state level.[80] Even in long-standing democracies, integrity can be undermined by gerrymandered district boundaries crafted to protect incumbents, by cartel party regulations designed to protect parliamentary parties, and by the constitutional, legal, and regulatory framework, established months and even years before an election is called.

When considering issues of timing, the cyclical model also emphasizes that each election contest is not de novo; it is useful to think of an "electoral stock" in any state. Contests are a cumulative experience, so that memories about the quality of a series of previous contests, as well as experience of democracy and human rights, have the potential to influence perceptions of subsequent elections. Thus mistrust borne from a long history of political corruption, intercommunal conflict, voter suppression, and litigious court challenges are likely to color views of each new contest. Following the July 2012 Mexican general election, for example, the losing candidate, López Obrador (Party of the Democratic Union, PRD) demanded a full recount, claiming widespread irregularities, including vote buying (using supermarket credit cards) and use of illicit funds by the Institutional Revolutionary Party (PRI), whose candidate, Enrique Peña Nieto, won with 38 percent of the vote. Claims of bribery were eventually rejected by the Electoral Tribunal on the grounds of insufficient evidence, and the OAS praised the conduct of the election as tranquil and orderly.[81] Nevertheless, opposition charges gained credence and resonated in a culture with low reservoirs of political trust, since they are likely to have triggered deeply ingrained memories of past electoral irregularities used by the PRI to maintain power during earlier decades.[82] Similarly, post-2000, the brouhaha over Florida has generated renewed interest in problems of American elections, whether framed by Republicans as a concern about electoral fraud or by Democrats as concern about voter suppression.[83]

Where?

Where are problems evident around the world and by type of regime? The most serious violations are commonly thought to arise in "electoral autocracies" – regimes with a façade of multiparty competition but with serious and persistent restrictions on human rights and democratic institutions, where power is disproportionately in the hands of the ruling party.[84] A growing body of research has sought to explain why authoritarian leaders risk the uncertainty of holding multiparty elections and how these contests function to legitimate ruling parties, deflect international criticism, and undermine opposition dissent.[85] It would be a serious mistake to assume that problems of electoral integrity are confined to these electoral autocracies, however, as certain types

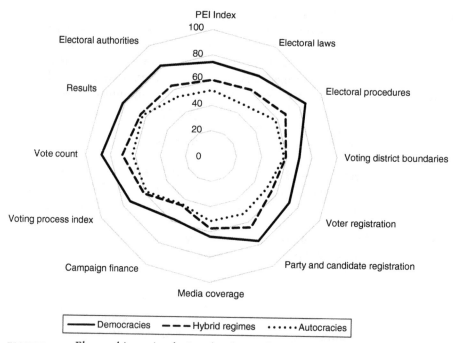

FIGURE 2.3. Electoral integrity during the electoral cycle by type of regime.
Note: The mean scores on each stage in the electoral cycle by type of regime. The classification of democratic (*free*), hybrid (*semi-free*), and authoritarian (*not free*) regimes from FH matched to the year of election.
Sources: Electoral Integrity Project. 2014. *The expert survey of Perceptions of Electoral Integrity*, Release 2.8 (PEI-2.8); Freedom House. *Freedom around the World* (various years).

of irregularities, including protests, occur most commonly in many hybrid regimes.[86] As Florida vividly illustrated, even mature democracies are not immune from flaws.[87]

For an overview, the results of the PEI Index are summarized by election in Figure 2.3. Not surprisingly, elections in the survey rated highly by experts include many long-established Northern European democracies and affluent post-industrial societies, including Norway, Germany, Iceland, the Netherlands, and Austria. These states have experienced a long succession of multiparty contests over many decades, as well as having developed effective institutions for democratic governance. Analysis of the subcomponents showed that these states scored exceptionally well for their electoral procedures, such as running effective and efficient voter registration and vote tabulation processes. It is also notable that all these countries are characterized by power-sharing institutions and "consensus" democracies, providing multiple checks and balances through coalition governments, providing further reason to test propositions arising from consociational theory. In general each country's historical reservoir of *democratic capital* (built from the length of time it has been democratic) is usually a strong predictor of contemporary levels of electoral integrity.[88] Practice over repeated contests seems commonly to strengthen electoral quality, by consolidating institutions and embedding support for democratic rules of the game in the political culture. Losers may be less likely to challenge a particular problem occurring in a specific contest if they believe that in general, procedures are usually legitimate and electoral authorities trustworthy and impartial.

Yet history is not destiny; electoral integrity is not simply due to the length of a country's stock of democratic capital. Several European states that only established multiparty systems and competitive elections following the fall of the Communism during the early 1990s also scored highly, according to the judgments of experts, in the quality of their contests, notably Costa Rica, the Czech Republic, Slovenia, and Lithuania. It is equally striking that despite decades or even centuries of holding multiparty elections, several mature democracies did not perform well according to the global comparison, including Italy and Japan. During the early 1990s, both countries experienced major political corruption scandals and the fragmentation of predominant one-party systems. Italy and Japan both revised their electoral systems in attempts to address these issues, but further institutional reforms continue to be debated in these societies.[89] This is illustrated in Table 2.6 showing the mean scores on the PEI Index by country in each of the types of regimes under comparison, as categorized by FH in the year of the election. It is apparent that although there is a relationship between the type of regime and the PEI score, nevertheless there is also considerable deviation around the mean. Thus, Balkan states such as Bulgaria, Montenegro, and Romania are categorized by FH as *free* or democratic regimes, although they score moderately in the quality of their elections, according to the PEI Index. By contrast, Cameroon, Rwanda, and Iran, which are classified by FH as autocracies, score around the same level as the Balkan states. Clearly, there is often a link between assessments of the quality of liberal democracy and elections, not least because these institutions are at the heart of contestation and participation. Yet elections alone are not sufficient for liberal democracy in the absence of other conditions, such as an effective parliament and independent judiciary, as well as respect for non-electoral rights.

It is also striking that the 2012 US presidential elections were ranked thirty-second out of ninety-seven states worldwide in the overall comparison of electoral integrity, a moderate level similar to many developing societies, such as Mexico, El Salvador, and Mongolia. Experts expressed concern about problems of US electoral laws, voter registration, and partisan gerrymandering in the process of drawing district boundaries, as well as the regulation of campaign finance. Issues of voter fraud and voter identification requirements have become increasingly polarized and litigious in the United States ever since the 2000 Florida debacle, generating growing controversy in statehouses and the courts.[90] Thus, Republican concern about the potential problem of citizens casting fraudulent or multiple ballots has been countered by Democrats

TABLE 2.6. *Electoral integrity by types of regimes*

Democracies		Hybrid regimes		Autocracies	
Norway	87	Tunisia	76	Rwanda	71
Costa Rica	84	Mexico	70	Cameroon	64
Germany	84	Bhutan	68	Iran	64
Sweden	84	Georgia	68	Guinea-Bissau	63
Iceland	83	Colombia	68	Mali	62
Netherlands	83	Indonesia	65	Azerbaijan	57
Lithuania	82	Bolivia	65	Jordan	57
Czech Republic	82	Sierra Leone	65	Swaziland	56
Austria	82	Honduras	64	Iraq	55
South Korea	81	Bosnia-Herzegovina	64	Mauritania	54
Slovenia	81	Maldives	64	Algeria	54
New Zealand	80	Paraguay	64	Turkmenistan	50
Slovakia	80	Ecuador	64	Egypt	48
Israel	80	Kuwait	64	Zimbabwe	48
Cyprus	79	Albania	64	Angola	48
Belgium	77	Fiji	63	Belarus	46
Latvia	77	Turkey	61	Cambodia	46
Brazil	77	Pakistan	60	Afghanistan	45
Australia	76	Philippines	59	Congo (Brazzaville)	45
Chile	74	Nepal	59	Tajikistan	43
Japan	74	Macedonia	58	Syria	42
Grenada	73	Malawi	58	Djibouti	40
Italy	73	Venezuela	58	Equatorial Guinea	39
Malta	72	Ukraine	56		
Botswana	72	Armenia	55		
Mongolia	72	Guinea	54		
Argentina	71	Kenya	53		
Micronesia	71	Burkina Faso	53		
South Africa	70	Madagascar	52		
United States	70	Bangladesh	51		
Barbados	70	Togo	50		
Panama	68	Malaysia	48		
El Salvador	67	Mozambique	46		
India	67				
Serbia	66				
Sao Tome & Principe	66				
Ghana	66				
Hungary	65				
Bulgaria	63				
Montenegro	60				
Romania	58				

Note: The mean score on the PEI-2.8 Index for types of regime, based on the annual FH classification of democracies (*free*), hybrid regimes (*semi-free*) and autocracies (*not free*) regimes matching the year of election.

Sources: Electoral Integrity Project. 2014. *The expert survey of Perceptions of Electoral Integrity*, Release 2.8 (PEI-2.8); Freedom House. *Freedom around the World.* Various years 2012–2014.

worried about the dangers of voter suppression through overly demanding voter identification requirements.[91] The PEI survey suggested deeper and more complex structural problems of American elections, notably the role of campaigns flooded with money, pervasive partisan gerrymandering, and state restrictions on ballot access for third party candidates.

By contrast, low integrity elections ranked at the bottom of the comparison are from diverse global regions, including several countries in sub-Saharan Africa (in Zimbabwe, Angola, the Republic of Congo, Equatorial Guinea, Burkina Faso, Djibouti, Togo, and Sierra Leone), which have experienced deep-rooted conflict and with weak state capacity. Other regimes scoring poorly, rated with low integrity, include one-party autocracies in post-Soviet Tajikistan and Belarus in Central Eurasia and, in Asia, Cambodia, Malaysia, and Bangladesh. In general, the observed pattern suggests that poor developing societies usually have significantly worse quality elections, lending some initial plausibility to the modernization thesis.[92] Again, however, this was far from a fixed pattern, since the developing societies of Rwanda, Mongolia, and Bhutan, for example, all scored relatively well.

Therefore, many important puzzles remain before scholars and practitioners can hope to understand the phenomenon of electoral integrity and malpractice. To build upon this framework, the next chapter starts to examine the evidence, including the impact of structural conditions such as ethnic divisions, deep-rooted poverty, and the "resource curse," which are commonly thought to provide challenging constraints for processes of democratization as well as, by extension, for holding contests meeting international standards of electoral integrity.

PART II

EXPLAINING FAILURES

3

Structural Constraints

Explanations based upon deep drivers in each society highlight the dangers of attempting to organize elections under a wide range of challenging conditions, including in poor and illiterate societies with scattered rural populations lacking access to modern communications and transportation, in deeply divided states emerging from years of conflict, and in countries with a long legacy of authoritarian rule and little, if any, experience of democratic practices.

The severe risks associated with attempting to hold popular contests that meet international standards of electoral integrity under the most difficult circumstances are perhaps best illustrated by contemporary events in Afghanistan. Successive elections for the presidency, lower house of parliament (the Wolesi Jirga), and provincial councils have been held in this country since 2004 despite a traditional political culture with tribal allegiances and rival forms of regional authority and elite patronage rooted in semifeudalism, poor communications and transportation infrastructure over a vast territory, low levels of literacy and schooling (with the 2013 UNDP Human Development Index ranking Afghanistan 175th lowest out of 186 countries worldwide, and second from the bottom in terms of the Gender Inequality Index), a murky politics characterized by endemic corruption and violence, and weakly institutionalized political parties, among peoples who have lived under violent conflict for decades. In 2009, widespread complaints about ballot stuffing led the Independent Election Commission to organize a complete recount. The second round of the 2014 Presidential elections saw more than 150 reported incidents of violence on polling day and, in the aftermath, the leading presidential contender, Abdullah Abdullah, demanded that the independent electoral commission should cease the count midway through due to alleged irregularities, an event followed by mass protests, the resignation of the chief commissioner, and delays in announcing the results. The results of the audit suggest that perhaps as many as 2 million fraudulent votes were cast out of 8 million in total. In the end, a brokered power-sharing agreement resolved the outcome but this also violated the spirit of the election. A detailed study of the Afghan experience over successive elections since 2004 concluded that the process strengthened the power of ruling elites but did little to develop representative democracy.[1]

To understand these types of problems, this chapter describes modernization theories of democratization, considers which structural factors from the previous research literature are plausible candidates to explain electoral integrity and malpractice, and then analyzes the cross-national evidence and selected cases. This chapter therefore focuses upon determining the direct impact, if any, of these structural constraints on electoral integrity (seen schematically as H[1] in Figure 1.3), while subsequent parts of the book examine any indirect impacts. The following chapters build upon this analysis by considering the role of international engagement and institutional designs.

I: Modernization Theories

The earliest approach to understanding successful transitions from autocracy and processes of democratization is rooted in theories of developmental studies, political economy, and political sociology, exemplified by the long tradition established by Seymour Martin Lipset in the mid-twentieth century.[2] The so-called Lipset thesis argues that democracies (and, by extension, levels of electoral integrity) flourish best in industrialized and postindustrial societies characterized by conditions of widespread literacy and education, with a substantial affluent professional middle class and a pluralistic range of civic associations serving as a buffer between citizens and the state.[3] The original claim by Lipset specified simply that: *"The more well-to-do a nation, the greater the chances that it will sustain democracy."*[4] Development consolidates democracy, Lipset theorized, by expanding access to information derived from literacy, schooling and the mass media, broadening the size of the middle classes, reducing the extremes of rural poverty, facilitating intermediary organizations such as labor unions, professional associations, and voluntary organizations, and promoting the cultural values of legitimacy, moderation, and social tolerance. The shift from agrarian to industrial capitalist production weakened the feudal grip of the traditional landed estates. Newly unionized urban workers and the middle class professional groups demanded access to the voting franchise and mobilized around rival parties reflecting their interests. Lipset emphasized that extreme social inequality maintained oligarchy or tyranny, but more egalitarian conditions, and in particular the swollen ranks of the middle classes, facilitated mass political participation and moderate political parties: *"Only in a wealthy society in which relatively few citizens lived in real poverty could a situation exist in which the mass of the population could intelligently participate in politics and could develop the self-restraint necessary to avoid succumbing to the appeals of irresponsible demagogues."*[5] During the 1970s, Dankwart Rustow reinforced the Lipset argument by claiming that the transition to democracy could be attributed to a predictable series of social changes accompanying economic development and societal modernization, as predicted by such indicators as per capita energy consumption, literacy, school enrollments, urbanization, life expectancy, infant mortality, the size of the industrial workforce, newspaper circulation, and radio and television ownership.[6]

The social determinism implicit in the more mechanical versions of modernization theories has been subject to considerable criticism, especially the neglect of the role of actors, institutions, social movements, and key historical events contributing to overturning dictatorships and founding democracies. After all, middle-income nations such as Russia, Venezuela, and Malaysia have experienced major problems with democracy and elections, which are not confined by any means to the world's poorest societies. Nevertheless, following in Lipset's footsteps, in subsequent decades the relationship between wealth and democracy has been subject to rigorous empirical inquiry. For more than half a century the association has withstood repeated empirical tests under a variety of different conditions, using cross-sectional and time-series data with a large sample of countries and years, and with increasingly sophisticated econometric models, as well as in many historical accounts of political developments occurring within particular nation states. Many studies have reported that wealth is associated with the standard indicators of democratization, although the precise estimates of effects are sensitive to each study's choice of time period, the selection of control variables specified in causal models, and the basic measurement of both democracy and economic growth.[7] Thus the Lipset hypothesis has been confirmed by successive studies conducted by Jackman (1973), Bollen (1979, 1983), Bollen and Jackman (1985), Brunk, Caldeira and Lewis-Beck (1987), Buckhart and Lewis-Beck (1994), Vanhanen (1997), Barro (1999), among others, as well as more recent work when Lipset revisited the original thesis (1993, 2004).[8] The major challenge to the conventional wisdom has arisen from the work of Adam Przeworski, Michael Alvarez, José Antonio Cheibub, and Fernando Limongi, who argue that greater economic development does not *cause* the downfall of autocracies and the initial steps toward democratization (which arise from multiple unknown causes, such as the death of a dictator, splits in the ruling party, or external invasion), although, after passing a certain threshold level, a comfortable level of economic development does *consolidate* democratic institutions and thereby serve as a buffer, preventing reversions to autocracy.[9]

In previous work I have used time-series cross-national data during the third wave era since the early 1970s and compared the impact of wealth (log per capita GDP) on four alternative measures of democratization (by Freedom House, Polity IV, Vanhanen and Przeworski et al./Cheibub and Gandhi), to double-check the robustness of the relationship, in well-specified models incorporating many structural controls.[10] The evidence confirmed that wealth was significantly positively associated with each measure of democracy, showing a robust relationship, as many previous studies have reported. The underlying reasons for this relationship continue to be debated but separate models testing the effects of education and literacy on democratization displayed a particularly strong link, as Barro highlighted earlier, suggesting that societies that invest in human capital are more likely to sustain democratic regimes.[11] Moreover, besides development, my earlier study concluded that many additional structural fixed conditions proved significant: "*Democracy was usually more probable in countries which shared an ex-British colonial legacy, in regions which had seen the spread of democracy, in states outside the Middle East, in ethnically homogeneous societies, and in countries with smaller populations...the models explained between half and two-thirds of the variance across the comparison, suggesting a relatively good fit, although...many outlier cases can be found among both rich autocracies and poor democracies.*"[12]

Structural Conditions and Electoral Integrity

Do similar structural conditions determine where elections succeed and fail? Since elections are a necessary condition for democratization, although far from sufficient, similar patterns can be expected to be observed. The modernization thesis can therefore be plausibly extended for our purposes to generate a series of testable propositions about the socioeconomic conditions thought most favorable to strengthening electoral integrity. Studies of fixed constraints typically focus on wealth and income (and thus indicators of economic growth, human development, and social inequality), as well as the role of physical geography (the size and location of a state), inherited colonial legacies, patterns of ethnic heterogeneity, deep-seated cultural attitudes and values, and the distribution of natural resources. Conditions in each society are regarded from the modernization perspective as largely static, or else as phenomena like human development and political culture, which are believed to evolve at a glacial pace over successive decades or even centuries.

As discussed in the opening chapter, contemporary multiparty elections, once largely the preserve of industrialized Western nations, have spread worldwide. They are attempted under many challenging social conditions today, including in extremely poor and divided developing societies, in fragile states, and in transitional or hybrid regimes lacking both the military control used to maintain order by fully authoritarian states, on the one hand, and the shared cultural values and accumulated experience of elections found in consolidated democracies, on the other. Since 2000, all but eleven countries worldwide have held national elections, and only a handful of states, such as Saudi Arabia, Qatar, and Oman, have never held direct parliamentary elections.[13] The number of popular referendums has also become more common to determine constitutional issues and state secession, such as in Montenegro (2006), South Sudan (2011), and Crimea (2014). The growth of decentralized governance has led to more contests for state and local office, and the number of contests has multiplied within the 28 EU member states due to direct elections to the European Parliament since 1979.

Therefore, one plausible theory seeking to explain the distribution of flawed and failed elections around the globe lies in structural or fixed conditions that make contests inherently risky enterprises. Skeptics highlighting the perils of elections can point to an earlier wave of institution building, when European-style parliaments were transplanted to many African societies during the winds-of-change era of decolonization, only to collapse as the military or big men usurped power.[14] As Dahl noted, where the underlying conditions are highly unfavorable, it is improbable that democracy can flourish under any institutional design. By contrast, if the underlying conditions reduce the risks, then democracy is likely to take root under almost any type of constitution.[15]

II: Evidence for the Impact of Structural Conditions on Electoral Integrity

Despite the plausibility of structural explanations, and the extensive body of political economy and sociological literature testing the effects of wealth and security on democratization, by contrast there is surprisingly little systematic evidence available to analyze the impact of structural conditions on the quality of elections. One notable exception is work by Sarah Birch that examined whether a range of sociopolitical conditions heightened risks of electoral malpractice, including levels of economic development, trade dependence, foreign direct investment, corruption, social inequality, and urbanization.[16] Each of these factors can be regarded as "structural" constraints on elections, since it is difficult to alter many of these conditions in the medium to short term, if at all; for example, countries cannot reinvent their histories, or easily avoid conflict and refugees flowing across their borders from neighboring states, although obviously states attempt to accelerate economic growth and human development, with greater or lesser degrees of success. Fully specified models should therefore control for a range of structural conditions. Such accounts are most powerful in explaining long-term trajectories of political development and the general probabilities of democratization worldwide. They are less helpful in accounting for the specific timing and particular type of short- or medium-term fluctuations in electoral integrity. The policy implications of fixed conditions for the international community are largely the need to be strategic in prioritizing the choice of country interventions, since high risks are associated with attempts to strengthen electoral integrity in the most challenging environments. A wide range of indicators has been developed by scholars, and these are consolidated for analysis in the cross-national time-series data sets assembled and distributed by the Quality of Government Institute based at the University of Gothenburg in Sweden.[17]

When analyzing the empirical evidence, it is important to consider conventional assumptions about the direction of causality in complex interactive processes. Ethnic heterogeneity, and population divisions by religious, linguistic, racial, and nationalist identities, for instance, are conventionally treated by researchers as enduring or "fixed" characteristics of societies. Yet constructivist accounts emphasize that the political salience and meaning of latent ethnic identities can be either heightened or moderated by the rhetorical appeals of party leaders – and thus by the institutional incentives to mobilize either ethnic or intercommunal appeals arising from the electoral rules.[18] The physical boundaries of the nation state are regarded from the structural perspective as largely stable, even though geographic distances for trade and access to Western markets are shrunk by developments in transportation, communications, and modern technologies. Similarly, the mapped boundary lines of the nation state are occasionally reshaped by secession and conquest, as in Eastern Ukraine, as well as by enlargement of regional associations, such as Romania (2007) and Croatia (2013) joining the European Union, and by broader processes of globalization and cosmopolitan communications, discussed in the next chapter.[19] Similarly access to the production of natural resources such as oil and natural gas have been transformed by technological developments, such as how hydraulic fracking has facilitated exploitation of new areas of hydrocarbons, while regulatory policies can either mitigate or exacerbate the impact of state capture of natural resources. Factors such as a culture of corruption can also be regarded as the effect of lack of electoral accountability, as much as a cause of why contests fail.

Despite these complex issues of interpretation, and the limits of the available longitudinal evidence, the effect of several long-term conditions that are genuinely independent of electoral integrity within the time-span of a specific contest – including the impact of physical geography, colonial legacies, and population size – are examined in this chapter. These conditions are properly specified as fixed in the models: holding elections in some of the world's largest countries, India, Nigeria, or Indonesia, for example, may plausibly provide more serious logistical and organizational challenges compared with contests in, say, Guatemala or Jamaica. Nevertheless, national elections per se cannot affect a country's physical geography or population size in the short term (although even here, a few notable exceptions exist, since previous secession referendums, such as in Bangladesh, Sudan and Crimea, can determine a country's contemporary national borders and electorate in subsequent contests).

Economic and Human Development

The core Lipset thesis concerns the role of economic development (conventionally monitored by each society's per capita GDP), which is closely associated with notions of societal modernization, including the spread of industrialization, urbanization, and education, as well as the related role of the broader notion of human development (as measured by UNDP, where longevity and education are added to the measure of per capita GDP). While it is commonly assumed that higher quality elections occur in richer nations, in fact the empirical evidence supporting this claim is not well established. In one of the most systematic comparative analysis, Birch used multivariate models to test the impact of a series of structural variables on electoral malpractice. The study found that GDP growth was not significantly correlated with many measures of election quality (by Freedom House, the Economist Intelligence Unit, and Kelley's Quality of Elections Dataset). Moreover, Birch also reported that growth was significantly related to her Index of Electoral Malpractices, but in a *positive* direction (suggesting that higher growth led to worse quality elections), for reasons that remain unclear.[20] The study did not test the direct effects of levels of economic development on malpractice, however, to avoid problems of multicollinearity in her models.[21] Any interpretation of the relationship also needs to consider using time lags to partially overcome possible issues of endogeneity. Chauvet and Collier reversed the relationship to test the impact of the frequency of holding elections (of any quality) on economic policies in developing countries. They reasoned that regular contests strengthened the incentive for governing parties to improve their economic performance, in order to win votes and retain office. The study reported that the more frequently elections are held, the better the policies, as measured by the World Bank Country Policy and Institutional Assessments.[22]

To start to describe the comparative evidence for ninety-six societies without any controls, Figure 3.1 shows the observed correlation between contemporary levels of electoral integrity measured by the summary PEI-2.8 Index and levels of economic development lagged by five years (to reduce the danger of endogeneity, since the quality of elections could affect income), measured by per capita GDP (in purchasing power parity) in 2009 from the World Development Indicators. The bivariate correlation without controls displays a significant and strong relationship (R = 0.583, P = 0.00); as expected affluent postindustrial societies, such as Norway, the Netherlands and Austria, also have the highest quality elections, according to the overall PEI-2.8 Index. By contrast, some of the poorest societies under comparison had the worst electoral performance, including Cambodia, Djibouti, and the Democratic Republic of Congo. Moreover, the results proved consistent when the subcomponents of the PEI survey were broken down further, revealing that wealth was significantly correlated (at the conventional 0.05 level) with all the indicators, with the exception of district boundaries (see Table 3.1).

Nevertheless, the best fit line displayed in Figure 3.1 is not linear but quadratic, *suggesting that a stepped shift occurs in the integrity of elections once a certain minimum level of moderate economic development is reached.* The estimate suggests that integrity is most likely once most countries achieve a per capita income of roughly $15,000 or more (in purchasing power parity and constant 2005 dollars). Thus, it can also be observed that many contests which experts rated positively as "high integrity" (ranked in the top third of the PEI Index) showed a wide scatter across the top oval. Therefore, contests in many middle-income nations scored well, such as Chile, Argentina, and Lithuania, all rated by experts as similar or better than the quality of elections in the United States. At the same time another cluster of poorer countries can be observed

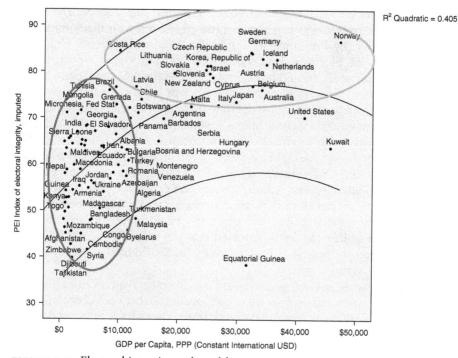

FIGURE 3.1. Electoral integrity and wealth.

Sources: PEI Index Electoral Integrity Project. 2014. *The expert survey of Perceptions of Electoral Integrity (PEI-2.8); Per capita GDP in purchasing power parity in 2009 from the World Development Indicators included in the Quality of Government Cross-National Dataset,* http://www.qog.pol.gu.se/data/.

with per capita income below $15,000 (in the bottom oval) and in this category societies varied sharply in the quality of their elections, ranging from low income Tajikistan and Djibouti, with flawed contests, compared with poor countries such as Mali, Bhutan, and Nepal, which had elections rated more highly by experts. The observational pattern suggests that there is a link – as expected, richer nations tend to have better quality elections – but the relationship is a stepped shift once a level of minimal level of wealth is reached in a society, and several exceptions such as Equatorial Guinea and Kuwait show that the links are far from deterministic. In this regard, the observed relationship is closer to the ACLP version of modernization theory rather than the classic Lipset thesis.[23] In subsequent OLS multivariate regression analysis, per capita GDP is transformed by estimating the square root in order to model the stepped shift more accurately.

To test the Lipset thesis further, the UNDP's Human Development Index arguably provides a superior measure of societal modernization, by combining wealth, longevity, and education. Reflecting Amartya Sen's notion of human

TABLE 3.1. *The PEI Index and its components correlated with economic indices*

	GDP per capita, PPP (constant international USD)	Human Development Index	Total natural resource rents (% of GDP)	Corruption Perceptions Index
PEI Index of electoral integrity	.594**	.662**	−.434**	.739**
Electoral laws index	.274**	.290**	−.387**	.463**
Electoral procedures index	.536**	.649**	−.417**	.676**
Voting district boundaries index	.228*	.384**	−.260*	.315**
Voter registration index	.595**	.640**	−.359**	.603**
Party & candidate registration	.482**	.526**	−.417**	.610**
Media coverage index	.311**	.280**	−.325**	.456**
Campaign finance index	.552**	.595**	−.368**	.628**
Voting process index	.528**	.656**	−.317**	.599**
Vote count index	.501**	.649**	−.488**	.631**
Results index	.556**	.660**	−.330**	.629**
Electoral authorities index	.504**	.571**	−.466**	.700**

Notes: **Correlation is significant at the 0.01 level (2-tailed). *Correlation is significant at the 0.05 level (2-tailed). N = 95 to 97 countries.

Sources: PEI Index and its subcomponents: Electoral Integrity Project. 2014. *The expert survey of Perceptions of Electoral Integrity* (PEI-2.8); CPI from the Quality of Government Cross-National Dataset, http://www.qog.pol.gu.se/data/; Total natural resource rents as % of GDP, 2012, from the World Bank, World Development Indicators.

development, this index monitors the quality of people's lives, not simply the success of the economy.[24] The series of annual UNDP Human Development Reports has convincingly demonstrated that many societies, such as Equatorial Guinea and Iraq, with moderate levels of median income at national level (derived from natural resources) lag behind in relative levels of schooling, longevity, and living conditions.[25] Education, in particular, provides cognitive skills, knowledge, and cultural attitudes that are widely regarded as vital for citizen's informed choices and active participation in civic affairs. The comparison observed in Figure 3.2, without controls, confirms that the Human Development Index is more strongly correlated with the quality of elections than GDP alone, although again contrasts can be observed between low development societies, such as Rwanda and Bhutan, with relatively positive scores in the quality of elections, and Djibouti and Angola, which perform poorly. The cubic line rather than a linear relationship provides the best overall fit,

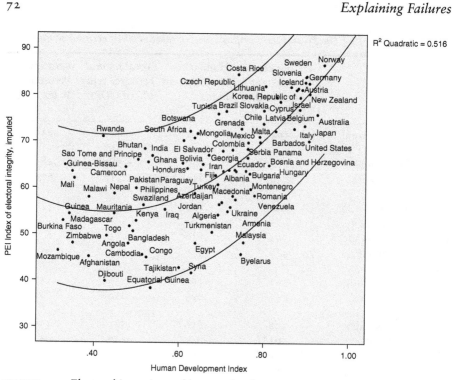

FIGURE 3.2. Electoral integrity and human development.

Sources: PEI Index Electoral Integrity Project. 2014. *The expert survey of Perceptions of Electoral Integrity (PEI-2.8); Human Development Index 2009 (combining income, longevity and education) from the UNDP included in the Quality of Government Cross-National Dataset,* http://www.qog.pol.gu.se/data/.

suggesting a far from straightforward progressive shift. Table 3.1 displays strong and significant correlations across all the eleven subcomponents of the electoral cycle.

Natural Resources and Corruption

There are also a couple of cases that can be observed as clear outliers in the relationship between wealth and electoral integrity – notably oil-rich (but human development poor) Equatorial Guinea. The well-known "resource curse" is another related structural explanation, suggesting that countries with GDP highly dependent upon abundant reserves of nonrenewable mineral resources, such as Kuwaiti oil, DRC gold, or Sierra Leone diamonds, usually produce less diversified and less competitive economies, more income inequality with less investment in social policies building human capital, and heightened danger of state capture and rent-seeking by ruling elites.[26] Lootable natural resources that can be smuggled across borders, such as diamonds, rare minerals, ivory, cocaine, and heroin, make countries particularly vulnerable to criminal cartels,

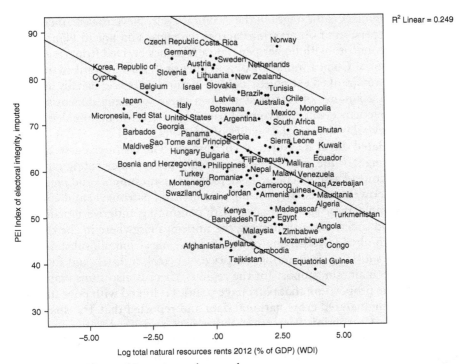

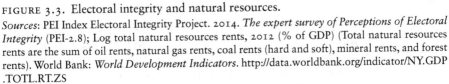

FIGURE 3.3. Electoral integrity and natural resources.

Sources: PEI Index Electoral Integrity Project. 2014. *The expert survey of Perceptions of Electoral Integrity* (PEI-2.8); Log total natural resources rents, 2012 (% of GDP) (Total natural resources rents are the sum of oil rents, natural gas rents, coal rents (hard and soft), mineral rents, and forest rents). World Bank: *World Development Indicators.* http://data.worldbank.org/indicator/NY.GDP .TOTL.RT.ZS

civil war, insurgency, and rebellion.[27] Assessing the degree to which an economy is dependent upon natural resources is not easy, however, especially the black market trade in illicit goods. To measure the distribution of natural resources, the study draws upon the World Bank's measure of total natural resources rents, 2012 (% of GDP), where these rents are the sum of oil, natural gas, coal, minerals, and forest. Given the unequal distribution of resources across countries, the measure is logged, for a better linear fit. "Rents" are estimated as the difference between the value of production of these resources at world prices and the total costs of production. "Rentier states" are those, like Saudi Arabia, which derive all or a substantial portion of their national revenues from the rent of indigenous resources to external clients.

Figure 3.3, without any prior controls for the wealth of a country, displays a strong negative correlation (R = −.450, P = .000) linking the distribution of natural resources and the PEI Index of electoral integrity. Further analysis in Table 3.1 confirms significant correlations linking resource rents with all of the PEI subindices from stages in the electoral cycle. Nevertheless, there is a substantial dispersion of observations across the regression line in Figure 3.3; for example, countries with higher per capita revenues derived from resources include Equatorial Guinea (ranked worst in integrity), Kuwait (ranked moderate), and Norway (ranked extremely highly). Natural resources usually appear to function in a number of rentier states as a curse for many dimensions of democratic governance, but reservoirs of natural resources in mature democracies do not inevitably depress the quality of elections.

What of related direct measures of corruption? The resource curse can be expected to heighten the risks of electoral malpractice, since ruling elites in rentier states control assets that can be deployed to gain support and maintain their grip on power, particularly through clientelism, patronage, and corruption. For example, in 2014 when faced with continuing antigovernment protests, riots, and social unrest following the uprisings elsewhere in the region, Bahrain, which obtains 90 percent of its state revenues from oil, substantially boosted state subsidies discounting the price of petrol, utilities, and food, in the attempt to maintain support for the regime. There is also some empirical support for the proposition that patronage politics is linked with poor quality elections; Birch analyzed cross-national data and reported that Transparency International's Corruption Perception Index was associated with incidence of electoral malpractice.[28] But care is needed when interpreting the direction of causality in this relationship. Acts such as the abuse of state employees, patronage politics, and vote-buying can clearly serve to undermine electoral integrity, especially where a pervasive culture of kleptocracy undermines public trust and confidence in electoral procedures and authorities. But it could also be argued that by breaking the chain of electoral accountability, so that crooked leaders can no longer be thrown out of office through the ballot box, corruption should be understood as primarily the product, rather than the cause, of poor quality contests. Thus again, it is important to lag the independent measure of corruption, as a partial control for problems of endogeneity in cross-national analysis.

Comparative evidence of the frequency of actual corrupt behavior is notoriously difficult to gather with any reliability, not least because these acts are often illicit and hidden. To monitor perceived corruption, as a close proxy, this chapter draws upon Transparency International's Corruption Perceptions Index (CPI), based on compiling many expert sources, first launched in 1995. There are questions about whether reported corruption perceptions reflect the lived experience and underlying reality of corruption, and whether such perceptions are uniform across cultures.[29] Nevertheless, the CPI is widely used scholars and by the international community, including being incorporated into the World Bank Institute's Good Governance indices.[30] One note of caution is in order. It would be expected that the expert perceptions of electoral integrity would probably closely reflect broader perceptions of corruption – not least because

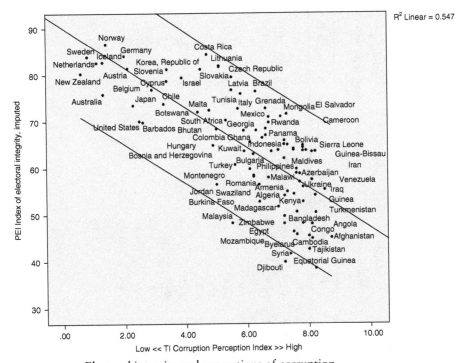

FIGURE 3.4. Electoral integrity and perceptions of corruption.

Sources: PEI Index Electoral Integrity Project. 2014. *The expert survey of Perceptions of Electoral Integrity* (PEI-2.8); *Corruption Perceptions Index 2009 included in the Quality of Government Cross-National Dataset*, http://www.qog.pol.gu.se/data/.

the composite PEI Index includes some related questions on political finance, although the term "corruption" was not used explicitly in the design of the PEI questionnaire (see Table 2.2). As a partial control for endogeneity, the CPI was measured in 2007–11, lagged before the year of the election. Figure 3.4 shows the correlation between the lagged CPI and the PEI Index of electoral integrity, without controls. The observed results confirms the existence of a strong and significant bivariate relationship (R = .726, P = .000). Moreover, the CPI was strongly and significantly linked with all the subcomponents of the PEI with one exception (voting boundaries). Like wealth, the quadratic line provided the best fit, suggesting a stepped shift or "plateau" effect. The simple correlations therefore suggest that perceptions of corruption (which are also strongly linked with the macrolevel distribution of resource rents) are associated with perceptions of electoral integrity.

Several of the observed relationships of the key economic factors can be tested more systematically by examining the multivariate analysis presented in the first model in Table 3.2. The remaining models add successive blocks of

TABLE 3.2. *Structural conditions and electoral integrity*

	Model 1 Economy		Model 2 And geography		Model 3 And ethnicity		Model 4 And colonial legacy		Model 5 And state history	
	B	S.E.	B	S.E.	B	S.E.	B	S.E.	B	S.E.
Economy										
Wealth (Sqrt per capita GDP ppp)	.120***	.019	.110***	.024	.075***	.025	.071**	.026	.023	.027
Natural resources (% GDP)	-1.67***	.546	-1.73***	.546	-1.54***	.544	-1.54**	.546	-.653	.559
Geography										
Population size (000s)			.001	.000	.001	.000	.001	.001	.001	.000
Latitude			3.76	6.01	12.88*	6.013	12.90*	6.42	13.22*	5.83
Area size (sq. km)			.001	.000	.001	.000	.001	.000	.001	.000
Ethnicity										
Linguistic fractionalization					.662	3.999	.583	4.07	3.08	4.03
Religious fractionalization					.047	4.490	-.008	4.84	2.65	4.60
Predominant Muslim society (0/1)					-6.20*	2.62	-5.96*	2.66	-3.14	2.65
Predominant Catholic society(0/1)					3.10	2.40	2.87	2.55	3.33	2.36
Predominant Orthodox society (0/1)					-7.92*	3.29	-7.28*	3.39	-4.76	3.25
Middle East Region (0/1)					-1.57	3.30	-1.85	3.49	3.53	3.79
Colonial legacy										

	(1)	(2)	(3)	(4)	(5)
Previous British colony (0/1)	.777	2.44	-.177	2.36	
Year of independence	-.008	.009	-.003	.009	
State history			.047***	.012	
History of democracy 1972–2010 (FH)			-.070	.085	
History of conflict 1972–2004 (UCDP)					
Constant	55.0	54.4	56.1	71.5	58.3
Adjusted R²	.432	.421	.502	.496	.566

Notes: OLS Regression analysis where the PEI Index is the dependent variable in 96 countries. All models used tolerance tests to check that they were free of problems of multicollinearity. See the technical appendix for more details about the selected indices. ***Correlation is significant at the 0.001 level. **Correlation is significant at the 0.01 level. *Correlation is significant at the 0.05 level.

Sources: PEI Index Electoral Integrity Project. 2014. *The expert survey of Perceptions of Electoral Integrity*, Release 2.8 (PEI-2.8); All other indices from the *Quality of Government Cross-National Dataset*, http://www.qog.pol.gu.se/data/.

factors, excluding any variables that cause problems of multicollinearity. Thus, models did not test for the effects of the UNDP's Human Development Index, since, not surprisingly, this index is strongly intercorrelated with wealth, by definition and construction. The models also excluded the TI subjective measure of perceptions of corruption, since this was so strongly related to per capita GDP and the objective measure of resource rents, generating similar problems of multicollinearity.[31]

The first model tests the effects of wealth (transformed by the square root of GDP per capita in purchasing power parity) and the measure of natural resource rents on the PEI Index in 96 countries. The results in Table 3.2 confirm that both wealth and natural resources were strongly and significantly related to the PEI Index; not surprisingly, *most richer countries had better quality elections, while at the same time resource-rich states usually tended to suffer from worse malpractices.* These two factors alone explained considerable variance in the PEI Index (Adjusted R^2 = .432). We will return to consider the reasons underlying this relationship in the chapter's conclusions.

Geography

Were other structural conditions also important? The physical geography of a country can be expected to matter for processes of democratization and development in several ways, including a state's location close to the equator (and thus vulnerability to tropical diseases and distance from access to global markets), the physical size and terrain of a state (and thus types of agricultural production and distances from the federal government), and the population size.[32] By extension, geographic factors are also plausible underlying conditions that could affect the quality of elections. At the simplest level, immense logistical challenges are raised when organizing elections in large and populous countries; in India, for example, over 814 million citizens were entitled to vote in 930,000 polling stations during the 2014 general elections, involving five million polling personnel and civil police force with nine staged phases of voting from 7 April to 12 May, with ballot boxes carried to and from remote communities in deserts and far-flung mountainous villages. The estimated total cost of the general election campaign was $5 billion, of which around US$577 million for running expenses comes from the public purse.[33] The logistical, financial, and technical challenges shrink to more manageable proportions in smaller states. Nevertheless the importance of the size of nations on electoral integrity needs testing empirically, not least because the role of physical geography as a deep driver of economic growth and development has been strongly debated among political economists, with some rival schools arguing that "institutions rule" in determining economic growth, especially the colonial legacy concerning the institutions of rule of law and private property.[34] Other aspects of physical geography, including the location of a country with neighboring states (and thus patterns of regional diffusion, the influence of hegemonic states, the spill-over effects of conflict, and the permeability to cross-border

communications) are treated in this study more properly as international influences upon elections and therefore discussed in the next chapter.

The results of the empirical analysis presented in Model 2 in Table 3.2 show
that despite the assumed importance of physical geography, contrary to expectations, in fact once models control for wealth and natural resources, *the population size and area size of a country are not significant predictors of electoral
integrity*. After all, despite the immense logistical hurdles that Indian elections
encounter, according to PEI, more severe problems occurred with contests in
the smaller states of neighboring Bangladesh and Pakistan. Debate about the
role of geography for development continues to rage in political economy,
following Easterly and Levine, as several scholars have emphasized that geographic latitude is critical for development as it serves as a proxy for many
other factors, including the type of agricultural crop production, distance to
global trade markets, ecological threats, vulnerability to tropical diseases, and
the existence of deep-rooted poverty.[35] The results of the analysis in Table 3.2
Models 2–4 suggest that for all these reasons, *the latitude of a state's location
also plays a role in increasing the dangers of electoral malpractice occurring in
states close to the equator*.

Ethnic Heterogeneity and Religious Cultures
Ethnic heterogeneity is widely regarded as another condition that heightens
the risks of failed elections – and indeed failed states and failed economies.[36]
Deeply divided societies with a high level of ethnic fractionalization among distinct religious, linguistic, nationalistic, or racial communities are also believed
to be most vulnerable to armed internal conflict.[37] Multiethnic societies are
widely assumed to face particularly serious challenges in holding democratic
elections, maintaining political stability, and accommodating rival communities. Hence, Mansfield and Snyder argue that holding early elections as part
of any peace-settlement in poor and conflict-ridden states can exacerbate tensions, by generating populist leaders seeking to heighten latent ethnic identities
to maximize their popular support.[38] In this view, it is important to follow a
sequential process in this context, first reconstructing the core functions of
the state to maintain security and manage the delivery of basic public services
before subsequently moving toward elections. Tensions among different ethnic communities are generally thought to undermine government legitimacy,
social tolerance, and interpersonal trust, all of which are believed to lubri-
cate the give-and-take of political bargaining and compromise that character-
ize democratic processes. In the worst cases, ethnic conflict may lead toward
deep-rooted and prolonged civil wars, and occasional cases of outright state failure, as exemplified by developments in Bosnia-Herzegovina, Rwanda, Sudan,
Azerbaijan, Chechnya, and Sri Lanka.[39] Ethnic heterogeneity is monitored in
the third model using Alesina et al.'s estimate of linguistic and religious fractionalization, since these types of social cleavages differ across world regions.[40]

It should be noted that although this data source provides comprehensive estimates for countries worldwide, it only gives an indication of the homogeneity or heterogeneity of a society using relatively crude measures, without attempting to assess the political salience and cultural meaning of these cleavages. The cross-national measurement of ethnic divisions remains a tricky and complex issue. For example, in the UK, Welsh nationalism is strongly tied to linguistic cultural identities, with roughly one-fifth of the population able to speak Welsh, whereas north of the border, the issue of Gaelic is less salient for feelings of Scottish nationalism, except on the islands. By contrast, Northern Ireland is divided between Protestants and Catholics, and by social class and income, not by language. Thus, the Alesina et al. measures, drawn from incomplete sources, capture only a very imperfect and limited dimension of all these types of identity politics in the British Isles.

In addition, debate continues about the importance of the predominant religious culture in a society, in particular whether the robustness of authoritarianism (and thus the failure of electoral integrity) to take root throughout most states in the Middle East, despite the Arab Uprising, can be attributed primarily to the rentier states and sharp social inequalities generated by oil-dependent economies in this region, or whether this is a broader phenomenon that can be attributed to deep-rooted cultural values dividing the Muslim world and the West.[41] The well-known "clash" thesis developed by Samuel Huntington also emphasized the enduring legacy of religious cultures on democratic values and beliefs throughout the world, including historical divisions within Europe into Protestant, Catholic, Muslim, and Orthodox states.[42] The role of predominant religious cultures is expected to leave a deep and enduring imprint on the democratic, economic, and social values that are widespread in contemporary societies, even though faith and active religious practices have faded in affluent secular societies.[43] Thus, even today Protestant Sweden and Catholic Italy are expected to show divergent values on many basic moral tenets, such as the value of marriage and the family, the role of the state, or willingness to obey the law and pay taxes voluntarily, even though regular churchgoing has been abandoned in the Nordic states and both societies share many similar characteristics as affluent postindustrial economies and European Union member states.

Accordingly, the third model entered the predominant religious tradition of each state, where Protestantism is treated as the default category. Finally, the Middle East is also entered as a dummy variable, to see if there is any residual impact from Arab states once controlling for Muslim cultures and the distribution of natural resources. The results in Model 3 in Table 3.2 show that once wealth and natural resources are controlled for, contrary to expectations, *linguistic and religious ethnic heterogeneity play insignificant roles as predictors of the PEI Index.* Societies can be relatively homogeneous or they can be divided into many ethnic communities, but the model suggests that this, in itself, based on these admittedly imperfect estimates, does not predict when elections fail. Nevertheless, the type of predominant faith does seem to leave a cultural imprint: *states in Eastern Europe with an Orthodox religious heritage, and also predominately Muslim societies, perform significantly worse in the quality of their elections than Protestant societies*, even after controlling for natural resources and levels of economic development. Moreover, it appears that, contrary to Stepan and Robertson,[44] it is a predominantly Muslim heritage, more than being located in the Middle East and North Africa, that has this effect.

Colonial Legacies

The historical imprint left from colonial legacies can also be expected to prove important for development and democratization, and by extension for electoral integrity as well.[45] An association between the past type of colonial rule and contemporary patterns of democracy has been noted by several observers; for example, Clague, Gleason, and Knack report that lasting democracies (characterized by contestation for government office) are most likely to emerge and persist among poor nation states in ex-British colonies, even controlling for levels of economic development, ethnic diversity, and the size of the population.[46] Under British rule, they suggest, colonies such as Canada, Australia, and India gained experience with electoral, legislative and judicial institutions, in contrast with countries under French or Spanish rule. Arguing along similar lines, Lipset, and Lakin also suggest that what mattered in ex-colonial states was whether the previous occupying power was itself democratic.[47] Settlers in the British colonies, they argue, inherited a pluralist and individualist culture, and legislative institutions of self-government, which would prove critical to the development of democracy, notably in the United States, Canada, India, and New Zealand. By contrast, colonists in Latin America were strongly influenced by the Spanish and Portuguese culture, with a more centrally controlled, hierarchical and paternalistic form of rule, at a time when the Spanish monarchy had few institutionalized checks on their power.

To examine the path-dependent role of the type of colonial legacies on contemporary patterns of electoral integrity, countries are coded for whether they were ex-British colonies or not. The year of national independence is also examined, on the grounds that longer experience of sovereignty is likely to consolidate institutions such as electoral systems, political parties, parliaments, and the courts over successive decades, whereas countries which have experienced more recent decolonization, such as Georgia's and Ukraine's independence from the USSR, and Timor-Leste's independence from Indonesia, as likely to have more fragile institutions. Thus, Model 4 in Table 3.2 adds colonial histories to the structural conditions already considered. Although there are many reasons to assume that these historical conditions should matter, in fact the results suggest that, contrary to expectations, *neither a British colonial legacy nor the year of independence proved a significant predictor of the quality of elections*.

State Histories: Fragile States and Democratic Stock

Finally, path-dependent accounts also emphasize that the historical traditions of a state will leave an enduring mark in other ways beyond colonial legacies. In particular, elections held in fragile states and deeply divided societies emerging from conflict are regarded as at particular risk of failure. Since the early 1990s, during the post–Cold War era, elections have become a standard part of the international community's peace-building blueprint.[48] It is widely hoped that elections will facilitate the emergence of democratic governments with popular legitimacy, and will encourage political parties to channel grievances through conventional political channels rather than armed conflict, and thus bring durable stability to deeply divided societies with a long history of bloodshed. Hence, UN peace-building missions assisted with organizing transitional elections in Cambodia, Timor-Leste, Burundi, Sri Lanka, Sierra Leone, DRC, Nepal, Liberia, and Sudan.[49] In the most positive cases, elections do appear to have contributed toward durable peace settlements and the establishment of legitimate and stable governments, such as in Mozambique, El Salvador, and Croatia.[50] Elsewhere, the efforts of the international community to hold elections have often proved less effective, however, and states have continued to struggle to contain violence.[51] This problem is exemplified by continuing unrest in the Central Africa Republic, the Democratic Republic of Congo, and Afghanistan, the three most fragile states ranked worldwide by the Center for Systemic Peace in 2013.[52] Renewed ethnic conflict that broke out in Iraq in 2014, despite national elections in 2005 and 2010, can now be added to this list.

Moreover, scholars warn that instead of building sustainable peace, elections attempted prematurely during regime transitions are likely to backfire.[53] Where party competition remains poorly institutionalized, Mansfield and Snyder argue that elections provide incentives for leaders to use ethnic and nationalist appeals when attempting to mobilize supporters and thereby gain power, indirectly intensifying the risks of intercommunal conflict. Instead of rushing into early elections, the authors recommend that a sequential process should be followed by peace-building missions – where the most urgent priorities are to establish rule of law and security, effective public sector services, and public administration reforms – before subsequently seeking to hold competitive and democratic elections.[54] For all these reasons, states that have experienced recent conflict are likely to have elections that are at highest risk of further bloodshed. By contrast, path-dependent accounts emphasize that states that have consolidated democratic institutions over an extended period of time will have accumulated a deep reservoir of democratic culture, including the values of trust and tolerance, which makes them more likely to manage to overcome any specific problems that may arise in a particular contest through peaceful mechanisms, such as the courts, rather than resorting to violence (Figure 3.5).

Accordingly as a final step, Model 5 in Table 3.2 includes a summary measure of each country's previous historical experience or "stock" of democracy

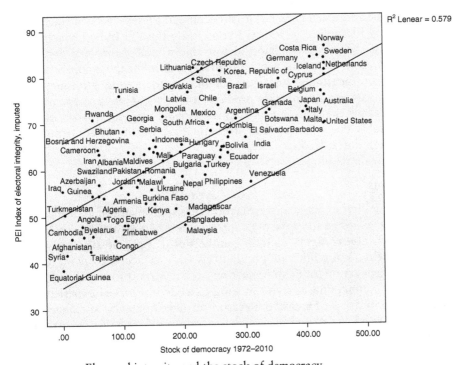

FIGURE 3.5. Electoral integrity and the stock of democracy.

Sources: PEI Index Electoral Integrity Project. 2014. *The expert survey of Perceptions of Electoral Integrity* (PEI-2.8); The stock of democracy is measured by estimating Freedom House's cumulating rating of political rights and civil liberties in each country since the start of the third wave era (from 1972 to 2010).

(the sum of the annual Freedom House annual scores for political rights and civil liberties from the third wave era in the early 1970s to 2010) and also each country's previous experience of civil conflict (the sum annual scores for internal conflict from UNDP-PRIO's dataset from 1972 to 2004). Here the results of the analysis do differ from the earlier models; in particular, *in Model 5 the historical stock of democracy proved to be a strong and significant predictor of contemporary levels of the PEI Index, while the economic indicators dropped out of the explanatory factors.* Thus, if a country had a strong record of political rights and civil liberties throughout the third wave era, contemporary elections were more likely to meet international standards of integrity. The evidence implies that a large part of any electoral success or failure may come not from the particular contest itself but from state institutions, cultural values, and political behaviors that evolve and consolidate over many decades. This is a path-dependency explanation, although at the same time it does leave numerous puzzles open, not least what drives the past success of democratic regimes in some places more than others? I have discussed this issue in detail elsewhere and it cannot be addressed here, not least because at present we lack consistent time-series data to explore historical trends using the PEI Index, which only started to be measured with election held in mid-2012.[55] Moreover, and contrary to expectations from the case-study literature, unlike the democratic record, the summary measure of historical conflict experienced by a country over recent decades was *not* a significant predictor of electoral integrity today. This somewhat weakens the path-dependency argument, suggesting past conflicts will not inevitably doom attempts to strengthen the quality of contemporary contests through the ballot box.

III: Conclusions

In accordance with the classic modernization thesis, problems of electoral malpractice can be expected to prove most intractable where structural conditions produce unfavorable contexts, including in the world's poorest societies, where contests are held among illiterate populations without access to news media, with poor infrastructure for communications and transport for managing polling and campaigning, and in states lacking extended historical experience of democratic contests. An extensive literature in developmental sociology and political economy has debated these claims over more than half a century. The idea that underlying structural conditions greatly heighten the risks of failed elections is also a pervasive assumption in much popular commentary. What does the empirical evidence suggest?

Three Key Findings Emerged From the Empirical Analysis

Firstly, *wealth matters for the quality of elections*; not surprisingly richer economies usually had better quality elections, according to the PEI Index. But *this process was observed to function primarily through a stepped shift rather than a linear development*. Once countries reached a minimal threshold of around $15,000 per capita GDP, then elections commonly tend to meet international standards. Among poorer countries falling below this threshold, however, elections are riskier operations and malpractice often becomes more common. The impact of wealth continued to prove significant predictor of the quality of elections across successive models with a progressively wider range of structural controls.

This finding is hardly surprising given the extensive research literature over the last half century linking wealth and democracy. Exactly why there are these contrasts between rich and poor societies, however, remains to be determined. On the one hand, sociological explanations in line with the classic Lipset argument suggest that more affluent societies expand the moderate middle classes, generate civic associations, labor unions, and professional organizational networks serving as a buffer between citizens and the state, strengthen access to information through literacy, schooling, and mass media, encourage cultural values of trust and tolerance associated with democracy, and reduce the extremes of rich and poor common in agrarian societies. On the other hand, an institutional account, developed further in subsequent chapters, suggests that more affluent nations have the resources – including human, financial and technical capital – that strengthen the capacity of electoral authorities to organize elections meeting international standards. Or possibly both propositions could be at work.

Secondly, *natural resources (measured by per capita oil exports) do usually appear to operate as a "curse" for the quality of election.* This is consistent with the well-documented effects of resources on broader processes of democratization. The pattern was found to persist despite controlling for many other related structural factors, notably countries with a predominantly Muslim religion. Thus, for Arab states, oil seems to trump the type of faith, although it remains to be seen whether this pattern persists once more elections are evaluated from the region. Nevertheless, this remains a probabilistic statement, not an inevitable destiny, which helps to explain the quality of contests in Equatorial Guinea and Turkmenistan more than an obvious outlier such as Norway. The main reasons underlying the relationship, we suggest, is that natural resources and oil-dependent economies often produce rentier states that are run by an affluent few and are characterized by stark socioeconomic inequalities, lack of investment in human capital and basic welfare services, many migrant workers and expatriate visitors lacking citizenship rights, and the patronage politics of crony state capitalism. Yet the contrasts observed between contests held in Kuwait and Equatorial Guinea suggest that nothing is inevitable and even oil-rich authoritarian states can still improve the quality of their elections.

Finally, once studies control for wealth and oil, many of the structural conditions that might be considered plausible candidates to explain the quality of elections around the world, including the physical size of countries, colonial legacies, and ethnic fractionalization, *were not observed to be significant predictors of contemporary patterns of electoral integrity.* The main exceptions to this generalization concern contests in states closer to the equator, and also those in countries with a predominant Orthodox or Muslim culture, were also often riskier propositions. In addition, the stock of democracy (measured by the history of democracy and autocracy in a country during the third wave era since the early to mid-1970s), proved important for the contemporary quality of elections – suggesting that democratic institutions and cultures consolidate over successive experience of electoral contests. Consolidation implies that even where specific irregularities occur – such as Florida – the reservoir of trust and confidence that institutions gradually accumulate over time is sufficient to overcome these problems through regular democratic channels, including resolving disputes through the courts and legal reforms, rather than through resorting to direct actions that destabilize the electoral process, such as violent protests or opposition election boycotts. Thus, the initial elections after the initial downfall of autocracies, and subsequent contests occurring during the early stages of democratization, are indeed risky enterprises as actors come to learn the rules of the game. This danger is perhaps illustrated most vividly in recent years by the experience of Egypt post-Mubarak, with the rise of the Muslim Brotherhood during the transitional multiparty elections, only to be followed by post-revolutionary instability and a backlash producing the popular election of a brutal dictatorship under General Sisi without respect for human rights. Yet from a policymaking perspective – as the cases of Slovenia, the Czech Republic, and Lithuania also illustrate – in some favorable circumstances middle-income societies that have lived for decades under authoritarian one-party rule can still develop effective electoral processes meeting international standards within just over a decade. One possible reason for the success of these cases could be the location of these countries close to the European Union, and thus the engagement of the international community in strengthening democracy in these states, compared with the realpolitik that dominates international aid flowing into Egypt. Developing countries can benefit from receiving technical assistance and international aid when organizing elections – and they face diplomatic pressures when they fail. Thus the next chapter turns to consider the role of the carrots and sticks developed by the international community and how far this has been effective in strengthening standards of electoral integrity.

4

International Forces

In recent decades, a growing body of literature in international relations and comparative politics has focused upon the role of external actors seeking to strengthen regime transitions, processes of democratization, and the quality of elections. This approach seeks to assess the impact arising from the engagement of an alphabet soup of the UN agencies and bureaus, regional intergovernmental organizations, and bilateral donors working on elections in many countries facing extremely challenging structural conditions. These organization deploy a range of "carrots and sticks" designed to build local capacity, to strengthen electoral authorities and processes, to incentivize recalcitrant rulers, to persuade disgruntled losers to accept the outcome without resort to violence, and to monitor that elections meet international norms of electoral integrity. The international perspective is essentially a model about "exporting" democracy, emphasizing the active role of the West (especially the foreign and developmental policies followed by the United States and Europe) over the rest.[1] But at the same time this approach is largely silent about the black box of exactly *what* is imported, how reforms are implemented, and what works.

The 4th March 2013 Kenyan general elections illustrate this process. The 2007 contests had attracted international concern due to the bloody violence that broke out in the immediate aftermath. Estimates suggest that up to 1300 Kenyans were killed and roughly six hundred thousand were displaced during the two-month conflict. The mayhem shocked the world and ultimately brought about a power-sharing agreement on 28 February 2008, brokered by former United Nations Secretary General Kofi Annan. The agreement ended the violence and mandated a formal coalition government, with Mwai Kibaki as President and Raila Odinga as prime minister. Formal indictments for crimes against humanity were later levied at the International Criminal Court against President Uhuru Kenyatta and Deputy President William Ruto. Enormous efforts were devoted to reconciling the ethnic divisions, resulting in a new constitution, agreed in 2010. Nevertheless, there remained widespread fears that the 2013 Kenyan general election would trigger renewed outbreaks of ethnic violence. To safeguard against problems, an Elections Donor Group was created to identify resource priorities and coordinate international donor aid, cochaired by USAID and the UK's Department for International Development (DfID), with contributions to the basket fund managed by the UNDP. The International Foundation for Electoral Systems (IFES) played a leading role in providing technical assistance. Programs were developed for conflict prevention, and civic education to engage women and young people, expanding the capacity and technical infrastructure of the newly formed Independent Election and Boundary Commission (IEBC), training domestic observer groups, technological procurement of voting equipment, and building consultative committees linking political parties and electoral authorities.[2] The European Union, African Union, the Carter Center, and the Commonwealth Secretariat all sent teams of observers to scrutinize the contest. Domestic election observers were also trained and organized, using a Parallel Vote Tabulation exercise. Ushadi provided a crowd-sourcing website platform for citizens to monitor and report any problems they encountered during the election. International monitors concluded that although there were disputes, the outcome was a credible victory for Uhuru Kenyatta, son of independence leader and first Kenyan President Jomo Kenyatta, who was elected as the fourth president of Kenya.[3] The process was largely peaceful, as all parties were careful to avoid a rerun of the 2007 conflict, with Odinga challenging the results through the courts. At the same, several technical irregularities occurred, including new biometric voting technologies that were purchased at considerable expense following an agreement with the Canadian government but which failed on polling day, due to delays in procurement, poor testing, and inadequate technical training of polling staff.[4]

To understand the effects of interventions by the international community, Part I in this chapter summarizes what is known from the previous research literature about each of the main types of international factors, which can be seen as a nested process, including the influence of cosmopolitan communications where information about global norms flows across national borders, the provision of technical assistance and development aid for capacity building, and the role of electoral observer missions. This chapter therefore focuses upon determining the direct impact, if any, of these external forces on electoral integrity (seen schematically as H^2 in Figure 1.3). Part II goes on to consider the challenges of research designed to assess the effects of these types of international factors on electoral integrity. It then examines new cross-national evidence predicting electoral integrity (monitored by PEI-2.5), using multivariate models controlling for economic development and natural resources, established as important structural constraints by the previous chapter. Part III illustrates this process in the case of the 2006 elections in the Democratic Republic of Congo, one of the most challenging contexts, where contests could not have been attempted without international engagement, although in the long term the initiative failed to achieve its ultimate objectives of building democratic legitimacy, stability, and peace. The conclusion summarizes the main lessons from the chapter and considers their implications.

I: Types of International Interventions

What is the role of international forces in shaping patterns of electoral integrity observed around the world? The quality of elections in a country may be expected to be affected by three types of external factors: cosmopolitan communications that diffuse global norms to strengthen international standards of electoral integrity, the provision of technical assistance and development aid to build local capacity, and the deployment of observer monitoring missions to strengthen transparency and accountability. These are related and complimentary types of interventions. They can be understood as nested components in a sequential process, where the diffusion of international standards through global information flows across national borders reflects the most general long-term factor, development aid and technical assistance are medium-term programmatic activities designed for institutional capacity building, while observer missions seeking to strengthen transparency, focused on specific contests, are far narrower in both scope and duration.

Theoretically, there are good reasons to believe that all these external forces may affect both general processes of democratization and, by implication, the quality of elections in any country. Nevertheless, this is an emerging field of study, evaluations of aid effectiveness raise complex methodological challenges, and studies often focus on determining project-level effects rather than larger processes. The debate raises politically sensitive issues. Proponents of democracy promotion argue that through this process Western states help to advance their values and uphold interna7tional principles of human rights, as well as strengthening other desirable developmental goals, such as prosperity, peace, and aid effectiveness.[5] By contrast, a more skeptical realist perspective, which is pervasive in the scholarly literature, suggests that bilateral donors such as the United States selectively advance their own national interests, by strengthening trade relations, strategic military relationships, arms deals, and security alliances, under the smokescreen of promoting democracy.[6] Hence the United States continues to give Egypt an annual aid package of $1.5bn, with the biggest chunk in military aid, despite the fact that the Sisi regime has brutally suppressed dissent, arrested journalists, and disregarded basic human rights, with the stated aim of stabilizing the region – or at least preventing further chaos.

Research assessing the complex effects of development efforts is equally divided, and so far little consensus has emerged in the literature. Hence, some studies of the impact of aid spending on democratization and regime change have argued that foreign assistance increases the likelihood of democratic transitions,[7] while others report that it decreases the likelihood,[8] or has no significant effect.⁹ Similarly, studies have attempted to assess the short-term impact of international observer missions, although scholars continue to disagree about whether the results of this activity have been largely beneficial by deterring abuses and also strengthening electoral integrity in subsequent contests, whether there are displacement effects so that acts of vote buying, ballot stuffing, or fraud move elsewhere to other polling stations without observers or to less visible types of malpractice occurring earlier during the electoral cycle, or whether any effects are conditional upon the use of diplomatic pressures following publication of observer reports.¹⁰ The research literature also commonly stops short of exploring in any depth what policies domestic regimes adopt to improve the quality of elections in response to development aid and technical assistance, nor does it seek to assess which types of domestic electoral reforms prove most successful under different types of structural constraints. For all these reasons, it is important to take a fresh look at the theories and evidence.

The Diffusion of International Standards and Global Information Flows

The broadest international process thought to effect electoral integrity arises from globalization and cosmopolitan communications. Theories of globalization suggest that cultural values flow increasingly rapidly across national borders, so that more cosmopolitan societies learn from each other, positively or negatively, due to the expansion of international markets and the flow of capital, labor, and goods, patterns of human migration, and technological developments in transportation and networked communications.¹¹ The diffusion of norms is thought to be particularly influential among neighboring states sharing similar historical cultures, languages and religions, media sources, strategic alliances, trade, financial and labor markets, peoples, and diplomatic links within each cultural region.¹² Cultural diffusion effects can be understood to occur in an active way, for example where states seek to use mass communications to spread democratic values, or where trade agreements and economic sanctions, or membership of regional organizations, are conditional upon member states' adherence to certain international standards. Or the effects may be expected to arise in a largely passive domino fashion, where information flows over national borders through processes of global communications, so that similar events occur successively through contagion and emulation within a cultural region. The "Color Revolutions" in post-Communist countries are often cited as examples of the diffusion processes, including the November 2003 people-power Rose Revolution that deposed veteran president Eduard Shevardnadze in Georgia, which is thought to have influenced events in Ukraine culminating in the Orange Revolution the following year.¹³ Counteracting negative phenomena include the role of President Putin in his attempts to reassert Russia's influence on the global stage, exemplified by events when Crimea seceded from Ukraine, tightening Russia's economic and military pressures on neighboring states. Similarly, during the Arab uprisings, the chain of events following the Tunisian overthrow of President Ben Ali strongly suggest a regional contagion effect in Libya, Egypt, Bahrain, Syria, Mali, Nigeria, and Iraq, with divergent influences on protest movements and contentious politics, state stability, regime change, and processes of democratization.[14] One reason why Tunisia seems to have moved more successfully toward democracy than many other states in the region may be close relations with France and Italy, as well as through economic cooperation with the European Union.

What may be the effects of the global flows of information on the adoption of international standards of electoral integrity? Previous theories of mass communications have usually assumed strong cultural influences arising from the globalization of the mass media, although scholars disagree normatively about the consequences. One common perspective suggests that "soft power" information flows can exert a positive role for democratization and human rights, especially where multilateral organizations, non-governmental organizations (NGOs), and bilateral actors actively seek to proselytize or spread democratic norms by advocating standards of electoral integrity, endorsing human rights conventions and treaties, requiring aid conditionality in return for democratic reforms, and/or providing targeted development assistance.[15] Alternative traditional theories of cultural imperialism, by contrast, have long claimed that this process is capable of exerting a powerful but negative influence, where the flow of information conveyed by the mass media controlled by major Western powers serves to threaten the traditional mores, habits, and cultural values in the developing world and peripheral societies.[16]

But do the global media actually exert a strong influence on local cultures, for good or ill, as commonly assumed by both proponents and critics? One way to understand this is through the concept of "cosmopolitan communications," which refers to the degree of information flowing across national borders, including how far people interact today within a single global community, or whether these networks remain more localized and parochial.[17] In previous work with Ronald Inglehart, we developed a "firewall model" of cosmopolitan communications that theorized that the effect of this process on changing domestic values, such as the spread of global norms of democracy and electoral integrity, is limited in more parochial societies due to several important barriers.[18] At societal level, the degree of trade integration determines whether countries are incorporated into global markets. The level of media freedom influences the availability of news and information within any state. And economic development shapes investment in modern communication infrastructures and thus penetration of the mass and social media, including how far societies have access to global messages. Each of these factors can be measured at macrolevel to generate a Cosmopolitan Communications Index. This helps to distinguish between the most cosmopolitan and the most parochial societies. Finally, at social–psychological level, local cultural values such as deference to strong authoritarian leaders and traditional elites, learned through traditional socialization processes in the family, school, and local community, may persist despite the foreign values communicated through imported communication flows. Thus, a series of "firewalls," individually and in combination, can serve to protect national cultural diversity from external influences. In practice, all contemporary societies reflect a mix of local and global information sources, but there is also a recognizable continuum stretching from the most isolated and parochial societies at the periphery of communication networks, at one extreme, exemplified by rural communities living in Myanmar (Burma), North Korea, and Mali, to others, such as the urban middle classes living in Switzerland, Luxembourg, and Sweden, which are densely interconnected with information flows from the rest of the world.[19]

The globalization thesis therefore suggest that cross-border information flows can have important effects on the acceptance of international norms of electoral integrity as appropriate standards within each society, although the reach of global communications may prove far more limited in the most parochial communities than in open societies. This thesis can be further examined empirically by measuring the permeability of states to information flows across national borders, through measures of political globalization, such as treaty endorsements, provided by KOF.[20] This allows us to test the empirical evidence for the first proposition in this chapter (H[2.1]), which predicts that *cosmopolitan societies are more likely than parochial societies to meet international standards of electoral integrity.*

Regional Effects

In addition to the information flows arising from access to global information flows, regional effects are also expected to be important in the diffusion of norms of electoral integrity, shaped passively by the dominant cultural norms that are pervasive in different parts of the world, and actively reinforced by the soft power influence of hegemonic states and by membership of regional intergovernmental organizations.[21]

Regional intergovernmental organizations have played an active role in promoting international principals of electoral integrity within their sphere of influence, including the European Union, the Organization of American States (OAS) in Latin America, the Organization for Security and Cooperation in Europe (OSCE), and, to a lesser extent, the African Union after member states endorsed the *African Charter on Democracy, Elections, and Governance.*[22] The impact of regional organizations is exemplified through the enlargement of membership of the European Union to eight Central and Eastern European countries in 2004, including Poland, Lithuania, and the Czech Republic, followed by expansion to Romania and Bulgaria in 2007.[23] States seeking EU membership are required to respect the "principles of liberty, democracy, respect for human rights and fundamental freedoms, and the rule of law" and the Copenhagen European Council set out the specific conditions that applicant states need to meet to qualify for membership. States seeking economic cooperation and trade with the EU have a strong incentive to introduce political reforms to meet these conditions, including improving the quality of electoral processes, although this mechanism weakens once states become members.

By contrast, other regional intergovernmental organizations, including the Association of South East Asian Nations (ASEAN) and the League of Arab States, have traditionally been less active in this area, giving greater priority to promoting free trade, security, and cultural relations. The role of regional bodies can be expected to reflect the predominant legacy of cultural norms found in different parts of the world, the values and interests of hegemonic powers (exemplified by the influence of Russia in Eurasia, China in South East Asia, Saudi Arabia in the Gulf states, and the United States in Central and South America), and the balance of democratic and autocratic regimes that constitute membership within each regional organization. Thus in the European Union, where the majority or plurality of member states is established democracies, then norms of electoral integrity are expected to be strongly reinforced among new member states. By contrast, in regions such as South East Asia, where the majority of ASEAN member states are autocracies (such as Brunei Darussalam, Myanmar, Singapore, Vietnam) or hybrid regimes (such as the Philippines and Indonesia), and where China exerts a strong diplomatic pressures as the predominant economic and military power, then no positive regional effects on electoral integrity are expected.

To test whether regional cultural norms influence the quality of elections, models can analyze empirical evidence for the second proposition ($H^{2.2}$), namely that *mean levels of electoral integrity within a world region will influence levels of electoral integrity within a country located in the region.*

Technical Assistance and Development Aid

The international community has invested growing resources in strengthening democratic governance, which has come to be understood as a vital component of human development.[24] This includes work by multilateral organizations including the United Nations, the United Nations Development Programme, and the Bretton Woods institutions, all of which have become increasingly active during the post–Cold War era in expanding electoral institutional capacity, exemplified by programs designed to support professional, impartial, and autonomous EMBs.[25] During this period, many bilateral donors in advanced industrialized countries have also channeled increasing resources into the promotion of democracy, "good governance," and human rights, for intrinsic reasons and on the instrumental grounds that an effective state is an essential partner for delivering development and reducing poverty. Thus, ministries of development have expanded programs in this area, including Norway's NORAD, Canada's CIDA, and USAID in America.[26] For example, in the decade since 1997, DfID more than tripled its financial resources for governance programs, from £85 million to £322 million.[27] It is also estimated that in recent years USAID has devoted around $2.5bn per year to strengthening democratic governance.[28] A recent report by Freedom House comparing ten democratic

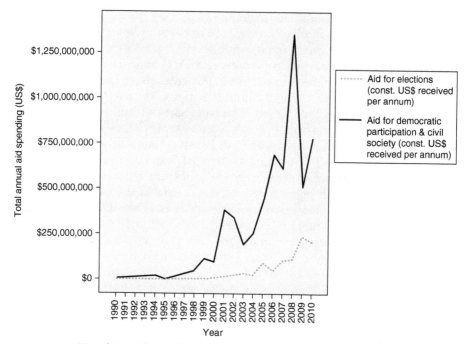

FIGURE 4.1. Trends in aid spending.
Source: AidData 3.0.

states concluded that nearly all have a systematic program of electoral support, whether through observation missions, assistance to electoral bodies, training and knowledge sharing, or condemnations of vote fraud. There is a near universal consensus that governments not chosen through honest and fair ballots are illegitimate. At the same time, the report noted that trade policies and strategic interests often trump human rights, for example in dealings with China.[29] AidData has compiled the most comprehensive and detailed estimates of aid spending (in constant US$) from a wide range of donor nations and multilateral organizations. Figure 4.1 shows how aid spending on both election programs and democratic participation expanded dramatically from 2000–10, with aid for all democratic participation programs peaking at US$1.25bn in 2008.

Many international Inter-governmental Organizations (IGOs) and NGOs also play leading advocacy roles promoting democratic values, human rights, and the quality of elections, and offering technical assistance and funding support in this area, exemplified by International IDEA, the Inter-Parliamentary Union, IFES (formerly the International Foundation for Election Systems), Human Rights Watch, the Open Society Institute, Amnesty International, Reporters without Borders, and Freedom House.[30] Networks of electoral observers are also linked across countries through organizations such as the Asian Network of Free Elections (ANFREL), the Global Network for Domestic

Electoral Monitors (GNDEM), and the Arab Election Watch.[31] Through the provision of technical assistance and aid, NGOs typically seek to strengthen the capacity of electoral authorities to hold contests meeting international standards, as well as sharing professional knowledge among officials through activities such as online networks, local workshops and international conferences, training manuals, professional guidelines, and providing expert consultants. The range of activities is exemplified by the ACE project Electoral Knowledge Network, the Quota Project, the iKNOW Politics network, the Global Elections Organization (GEO) annual conference, the Association of European Electoral Officials (ACEEEO), the Electoral Institute for Sustainable Democracy in Africa (EISA), and the BRIDGE training workshops for electoral administrators.[32] As one IFES guide emphasizes: *"Electoral management is a complex and large-scale set of operations. It involves a multitude of activities and sub-activities, complicated scheduling, training, employment and deployment of large masses of workers, simultaneous use of resources, logistical means and organizational assets and intricate monitoring of multiple activities. Further complexities arise with time-bound activities that must strictly comply with existing electoral legislation, and are often subjected to rigorous external scrutiny. In addition to the above, electoral management also spans multiple and diverse fields of operation: human resources, office administration, nationwide logistical operations, delivery of professional training to thousands of electoral officers, financial control, procuring enormous quantities of electoral materials and supplies, writing regulations, enacting legal reform, registering voters, monitoring political campaigns, developing voting and counting procedures, designing and implementing civic and voter education campaigns, liaising with stakeholders, dealing with security, adjudicating electoral disputes and much more."*[33]

The investment in all these processes can be substantial. For example, the $190 million price tag for the 2004 Afghan elections was financed completely by foreign donors, as was the $48 million spent on the 2004–5 Haitian elections.[34] Elections in developing countries routinely receive technical assistance from a range of agencies and bilateral donors in the international community. The strengths and weaknesses of technical assistance for elections are illustrated by the activities of the UNDP. The UNDP has been the largest provider of electoral assistance within the United Nations system. During the last two decades, UNDP has provided electoral assistance to more than a hundred member states, typically through strengthening electoral administration capacity, fostering inclusive participation for women, youth, and other underrepresented groups, and coordinating donor support for electoral assistance.[35] This program is part of the larger UNDP democratic governance practice. In total, in 2012 around US$1.2bn (one quarter of the UNDP's annual budget) was invested by UNDP in a wide variety of democratic governance programs in more than 170 countries.[36] The primary activities have sought to foster inclusive forms of participation, to strengthen civil society associations and the independence of the news media, to build state capacity through public administration reforms, to improve the transparency, accountability, and efficiency of the executive branch at national and sub-national levels, to strengthen the power of elected legislatures, to reinforce rule of law and access to justice through the judiciary, to develop the capacity of local communities to determine their own lives through decentralized governance, to monitor and protect human rights, as well as to integrate principles of gender equality into governance.[37]

As one of the largest organizations working on elections in developing countries, the number of countries assisted by the UNDP rose from 24 in 2004 to 62 in 2011, with the organization collaborating with many partners, such as IFES and International IDEA. UNDP has typically sought to improve the quality of elections through providing assistance for electoral system reform, strengthening electoral administration, building sustainable electoral processes, mobilizing resources, strengthening civic education, supporting electoral dispute resolution mechanisms, expanding the capacity of domestic observer organizations, working with political parties, media strengthening, and encouraging gender equality in elected office. This work is supplemented by many other agencies, exemplified by the Carter Center, OAS, and OSCE, which have given more emphasis to organizing international observer missions, with the aim of deterring abuses and monitoring problems.[38] Both technical assistance and observer missions can play a complementary role, but it is advisable for organizations to differentiate their functions, to avoid potential conflicts of interest if evaluation is undertaken by an administrative agency.

One of the most detailed and thorough independent evaluation of the UNDP's program on electoral systems and processes concluded that the organization was generally most effective at providing technical assistance that strengthened the work of electoral management bodies and helped to meet the large-scale needs of procurement, technology, logistics, security and training, especially in challenging cases of large post-conflict contests such as in Afghanistan, Sudan, and the Liberia.[39] The UNDP has the capacity to pool and coordinate donor assistance and to channel a basket of funds into local needs. When invited by the government to assist, the UNDP is a trusted partner that can share global experiences and detailed knowledge of elections gained from a wide range of developing societies. In line with agreed human rights frameworks, the organization has also encouraged more inclusive electoral processes for women, young people, and other marginalized groups, such as by strengthening electoral registration, voter participation, and civic education programs and sharing knowledge about candidate training and the use of gender quotas for elected office. Yet the UNDP evaluation concluded that the organization has been less effective in promoting the normative values of free and fair contests, especially where local UNDP country offices regard their job as primarily supporting state capacity rather than promoting and upholding international standards.[40]

It remains difficult to know how far these lessons can be extended to other intergovernmental organizations and bilateral developmental agencies, however, and illustrative case studies of success and failure are often "cherry-picked" by both proponents and critics in debates about the effectiveness of democracy aid. To assess the evidence more systematically, using estimates provided by AidData, we can test the third proposition (H[2.3]), namely that *contemporary levels of electoral integrity will be affected by the historical stock of election aid received by developing countries.*[41] Aid spending can be analyzed for programs on elections (including for EMBs and processes, election observation, and voter education) and for the broader category of democratic participation and civil society. Since elections are only part of the state institutions that need to be strengthened in regime transitions and the consolidation of democracy, related programs may also be expected to also improve the quality of elections, for example by strengthening political parties and civil society organizations, building the capacity of the courts and legislatures, and anti-corruption and public administration reforms. Controlling for other factors, the fourth related proposition (H[2.4]) therefore suggests that *contemporary electoral integrity will be affected by the historical stock of aid spending for democratic participation and civil society in a country.* The simplest assumption is that the greater the past investment of technical aid and assistance in a country, the better the quality of contemporary contests. Nevertheless, it should be emphasized that cross-national comparative evidence provides a strictly limited test of this claim, as potential problems of endogeneity arise in interpreting this relationship; countries with worse records of democratic elections may well be prioritized by international agencies to receive more aid. In addition, many other factors drive priorities for international aid, notably the immense spending by USAID and other bilateral donors and multilateral agencies on elections following conflicts in Iraq, Afghanistan, Sudan, and the Democratic Republic of Congo.

Observer Monitoring Missions

In addition to the general effects of globalization and the provision of technical assistance, during the post–Cold War era it has become increasingly common for many international organizations to dispatch observer missions to monitor campaigns. A growing body of research has sought to evaluate the impact of this activity.[42] Regional organizations and development agencies have aimed to strengthen the transparency of election procedures and to monitor the implementation of internationally agreed standards and principles. Thousands of international and domestic observers have been deployed in election missions, most commonly by regional organizations, including the Carter Center, IFES, the Organization for Security and Cooperation in Europe (OSCE), the African Union, the European Union, and the OAS.[43] Local election watch and media watch NGOs supplement these activities, along with attempts to strengthen the independent media and civil society organizations. The number of electoral observer missions has gradually grown from the start of the third wave era in the mid-1970s, followed by a sharp increase during the late-1980s.[44]

Today, relatively few elections have no international observer missions. Most missions focus upon the campaign period and polling day, with the aim of deterring incumbents from committing electoral irregularities such as ballot box fraud and vote tabulation miscounts, although many organizations recognize the need for long-term observation and also follow-up from one mission to the next.

Researchers have sought to determine the effectiveness of this development, in particular whether the presence of observers in certain electoral districts successfully reduces, or else simply displaces, fraudulent practices within particular countries.[45] Hyde documented the growth of international electoral observer missions during the 1980s and 1990s, arguing that this development reflects the spread of a new global norm.[46] She also sought to test the effects of this activity in a field experiment by comparing Indonesian polling stations with and without observers, where she found that the presence of observers helped to deter fraud within a country.[47] In another major study, Kelley examined the reports of several regional organization that monitored elections from 1975 to 2004.[48] Her research reported that international monitors can improve the quality of elections by making fraud more transparent, reducing incentives to cheat, increasing pressures for clean elections from local actors and the international community, and generating technical assistance designed to improve electoral procedures and processes. The study concluded that for all these reasons, monitoring missions did improve the quality of elections, but nevertheless substantial improvements require repeated missions over a long series of contests. In another related study, Donno argues that when international election observer monitoring is combined with the use of international leverage mechanisms by bilateral donors this is an effective way of promoting democratic norms.[49] She contends that bilateral actors and regional organizations respond to the signals provided by election observer reports and then seek to apply diplomatic pressure, incentives, and diplomatic persuasion to states that violate global norms of electoral integrity.[50] The study found that a consistently poor record of elections, as documented through a series of critical observer reports, serves to legitimate and encourage enforcement by regional organizations and bilateral agencies.[51] Experimental studies have also detected spill-over effects; Ichino and Schuendeln concluded that although fraud declined in polling stations in Ghana where observers were present, malpractice was displaced to other districts around the country.[52] As mentioned earlier, moreover, any effects arising from international monitoring may have weakened during the last decade, as the picture provided by observer reports has become increasingly muddied by the proliferation of international election monitoring groups, producing divergent assessments of the same contest. Hence, unfavorable reports by the OSCE or European Union can be more easily discounted where countries can call on friendlier and less critical endorsements provided by rival missions.[53]

Following Kelley, this study assumes that any medium-term effects from monitoring activity on the quality of elections at country level probably arise from successive observer visits, rather than from a single report.[54] All other things being equal, if there is a cumulative effect, then the fifth proposition (H[2.5]) suggests that *states with a long series of observer missions over successive contests should have higher levels of contemporary electoral integrity.*

II: Evidence for the Impact of International Engagement on Electoral Integrity

It remains difficult to assess the long-term impact of external actors on strengthening electoral integrity with any degree of confidence. Much work has been qualitative in approach, such as the UNDP evaluation report already described, using selected case studies at project level to assess the outputs from technical assistance provided by a specific national development agency or program, such as evaluations of training workshops assessed through participant surveys or performance indicators.[55]

Lab experiments, field experiments with randomized control tests, and natural experiments provide the "gold standard" for project evaluation of specific interventions and a rigorous approach used to determine the causal effects of particular initiatives.[56] Thus, field experiments gauge the effects of an actual program or intervention on randomized subjects where the outcomes are measured in an unobtrusive way. Experimental studies related to elections and governance have typically studied the effects of transparency, participation, corruption, and rule of law on ordinary citizens' attitudes or behaviors.[57] This approach is exemplified by evaluations of the role of international or domestic observers deployed across a randomized selection of polling places in Afghanistan, Ghana, and Indonesia.[58] Yet even with the most systematic and careful studies, it also remains hazardous to generalize from the specific results detected by a particular experimental intervention at project level to determine whether the similar effects are likely to be observed if interventions are up-scaled and rolled out in other types of related programs and political contexts. Repeated experimental tests under varying conditions are needed for more reliable generalizations. Moreover, experimental designs are most suitable for projects where the treatment can be randomized. Unfortunately, for all sorts of practical reasons, many important types of policy interventions do not lend themselves easily to randomized control treatments, and "natural" experiments need to be treated cautiously.[59] In addition, while the best-designed randomized control experiments can determine short-term effects from specific projects with a reasonable level of confidence, the process of strengthening the quality of elections is a gradual process of institution building involving a series of programs over several years. Project evaluations typically monitor outputs, but medium-term outcomes, and long-term sustained impacts at societal level, are far more complex to assess.

More comprehensive econometric analysis is the main alternative strategy comparing the observed effects of electoral aid and assistance at country level.[60]

A few studies have attempted to compare the effects of international electoral assistance on the quality of elections across a broad range of countries, using standard econometric techniques. One of the most thorough evaluation exercises for the democracy promotion work of USAID worldwide from 1990 to 2003, using well-specified growth models, concluded that spending by the agency on elections and political processes has a strong and significant contemporary effect on the quality of free and competitive elections, as well as positive impacts for more general processes of democratization.[61] By contrast, however, Birch compared patterns of malpractice and reported that the quality of elections was unaffected by overall levels of "government and civil society assistance," as monitored by the OECD Development Assistance data.[62]

Unfortunately, large-N cross-national time-series comparisons are also hampered by many technical problems, including, until recently, the lack of sufficiently fine-grained standardized cross-national and time-series data on development aid disaggregated by project sector, and thin measures of the quality of elections, as well the difficulties of isolating the complex effects of specific programmatic initiatives to strengthen elections from broader processes of regime transitions, democratization, and peace building.[63] Models are also commonly underspecified, by failing to incorporate a full battery of controls. In the attempt to overcome this problem, econometric analysis has also commonly focused upon comparing the quality of elections among similar countries within a specific regional context, such as Latin America or sub-Saharan Africa, although this strategy makes it hazardous to draw broader lessons for other contexts or cultures. The limits of observational data are that econometric models often prove highly sensitive to the particular specification and measures that are employed, and vulnerable to problems of missing data, which limits country coverage, rather than generating robust and reliable assessments. In the attempt to improve on this approach, and to reexamine the cross-national evidence, the PEI Index and its subcomponents can again form the key measures for the dependent variables, measuring the quality of elections in more detail and more comprehensively than previous studies, as outlined in Chapter 3. Multivariate regression models examine the impact on electoral integrity arising from globalization and regional norms, the stock of election development aid spending, and the past deployment of observer missions, all of which may be expected to strengthen contemporary levels of electoral integrity in a society.

Globalization, Information Flows, and Regional Norms

The degree of globalization is believed to be important for electoral integrity. As argued earlier, cosmopolitan societies that are highly integrated into global communications networks, with low barriers to cross-border information flows, such as Switzerland, Sweden, Latvia, and South Korea, are likely to be open to the diffusion of global norms of electoral integrity. By contrast, more parochial and isolated countries, such as Bhutan, Myanmar, and North

Korea, which are poorly integrated with the world through global links of trade, communications, and transportation, are less likely to be influenced by international norms. External barriers include the degree to which national borders are open or closed, whether imports of cultural goods and services are limited by tariffs, taxes, or domestic subsidies, and how far there are restrictions on the movement of people through international travel, tourism, and labor mobility. To compare how far countries are integrated into international networks, we draw upon the KOF Political Globalization Index. This provides comprehensive annual indicators of the degree of political globalization in 207 countries around the world since the 1970.[64] This is monitored through indicators such as membership in international organizations and endorsements of international treaties.

In addition, economic underdevelopment may also prove to be an important barrier to information; poorer nations commonly lack modern communication infrastructures, such as an efficient telecommunication sector and a well-developed multichannel broadcasting service, and large sectors of the population in these countries often do not have the resources or skills to access media technologies. To compare national levels of economic development, models continue to include per capita GDP in purchasing power parity. The previous chapter established that economic development is significantly and consistently linked with electoral integrity. Building upon this finding, this chapter suggests that one of the underlying mechanisms behind this pattern may be the way that economic development is closely correlated with patterns of globalization, through access to trade and markets, integration with information networks, and links through international organizations. Above and beyond patterns of globalization, regional effects are also expected, due to the cultural norms, the influence of hegemonic powers, and the role of multilateral organizations within each world region. The predominant standards of electoral integrity among countries within a world region can be measured by using the mean PEI Index in a global region.

The first model in Table 4.1 replicates the two structural factors that were found earlier to have strong and consistently significant effects on the quality of elections, namely wealth (a society's per capita GDP in purchasing power parity) and natural resources (a country's logged total natural resource rents as a proportion of GDP). The first model shows similar coefficients to those presented earlier. Model 2 then enters the KOF index of political globalization and regional mean levels of electoral integrity. The results demonstrate that natural resources continue to have a significant negative effect on electoral integrity, for the reasons discussed earlier, where patronage politics, clientelism, and bribery common in rentier states depress the quality of elections. Economic development continues to have a consistently positive effect on electoral integrity, as noted in the previous chapter.

Even with these structural controls, the international forces arising from levels of political globalization, and especially the mean regional level of the

TABLE 4.1. *Electoral integrity and international forces*

	Model 1 Economy		Model 2 And globalization		Model 3 And aid spending		Model 4 And observer missions	
	B	S.E.	B	S.E.	B	S.E.	B	S.E.
Economy								
Wealth (Sqrt Per capita GDP ppp)	.109***	.018	.072**	.021	.063**	.022	.058*	.028
Natural resources (Rents as % GDP)	-1.84***	.472	-1.67***	.457	-1.68***	.481	-1.66***	.465
Cosmopolitan communications								
Index of political globalization			.106*	.044	.109*	.044	.104*	.045
Mean PEI by region			.322*	.172	.329*	.172	.326*	.163
Aid spending								
On elections (5 year avg)					.001	.000	.001	.000
On democratic participation (5 year avg)					.001	.000	.000	.000
Observer missions								
Stock of observer missions (% elec 2000–10)							-1.60	2.89
Constant	56.0		31.6		32.2		34.3	
Adjusted R²	.468		.520		.523		.519	

Notes: OLS Regression analysis where the PEI Index is the dependent variable in eighty-eight countries. All models used tolerance tests to check that they were free of problems of multicollinearity. See the technical appendix for more details about all the selected indices. ******Correlation is significant at the 0.001 level. ******Correlation is significant at the 0.01 level. *Correlation is significant at the 0.05 level.

Sources: PEI Index: Electoral Integrity Project. 2014 (PEI-2.8); *KOF Globalization index from the Quality of Government Cross-National Dataset,* http://www.qog.pol.gu.se/data/; AidData 3.0; *Election observers Hyde and Marinov NELDA.*

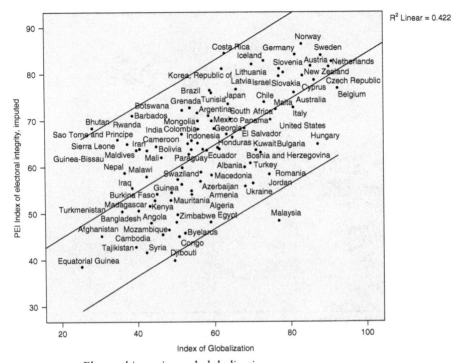

FIGURE 4.2. Electoral integrity and globalization.

Source: PEI Index and its subcomponents: Electoral Integrity Project. 2014. *The expert survey of Perceptions of Electoral Integrity*, (PEI-2.8); KOF Globalization index from the Quality of Government Cross-National Dataset, http://www.qog.pol.gu.se/data/.

PEI Index, have significantly *positive* effects on electoral integrity in each country. Thus, as shown in Figure 4.2, countries that are more open to information flows across their national borders, such as the Czech Republic, Slovakia, and Chile, are more likely to conform to global norms, accepting international standards of electoral integrity. Countries that are more isolated from world communication channels, trade routes, and diplomatic networks, such as Equatorial Guinea, Tajikistan, and Cambodia, are more likely to violate international standards in their elections. Regional norms are also influential on electoral integrity; as shown by the EU, countries adapt to the predominant political norms and standards for the quality of elections among neighboring states within their part of the world.

To test these relationships further, the links between the Norris–Inglehart Cosmopolitan Communications Index and electoral integrity are further explored in Figure 4.3. The Cosmopolitan Communication Index is designed to measure the degree to which information flows freely across and within societies, and it combines standardized measures of globalization, economic development (as a proxy for access to the mass and social media), and freedom

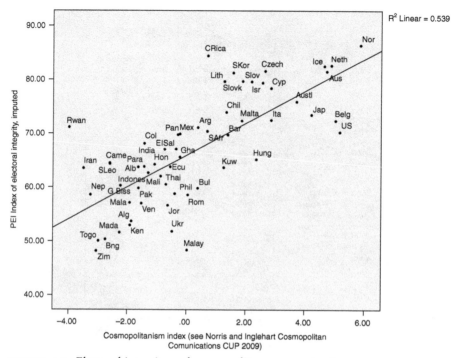

FIGURE 4.3. Electoral integrity and cosmopolitan communications.

Sources: PEI Index and its subcomponents: Electoral Integrity Project. 2014. *The expert survey of Perceptions of Electoral Integrity*, (PEI-2.5); Cosmopolitan Communication Index from Pippa Norris and Ronald Inglehart. 2009. *Cosmopolitan Communications*. New York: Cambridge University Press.

of the press in each society.[65] The results in Figure 4.3 confirm a strong and significant association with the PEI Index (R = .539, p = .000). Countries such as South Korea, the Czech Republic, and Slovakia are relatively open and cosmopolitan societies penetrated by transborder information flows and also with high quality elections today. By contrast, countries that are more isolated and closed include Zimbabwe, Togo, and Bangladesh, all with far worse records of flawed elections, according to the PEI Index. We will return to the role of the free press in the next chapter, as an important institution, when we consider checks and balances on the power of the executive.

Development Aid and Technical Assistance

What of the provision of development aid and technical assistance, which is typically designed to strengthen the capacity and resources of electoral authorities, to improve the administration of electoral processes, to build political party organizations, and to improve civic education and voter participation? Clearly, spending is only one proxy measure for these efforts and it may not be an accurate predictor of the effectiveness of interventions. For example, the typical costs of workshops used for training the core employees in the central electoral commission, or the cost of technical assistance for legislative committees and staff drafting new electoral laws, are usually relatively modest compared with the massive investment required in larger states and transitional regimes for compiling and verifying accurate voter registers and issuing voter identification cards, organizing and staffing hundreds of polling places with working ballot machinery, and managing complex logistical operations for security, transportation, and vote counting procedures.[66] Nevertheless, each step in the electoral cycle needs to work for efficient and effective operations. The AidData 3.0 project compiles comprehensive records for official development assistance, remittances, and foreign direct investment from 1946 to 2013, gathered the OECD Creditor Reporting System (CRS) database, donor annual reports, and project documents from both bilateral and multilateral aid agencies.[67] This provides the most complete picture currently available for the total resources available for recipient countries. The dataset can be broken down for analysis by project donors, sector/purpose/ activity codes, countries, and years. AidData attempts to capture the overall purpose and each individual activity taking place as part of the development project. For analysis, this study focuses upon the total aid for democratic participation and civil society, as the dominant sector targeted by the project, as well as a separate more granular code available to isolate election projects, including those for electoral management bodies, electoral processes, and voter education. The annual estimates in constant US$ are measured as rolling averages calculated for disbursements (not commitments) during the previous five years, to overcome the sharp fluctuations in spending in this sector caused by the periodicity of major election events. The aid data are also standardized to per capita spending, to compare levels of aid on a consistent basis across large and small countries. Model 3 in Table 4.1 adds the five-year average aid remittances for democratic participation and civil society and for elections.[68]

What emerges is that neither of their coefficients for aid spending proves to be statistically significant for the PEI Index. Figure 4.4 shows the wide scatter of developing countries which received international aid for elections in constant US$ ranging from modest amounts up to almost one billion allocated for Afghanistan. Clearly many other factors may be driving which elections receive massive contributions of aid and assistance, including levels of poverty and development, attempts at peace-building transitional elections in countries with a recent history of conflict, and the foreign policy interests and diplomatic relationships with donor countries. Further scrutiny of the relationship between election aid and the subcomponents of PEI in Table 4.2, without prior controls, shows that there are statistically significant correlations between election aid spending and indices for the quality of voting processes, the vote count, and the results stages of the electoral cycle, but all in a *negative* direction.

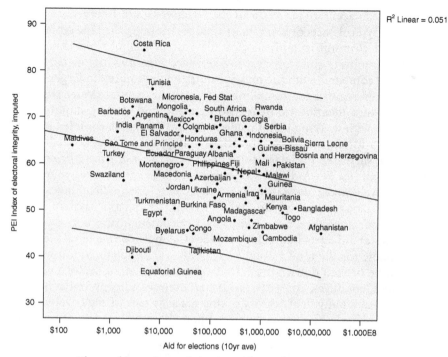

FIGURE 4.4. Electoral integrity and election aid spending.
Note: Only comparing countries which receive *any* aid spending on elections (10 year average).
Sources: PEI Index and its subcomponents: Electoral Integrity Project. 2014. *The expert survey of Perceptions of Electoral Integrity,* (PEI-2.8); AidData 3.0.

Several reasons can be suggested for this pattern. The most plausible interpretation is selection effects determining priorities about where to intervene based on needs assessments, not risk assessments: development aid flows most commonly to countries with a long history of flawed processes of electoral administration and poor capacity. In this regard, rather than strategic bets, the development community invests the highest stakes in the most hazardous cases, such as Afghanistan. In addition, the total amount of spending may have little relationship with the effectiveness of the aid; the cost of several steps in the electoral cycle varies substantially, for example managing an accurate electoral register is a massive logistical operation for any country, especially populous ones without standard official records, whereas designing the electoral laws and reforming administrative procedures is largely a technical and managerial issue requiring political will and expertize, but much lower financial costs. Although more development aid and technical assistance invested in the electoral process should be associated with improvements in the quality of elections, if aid works as intended, this cross-national evidence fails to demonstrate any positive linkages. Yet this should not be interpreted to mean

TABLE 4.2. *PEI Index and its components correlated with international indices*

Indices	Globalization index (0–100)	Regional Mean PEI (0–100)	Aid for democratic participation Avg 5 yr US$	Aid for elections Avg 5 yr US$	% elections with int. observers 2000–10
PEI	.650**	.601**	–.144	–.280**	–.467**
Electoral laws	.379**	.383**	.001	–.013	–.287*
Electoral procedures	.575**	.571**	–.170	–.340**	–.427**
Voting district boundaries	.280**	.394**	.001	–.103	–.234*
Voter registration	.566**	.584**	–.190	–.251*	–.417**
Party & candidate reg.	.604**	.509**	–.089	–.198	–.326**
Media coverage	.302**	.361**	.009	.082	–.374**
Campaign finance	.533**	.551**	–.160	–.149	–.489**
Voting process	.591**	.587**	–.116	–.245*	–.415**
Vote count	.611**	.570**	–.143	–.265**	–.378**
Results	.519**	.514**	–.203*	–.354**	–.484**
Electoral authorities	.574**	.543**	–.100	–.208*	–.421**

Notes: **Correlation is significant at the 0.01 level (2-tailed). *Correlation is significant at the 0.05 level (2-tailed). N countries 97.

Sources: PEI Index and its subcomponents: Electoral Integrity Project. 2014. *The expert survey of Perceptions of Electoral Integrity*, (PEI-2.8); *KOF Globalization index from the Quality of Government Cross-National Dataset*, http://www.qog.pol.gu.se/data/; AidData 3.0; Election observers Hyde and Marinov NELDA.

that there are no effects, and additional research on the impact of aid will be presented in the final volume of the trilogy. Time-series data and randomized control experimental trials are needed to examine this issue further and, in particular, whether election aid and technical assistance prior to contests generates subsequent improvements in their quality.

Observer Missions

Finally, what is the role of a series of observer missions in gradually improving the quality of elections? To examine the fifth proposition, we can draw upon data from the Hyde and Marinov NELDA dataset, which coded whether international missions were present in a series of elections. By coding how many elections in a country in 2000–10 have had international observer missions, we can test whether this activity has had a cumulative effect upon contemporary levels of electoral integrity. The results of adding the proportion of elections with observer missions to Model 4 in Table 4.1 shows a negative relationship to contemporary levels of electoral integrity, although this is not statistically significant. Comparison between the proportion of election with international observer missions and the sub-indices of electoral quality in Table 4.2, without controls, shows significant negative correlations.

Nevertheless, like the analysis of aid spending, cross-national comparative evidence provides a strictly limited test of this core claim, since potential problems of endogeneity arise in interpreting this relationship. In particular, countries with worse records of democratic elections and at high risk of malpractice may well be prioritized by international agencies to receive monitoring missions. Given limited resources, agencies commonly conduct a needs-assessment exercise prior to the deploying missions, so that contests that are seen as relatively unproblematic in emerging democracies are less likely to receive a full observer mission from the international community. Conversely, the most repressive states also continue to restrict Western observers from monitoring their elections, so there are likely to be both "ceiling effects" and "floor effects." Thus again, other methods, including time-series data, are needed to monitor the cumulative effect of this activity, rather than the cross-national measurements currently available from the PEI Index. Overall, the second model is therefore the strongest fit for the data, excluding international factors that proved to be insignificant, while identifying cosmopolitan communications as an additional factor, beyond development and natural resources, that contributes toward understanding of why elections succeed or fail.

III: The Role of the International Community in DRC Elections

To understand the process of external intervention in more depth, this can be illustrated by the international community's extensive involvement in assisting the Democratic Republic of Congo (DRC) hold general elections in July and October 2006, the first multiparty contests occurring in the country in four decades. This country exemplifies the riskiest conditions in which to hold elections. The equatorial Great Lakes region of Central Africa, bordered by DRC (formerly Zaire), the Central African Republic, Rwanda, Burundi, Uganda, Angola, and South Sudan, has been the site of extended conflict and humanitarian devastation, with displaced populations destabilizing neighboring states. The second largest country in Africa, Francophone DRC has territories the size of Western Europe, despite sparse transportation and communication networks, with an estimated population of 75 million divided into around 250 ethnolinguistic groups. Mineral rich (cobalt ore, diamonds, copper) and development poor, the DRC ranked as the second worst performer in the 2013 UNDPs Human Development Index (186th out of 187), making no real gains during the last three decades.[69]

The Second Congo war, starting in 1998, engaged nine nations and twenty armed groups, leaving millions dead from a combination of violence, malnutrition, and fatal illnesses.[70] After decades of armed conflict, President Laurent Kabila was assassinated in 2001 and replaced by his son, Joseph Kabila, who began to attempt reconciliation between the opposing sides. The main rebel groups signed a peace accord in 2002, followed by agreement over a transitional constitution the following year. The interim deal was monitored by largest contingent of UN peace-keepers (MONUC) ever deployed, involving nearly 20,000 combined uniformed and civilian personnel with an annual budget of approximately US \$1 billion.[71] A new constitution to establish a presidential republic was agreed by parliament in 2005 and endorsed by voters. As a result, in July 2006 electors went to the polls to elect the President of the Republic and the National Assembly, the lower house of the Parliament. The presidential contest uses a second ballot majoritarian electoral system, following the tradition inherited throughout much of Francophone Africa, despite the additional logistical and financial costs of holding two successive ballots and the risks of winner-take-all systems in divided societies, while the legislative contest used party list PR.

The elections were largely funded and supervised by the international community with significant political, military, and financial investment by the European Union, the United Nations, and donors like the United Kingdom and France that contributed toward the Congolese peace process. International elections support – political, technical, and financial – was coordinated by MONUC. The international community established a basket fund of roughly US\$267 million, managed by the UNDP. The DRC provided US \$40 million, roughly one-tenth of the total cost of the elections. The European Union sought to play a leading role in assisting the contests, although the effectiveness of their involvement has been criticized.[72] The sheer scale of electoral assistance mobilized in DRC is exceptional. Estimates of levels of international aid worldwide suggest that during the last decade DRC received the third highest share of funds for EMBs and processes, election observation, and voter education, just behind Afghanistan and Sudan.[73]

The logistics of mounting elections were formidable. The United Nations and Commission Electoral Indépendante (CEI) delivered voting materials to more than 50,000 polling stations by air, water, and road. Almost three dozen presidential candidates and numerous parliamentary candidates contested the first round of the election, generating an unwieldy and bewilderingly complex ballot paper in some districts; in the largest, in several Kinshasa districts, voters could choose from among 864 candidates. About 250,000 local polling workers had to be recruited, trained, managed, and paid by the CEI. Security concerns were triggered by sporadic violence by spoilers, although the United Nations blue helmets and diplomatic pressures managed to keep a lid on the tensions and avoid an escalation of the conflict during the campaign and polling day.[74] The two-round electoral system doubled the work, as well as generating a winner-takes-all majoritarian contest, which heightened the stakes. With no majority achieved in the first round of the presidential vote, incumbent leader Joseph Kabila (with 44.8% of the vote) and the opposition candidate in second place, Jean-Pierre Bemba (with 20%), contested a run-off poll on 29 October. President Kabila eventually won with a decisive 58% of the final vote. His governing alliance, the Alliance de la Majorité Présidentielle (AMP), also won the majority of seats in the national assembly and in seven of eleven provincial assemblies. Bemba claimed irregularities, but the DRC Supreme Court confirmed the results.

Did the contests, held in such difficult circumstances, meet international standards? The Carter Center mission sent long- and short-term observers. Their final report concluded diplomatically that *"Election procedures were, for the most part, well implemented despite a range of limitations and irregularities."*[75] The first round vote count had procedural shortcomings, although the team of observers noted that corrections were introduced by electoral authorities for the final round. The observer mission also reported the abuse of voter registers and other technical problems, although endorsing the outcome overall as "credible." This means that any irregularities were not of sufficient scale to throw the outcome into doubt. Despite the logistical hurdles, other reports by bilateral donors who had invested in the basket of funds were similarly largely positive in their reviews; for example, DfID in the UK concluded optimistically: *"Although these elections were not without flaws, they were perceived to be acceptably fair and representative of the general will of the Congolese people, and to have met their major objectives of re-establishing legitimate government in the DRC and contributing to durable peace."*[76] Nevertheless, renewed intercommunal clashes occurred barely a month after the election, and in 2008 outbreaks of heavy violence became more sustained. Today the DRC continues to be plagued by armed rebellion, marauding militia, sexual violence, renewed clashes, displaced populations, widespread corruption, and instability.[77] The next round of presidential and legislative elections, in 2011, received less international aid and assistance. Polling day was characterized by chaotic voting, incidents of violence, delays, and multiple irregularities of lost or mishandled ballots, leading to widespread criticism by teams of monitoring observers and the UN peacekeeping mission. The Carter Center concluded that the 2011 results were not credible, as it was not possible to determine the legitimate winner.[78]

Given the long history of poverty and violence in the country, perhaps the surprising fact, in retrospect, is less the continuing conflict and subsequent major flaws occurring during the 2011 elections, but the pervasive assumption that the 2006 elections could turn the tide of history and build peace through establishing a legitimate and democratic presidential republic after three decades of bloody war and authoritarian government. Reflecting these optimistic hopes, a 2013 UNDP report on African elections counted the 2006 DRC elections in the success column: "...elections in Mozambique in 1994, Sierra Leone in 2002, Liberia in 2005 and DRC in 2006, all ... marked an end to decades of civil conflict."[79] Despite this claim, the most recent (2014)

Fragile States Index ranks the DRC as the fourth riskiest state in the world (behind South Sudan, Somalia, and the Central African Republic).[80] Human Rights Watch assessed the contemporary situation as dangerous: *"Armed conflict continued in eastern Democratic Republic of Congo, with Congolese security forces and non-state armed groups responsible for serious abuses against civilians. The Rwandan-backed M23 armed group committed widespread war crimes, including summary executions, rapes, and forced recruitment of children in 2012 and 2013.... As the military focused attention on defeating the M23, many other armed groups filled the security vacuum. These groups continue to carry out brutal attacks on civilians across eastern Congo. In Kinshasa and elsewhere, government authorities have sought to silence dissent with threats, violence, and arbitrary arrests against human rights activists, journalists, and opposition political party leaders and supporters who were critical of government officials or participated in anti-government demonstrations."*[81] Despite the obvious risks, the United Nations and its partners probably had to support the new Congolese constitution and the government's requests to provide technical assistance for the 2006 elections, as this provided a critical opportunity to resolve the three-decade long war. The investment in the 2006 electoral process, while relatively expensive, paled into insignificance compared with the annual costs to the international community of maintaining the peace-keeping blue helmets. The quarter billion price tag for the 2006 elections produced only a temporary lull in violence in DRC, disappointing the hopes that this would contribute toward a sustainable democratic transition and enduring peace building. In short, DRC exemplifies all the problems that we have seen heighten the risks of failed elections, including the structural conditions of deep-rooted poverty and widespread corruption in a rentier state, combined with a long history of bloody conflict, isolation from the world community, and lack of stable democracies in the region. The international community was committed to try to strengthen reconciliation and a legitimate government through supporting the Congolese transitional elections, as an important opportunity to build a more peaceful future in the Great Lakes region – but in the circumstances, despite an enormous investment of aid and technical assistance, the risks of failure were always high.

IV: Conclusions

During recent decades, therefore, the international flow of information arising from processes of globalization is expected to have strengthened the diffusion of global norms and international standards of electoral integrity. The development community has also expanded its attempts to strengthen multiparty elections as an integral part of democratic governance, especially through providing development aid and technical assistance designed to strengthen the technical capacity of central EMBs and local electoral officials tasked with running elections. Finally, during recent decades, agencies have also deployed observer missions in many countries to monitor how far the quality of elections meets international standards.

The Evidence in this Chapter Suggests Three Main Findings

Firstly, *globalization does have an impact on electoral integrity*, with cosmopolitan societies more likely to hold contests which meet international standards. By strengthening the flow of international information across national borders, through ties of trade interdependence, communication flows, membership of multilateral organizations, this process spreads global norms and international standards of electoral integrity.

Secondly, for similar reasons, *the quality of elections in a world region also influences electoral integrity within countries*. The positive effects of this process are most easily exemplified by the explicit democratic condition required before states are accepted for membership in the European Union. But negative effects can also be observed, such as Russia's role in destabilizing elections in Eastern Ukraine. Once globalization and regional effects are entered into the models, the earlier structural factors of economic development and natural resources continue to play a significant role.

Finally, although election aid and electoral observers are two of the most commonly used instruments that are designed to strengthen elections, the cross-national evidence compared in this chapter was *unable to establish a significant link at aggregate level between these interventions and the contemporary quality of elections around the world*. A cautious and agnostic conclusion is the most appropriate interpretation, however, reflecting the Scottish verdict of "not proven," due to the role of selection effects in determining which elections receive the most attention from the development community. Further analysis is required, using such methods as time-series cross-national models and field experiment evaluations, for systematic exploration of these issues. But in addition, what may be the role of power-sharing domestic institutions, and the indirect effects when the international community provides constitutional advice about the most effective design for electoral integrity? It is to these issues that we now turn in the next chapter.

5

Institutional Checks

By contrast to both theories already considered, research on comparative political institutions focuses upon the constitutional design, the powers and capacity of the core agencies for electoral administration, and the incentives and constraints that arise from these arrangements. To lay the foundations for these arguments, the chapter first identifies alternative arrangements of power-sharing and majoritarian forms of electoral governance conceptualized as ideal types, with the United States and France selected as case studies, to highlight the contrasts. Part II summarizes rival claims about the pros and cons of each type of electoral governance and, in particular, arguments suggesting that power sharing strengthens democratization and, by implication, processes of electoral integrity. Institutional checks and balances preventing the abuse of power, building stakeholder trust, and reducing the incentives for malpractice, are believed to reinforce electoral integrity. Nevertheless, these potential benefits may come at the expense of some loss of accountability, coordinated policymaking, and administrative efficiency. To test empirical support for the arguments, Part III operationalizes the core concepts and considers the evidence for the links between four political institutions (the type of electoral system, the independence of the judiciary, strong parliaments, and freedom of the press) and patterns of electoral integrity, controlling for the key structural and international factors found to be important in previous chapters. The analysis draws upon the cross-national indicators (PEI) to measure electoral integrity and its components in the eleven step electoral cycle. The conclusion summarizes the main findings, and considers the overall implications.

I: Typology of Electoral Governance

The concept of "electoral governance" is understood as: "...*the interaction of constitutional, legal, and institutional rules and organizational practices that determine the basic rules for election procedures and electoral competition;*

organize campaigns, voter registration, and election-day tallies; and resolve disputes and certify results."[1] The notion therefore refers to the organizational bodies exercising decision-making and administrative authority over electoral laws and procedures. The idea encompasses two distinct levels: the higher constitutional arrangements in any regime and the more specific functions of administrative agencies responsible for implementing electoral regulations and detailed procedures governing different stages of the electoral cycle (discussed fully in the next chapter). Political institutions can be understood as the formal rules and the informal social norms structuring the workings of any regime. Formal rules include the legislative framework governing constitutions, as embodied in official documents, constitutional conventions, legal statutes, codes of conduct, and administrative procedures, authorized by law and enforceable by courts. Institutions provide incentives and sanctions that constrain human behavior. It is neither necessary nor sufficient for rules to be embodied in the legal system to be effective; social norms, informal patterns of behavior, and social prohibitions also create shared mutual expectations among political actors which can exert a powerful influence. Hence, a pervasive culture of corruption can trump any number of legal deterrents. Nevertheless, this study focuses most attention upon the formal rules, as these represent the core instruments of public policy that are open to reform and amendment through legislation, executive order, constitutional revision, administrative decisions, judicial review, or bureaucratic decree.[2]

The constitution in any state provides the broadest context for electoral governance. This includes, in particular, types of electoral system, as well as the role and powers of national parliaments, the capacity and independence of the courts and judiciary, and freedom of the mass media. Each of these can provide checks and balances countering the potential abuse of power of the executive. The structure and responsibilities of electoral authorities and regulatory agencies – commonly known as EMB – are the core administrative agencies implementing policies but their work is embedded within this wider institutional environment.[3]

The arrangements for electoral governance vary substantially around the world.[4] The type of majoritarian or proportional electoral systems, in particular, can be expected to shape the incentives for individual candidates to try to manipulate the district outcomes and the opportunities for gerrymandering and malapportionment.[5] In general, effective parliaments can serve as an important check on executive power, strengthening processes of democratization.[6] Countries differ in the exact roles that legislative and executive agencies play in the electoral process, including which branch is responsible for setting the legal and regulatory framework, overseeing electoral authorities, allocating budgetary resources, and appointing senior electoral commissioners. In some countries, for example in France, these functions are mainly the responsibility of a central government department, such as the Ministry of Interior, while elsewhere, such as in the United States, federal and state legislatures play a stronger oversight role. Similarly the courts, tribunals, and judiciary, including the highest constitutional authorities, influence electoral process through the interpretation of electoral laws and regulations, the resolution of disputes, the punishment for criminal acts, and the adjudication of complaints and appeals procedures, although in some countries some of these functions are shared with election management bodies and other specialist agencies.[7] Beyond the role of state institutions, a range of NGOs in civil society can also be expected to serve important functions for strengthening transparency in the electoral process, including the roles of the independent news media, as well as social media networks, domestic observer organizations, election-watch NGOs, and human rights advocacy groups. These actors ideally strengthen an informed citizenry, such as where watchdog reporting highlights cases of fraud or maladministration, thereby helping to hold electoral authorities to account for their performance. Electoral administrative agencies work within this institutional environment. It follows that research which focuses too narrowly upon comparing the organizational structure, powers, and legal autonomy of electoral authorities or EMBs, without taking this wider context into account, is in danger of neglecting the broader picture. Even the best designed EMB, which is given considerable autonomy, organizational resources, and technical capacity to run elections, is unlikely to succeed in electoral autocracies such as Zimbabwe, Turkmenistan, or Equatorial Guinea if electoral officials are marginalized and overruled by governing elites.

To make sense of diverse constitutional and administrative arrangements, forms of electoral governance can be classified into power-sharing and majoritarian ideal types. In practice, countries often fall somewhere in the middle of the spectrum, with mixed arrangements, but nevertheless the use of ideal types helps clarify the most important contrasts.

Power-Sharing Arrangements for Electoral Governance

"Power-sharing" forms of electoral governance are understood in this study most simply as those institutional arrangements where decision-making authority over election laws and procedures is dispersed among multiple branches of government, levels of government, and specialized administrative agencies. Power-sharing constitutional arrangements are typically characterized by proportional representation electoral systems with large multimember districts and low thresholds (generating multiparty representation in parliament and coalition cabinets), strong parliamentary powers counterbalancing those of the executive, an independent judiciary, and a pluralistic range of civil society organizations, including a free press with the capacity to report fraud and malfeasance. Similarly at the implementation level, responsibilities in power-sharing arrangements tend to be further divided among multiple specialized administrative agencies, for example where separate bodies are responsible for regulating political finance, delimiting electoral boundaries, regulating political broadcasts, maintaining polling place security,

investigating and adjudicating complaints, and running elections. As discussed later, this design aims to prevent capture and manipulation of the electoral process by any single leader, party, or party coalition, whether in government or opposition; to promote trust among multiple stakeholders; and to reduce the incentives for malpractice.

US Decentralization

The United States illustrates types of fragmented power-sharing arrangements for electoral governance despite using single member plurality elections for the legislature and having a two-party system. The American constitution maintains a strict separation of powers among the executive, legislative, and judicial branches of the federal government in Washington DC, with elaborate checks and balances that avoid the concentration of authority in any single branch, as well as the dispersal of federal powers and responsibilities to states and local counties and municipalities. In terms of running elections, Article I, section 4, of the constitution grants state legislatures the authority to regulate the timing, place, and manner of holding elections for Congress. The state legislatures remain the predominant source of legal regulations for elections, generating a complex patchwork quilt of arrangements even for basic matters, such as the hours that polling places are open, the requirements for voter registration and voter identification, and facilities for advance or postal voting.[8] To add a further layer of complexity, the operational procedures are then implemented in around 13,000 countries and municipalities across America, where local officials determine many practical arrangements, such as the location of polling places and ballot designs. Congress has the formal constitutional authority to "make or alter" state rules, although most federal laws are restricted to the rights to vote and the regulation of political finance.

At national level, the Federal Election Commission was created in 1974 to regulate and monitor how money is raised and spent in national elections, and to administer public funds in presidential contests. The FEC has strengthened transparency but over the years it has become an increasingly weak and ineffectual body, with the leadership mired in partisan gridlock and unable to propose reforms with any realistic chance of passing into law. The six member commission is divided by law so that no more than three commissioners can be members of the same political party and at least four votes are required for any official commission action. In practice, this has meant that as Democrat and Republican parties have become increasingly polarized over issues of political finance reform, the commission has become permanently gridlocked and marginalized, at a time when campaigns are awash with money and Supreme Court decisions have loosened major parts of the regulatory framework and donor limits. Indeed, even the process of replacing FEC members has become increasingly ineffective due to Senate veto over presidential nominees.[9] The major decisions altering the regulation of campaign finance have come from a series of decisions by the Supreme Court. In 2002 the Help America Vote Act created a new national oversight and advisory body, the Electoral Assistance Commission, designed to monitor minimum standards of administrative performance, but primary responsibility for running elections continues to rest with agencies at state and local levels.[10] The result of the fragmented nature of American electoral governance is a bewildering hodge-podge of state laws and local procedures determining some of the most basic electoral procedures that vary from place to place, such as the requirements for voter registration, for identification in polling places, and for casting absentee or advance ballots.[11] Where problems arise, such as Florida in 2000, accountability is weakened among multiple levels of government and the multiplication of veto points hinders the introduction of any sweeping procedural reforms. At the same time, states and localities have considerable authority to introduce a variety of new voting procedures, if these are interpreted by the courts as meeting broader constitutional and legal rights.

Majoritarian Electoral Governance

By contrast, in *majoritarian* forms of electoral governance, constitutional arrangements favor single member plurality "winner-take-all" electoral systems, moderate patterns of party competition, and unitary states, which thereby concentrate control over the electoral governance in the hands of the single largest party holding the reins of cabinet power in the central government. Under majoritarian electoral systems, smaller parties typically need to overcome substantial hurdles and effective vote thresholds to gain elected office. If smaller parties manage to win parliamentary seats, their elected representatives have opportunities to debate legislation and to scrutinize government actions, but not to share the spoils of ministerial office in governing coalitions. These forms of electoral governance typically have constitutional and legal arrangements based on majoritarian electoral systems, single party executives, weaker legislatures compared with the powers of the executive, and unitary states so that regional and local government are subordinate to central government.

Moreover, in terms of the electoral administrative agencies, decision-making and implementation authority over laws and procedures is concentrated largely within a single body. In practice, this arrangement is exemplified by centralized electoral authorities located in ministerial departments and administrative arrangements where most of the core tasks for organizing elections are the responsibility of a national or regional EMB (falling under what International IDEA terms the "governmental" model). The EMB is staffed by permanent civil servants located within an official department of state, such as the Department of Home Affairs, the Justice Ministry, or the Ministry of the Interior, reporting directly to cabinet and indirectly to parliament, with regulations and standardized procedures implemented at operational level by local and regional agencies accountable to the central authorities.

French Centralization

France exemplifies this type of electoral governance, where the regulation of electoral governance rests largely in a central government department based in Paris headed by a government minister, with several official bodies responsible for regulating aspects such as the publication of opinion polls, the allocation of broadcast time before and during the campaign, and the regulation of political finance. The day-to-day administration and implementation of electoral procedures is the responsibility of local government authorities, and a judicial council oversees the process. In the Bonapartist tradition, electoral governance is centrally regulated by state agencies. The result is a system of electoral governance in France with few independent checks and balances, but which is recognized by most observers as efficient, coordinated, and professional.[12] The model was inherited in francophone Africa, where electoral administration in former French colonies such as Cote d'Ivoire, Cameroon, and Djibouti rested in the Ministry of the Interior, although the effect of nonautonomous EMBs has proved problematic for processes of democratization in these countries.[13]

In France, the Ministry of the Interior, Overseas, Local Authorities and Immigration in Paris is responsible for technical and logistical administration of the election, as well as general domestic security and policing. The department is composed of permanent civil servants and is headed by a senior cabinet minister. The ministry issues instructions to 101 prefectures that represent the state at the department level, which in turn liaise with approximately 36,000 mairies (local government authorities) at the commune level. Mairies are responsible for managing the work of approximately 65,000 polling stations and for detailed aspects of electoral administration, such as maintaining the voter registry. Under the constitution of the Fifth Republic (1958), every five years presidential elections use a second ballot electoral system, where to be elected, candidates need to receive an absolute majority (50%+) of the valid ballots cast. If no candidate passes this threshold in the first round, a second ballot is held two weeks later between the top two candidates. Elections for 577 members of the Chamber of Deputies in the National Assembly follow a similar second ballot majoritarian system in single member districts, although proportional representation is used for European and some local elections. In addition, matters such as campaign materials and rallies during the election campaign are supervised by the National Commission for Control of the Electoral Campaign, a temporary body that consists of five members and is led by the Vice-President of the Council of State. The Commission for Opinion Polls, an independent body comprising representatives of the Council of State and assisted by expert staff, is tasked with reviewing published opinion polls to ensure that pollsters use a reputable methodology. Political finance is subject to extensive regulation supervised by another official body, the National Commission for Control of Electoral Accounts and Political Finance. The Supreme Audiovisual Council strictly regulates campaign coverage by broadcast media, both public and private. For example, during the official campaign period, all candidates need to be granted "equal" airtime and direct speech on all broadcasters. Additionally, each candidate is entitled to broadcast free spots on public television during the official campaign period.

General oversight of the results of French elections is vested with the Constitutional Council. Direct Constitutional Council involvement in the electoral process focuses upon the registration of candidates and the announcement of results. The Constitutional Council also reviews and advises on election-related legislation and adjudicates election-related complaints and appeals. The body is composed of nine members appointed for nine-year non-renewable terms, in addition to all former Presidents. The current president appoints three members of the Constitutional Council, including its head. The Presidents of the Senate and the National Assembly each appoints three members. One third of the appointed members are replaced every three years. It also receives reports from some 1,400 magistrates who are delegated by the Court of Cassation (the highest court) to ensure that election-day proceedings are in line with the law. Direct Constitutional Council involvement in the electoral process is limited to the registration of presidential candidates and the announcement of results. Thus, in France elections are strongly regulated, both through the constitution and by law, by several official government bodies, headed by the Ministry of Interior, with detailed procedures implemented by local governments. There is no independent electoral commission separate from government departments. Despite the potential risks inherent in this model, observer reports from the OSCE suggest that electoral administration is conducted impartially and professionally in France, with transparent procedures, and political parties and candidates lodge relatively few official complaints or legal disputes.[14]

II: Arguments about Power-Sharing Electoral Governance

What are the claims about the potential risks and benefits of these alternative ideal types of electoral governance? What are the pros and cons of either concentrating powers and responsibilities for elections in a single unified body located within a department of state, under a minister accountable to the cabinet and parliament, with local levels mainly implementing directives issued by the central office as in France, or else dispersing responsibilities for electoral decision making across a wide range of agencies and levels of governance, as in the United States? Conventional wisdom suggests that electoral administrative bodies should be autonomous of the executive, but the empirical evidence does not necessarily support such clear-cut conclusions.[15] In fact, extreme versions of either the majoritarian or the power-sharing model are likely to generate problems, for different reasons, so the ideal is probably somewhere in the middle of the spectrum. But exactly where the balance lies has not been clearly determined through previous research.

To make sense of the normative arguments, drawing once more upon the broader literature on democratization, insights can be derived from traditional theories of "power-sharing" constitutions. This general perspective has a long and distinguished intellectual pedigree, rooted in the theory of "consociational" and "consensus" democracy developed by Arend Lijphart, updated more recently in veto-player theory by George Tsebelis, among others, although it has also been subject to persistent criticism.[16]

Checks and Balances Limit the Potential Abuse of Power

The first claim for power sharing is that institutional checks and balances maximize the number of institutional veto-players in the policy process and thereby avoid the potential risks of power exercised by any single party, especially ruling parties controlling the executive. The common argument is that power sharing limits the capacity of incumbents to rig the rules of the electoral game through any of the techniques already discussed, such as by manipulating the procedural rules at any stage of the electoral cycle through gerrymandering and malapportionment of district boundaries, restrictions on ballot access, the abuse of state resources, the deployment of security forces to intimidate opposition supporters, appointing partisan sympathizers and acolytes to electoral commissions and courts, or, even more crudely, putting a thumb on the scales and stuffing the ballot count. Where the national election management body is located within a government department, subject directly to ministerial control, then the potential danger is that electoral authorities may fail to resolve electoral disputes or abuses of electoral rights in a neutral and timely manner, or, even if impartial, may fail to be regarded as trustworthy in their rulings. Thus, risks of the French model of government regulation of electoral administration are particularly strong if used in autocratic states where the governing party holds an absolute majority in the legislature, and in presidential republics where "rubber stamp" assemblies have weak legislative powers and autonomy, as opposition parties may then be unable to counterbalance and check any abuse of powers and manipulation of electoral rules by the executive. Manipulation may limit political competition to established parliamentary parties, in a cartel arrangement, or benefit just the dominant party.

By contrast, under power-sharing constitutions, coalition multiparty cabinets provide internal checks and balances on the power of any single party in government and thereby limit the capacity of the executive to manipulate the electoral rules or to nominate and appoint partisan senior commissioners in their pockets. Strong and independent legislatures with powers of oversight, where opposition parties can hold electoral authorities to account, provide an additional safeguard over the integrity of electoral laws and procedures, as well as the over the appointment and nomination process of electoral authorities. Beyond state institutions, independent reporting by the free press, which can provide watchdog reporting to highlight of any cases of electoral abuse or attempts at fraud or ballot rigging, provides another important check on the potential abuse of powers by governing or opposition parties.[17] In an earlier study, Birch found that lack of press freedom was significantly linked with problems of electoral administration and the manipulation of vote choice.[18]

Power Sharing Builds Trust and Stakeholder Buy-In

In addition to negative safeguards, advocates also argue that there may also be several positive consequences of power-sharing arrangements. In particular, proportional electoral systems maximize the number of "winners" elected to parliament and cabinet office, while federalism and decentralization promotes local and regional governance for national and ethnic communities. Through these sorts of mechanisms, inclusive power-sharing arrangements are thought to have a broader impact by building feelings of political trust, social tolerance, and legitimacy, long regarded as the foundations for a civic culture and stable democratic states.[19] A series of studies has demonstrated that those voters who support the electoral "winners" are far more likely to trust democracy and have confidence in institutions than those backing the losing side.[20] The previous volume in this trilogy confirmed this pattern for elections: compared with "losers", citizens who supported the winning party expressed far greater confidence and faith in the integrity of the electoral process.[21] Accordingly, institutional arrangements maximizing the number of party winners represented in parliamentary bodies or in coalition cabinets are likely to strengthen confidence in the political system. Proportional representation electoral systems (including variants such as mixed member proportional systems) lower the threshold for translating votes into seats, facilitating the election of many smaller parliamentary parties and also usually producing multiparty government coalitions. By maximizing the number of winners, political party elites with a stake in the legislature and executive are more likely to consent to the legitimacy of the electoral process, increasing trust in electoral procedures and rules among their supporters.

By contrast, majoritarian electoral systems concentrate the spoils of office in the hands of the winners, exaggerating the seat share for the largest party through a systematic "winner's bonus," while disproportionately penalizing geographically dispersed smaller parties through high vote-seat thresholds. As a result of majoritarian rules, party elites that are excluded from parliaments and cabinet office have a strong incentive to criticize the fairness of the electoral results, the rules of the game, and the electoral authorities, or to cry fraud following an election, thereby reducing confidence in the process among their members and voting supporters. Sustainable electoral rules and processes require that all actors with the power to challenge and disrupt the proceedings, whether incumbents who cling to office despite defeat or challengers deploying force, choose instead to respect and honor the rules and outcome.[22] By providing all parties with a stake in the process, power-sharing forms of electoral governance are likely to maximize the legitimacy of the process and outcome.

Single Member Districts Heighten the Incentives for Ballot Box Fraud
Power sharing concerns all the constitutional arrangements but the design of electoral systems, in particular, may be expected to prove critical for integrity. The main claim is that majoritarian electoral rules are believed to heighten the incentives for individual candidates to engage in several common malpractices; in particular, single member districts (SMDs) may exacerbate the risks of vote buying and ballot box stuffing.[23] The reason is that in highly competitive marginal districts, in particular, under winner-takes-all rules, even one vote may make the difference between victory and defeat. Lehoucq Molina reports that in Costa Rica, plurality districts generated more complaints about electoral fraud than multimember PR districts.[24] Compared with representatives in closed-list multimember PR districts, elected officials in SMDs are more likely to engage in clientelism, patronage politics, rent seeking, and other corrupt acts, delivering pork to constituents.[25] Large multimember districts with proportional representation, however, are expected to guard against these dangers, since many more ballots would need to be manipulated to change the winner. In closed-list PR systems, citizens cast a ballot for collective political party lists, not expressing preferences for individual candidates. Birch points out that candidates in SMD systems have more to gain from individual efforts to manipulate elections than is the case for candidates in (closed-list) PR contests; and malfeasance is more efficient under SMD rules.[26] At the same time, of course, this does not rule out the use of electoral malpractices or corruption by collective political parties earlier during the electoral cycle, for example through packing membership in the EMB, restricting ballot access, or suppressing voter registration.

Large Multimember Districts Reduce, or Even Eliminate, Gerrymandering
Moreover, SMDs also raise the risks of partisan gerrymandering and malapportionment, if district boundaries are drawn to favor one party (usually incumbent office holders) or a specific demographic group, such as minority populations.[27] The process works by packing voters of one type into a single electoral district, thereby seeking to ensure a safe seat and reduce competition, diminishing the impact of this group elsewhere. In Singapore, for example, the ruling People's Action Party has been criticized for using this technique to secure its parliamentary majority.[28] In the 2013 Malaysian general election, as well, the ruling coalition, which had been in power since 1957, Barisan Nasional (BN), won 47% of the vote but took 60% of the parliamentary seats. The opposition coalition, Pakatan Rakyat (PR), won a majority of the popular vote (51%) – but only 40% of the seats. The opposition ethnic-Chinese support is concentrated in densely populated urban seats, with far larger electorates, so that the opposition gets fewer MPs for every vote cast. The result of the malapportionment is to undermine the principle of equal votes. In the PEI expert survey, experts rated Malaysia worst on the item "Boundaries discriminate against some parties" among the eighty-six countries under comparison, although the

United States, Zimbabwe, and Togo also came out poorly by this measure. Similar gerrymandering favoring the governing party has been observed in many other places, such as Cameroon.[29] Parties can thereby win a higher number of seats without increasing their share of the vote. These dangers are particularly common where elected politicians and the dominant party control the process of drawing constituency boundaries. They may diminish if the process is in the hands of nonpartisan officials, such as judges, independent commissions, or boards. By contrast, large multimember districts in PR systems reduce, or sometimes even eliminate, the need for any redistricting, for example if fixed district boundaries reflect administrative regions. Worldwide in around fifty countries, such as Norway, Portugal, and Russia, existing regional or provincial boundaries are used to delimit election districts in the lower house of the national legislature.[30] Some empirical support for these propositions has been demonstrated; for example, when comparing varied electoral systems in two dozen post-Communist states, Birch found that electoral misconduct was associated with the proportion of SMD seats in a country.[31]

Despite these plausible arguments, power-sharing arrangements may also have several significant *dis*advantages. The general benefits have long been strongly challenged by proponents of majoritarian arrangements. Donald Horowitz argues that in general, power-sharing constitutional arrangements may, in fact, unintentionally serve to heighten latent ethnic identities, strengthen party extremism and fragmentation, and freeze community boundaries, failing in the long term to generate the conditions of social tolerance and moderation where democracy flourishes.[32] Potential costs may involve a loss of consistent standards and procedures in electoral administration, generating inequalities of voting rights within a country.

Power Sharing Weakens Accountability, "Joined-Up" Governance, and Consistent Standards

Where electoral authorities are dispersed horizontally and vertically among multiple agencies, so that if there are procedural problems and administrative short-comings requiring reforms, it becomes unclear which agency is responsible ("where the buck stops") and multiple veto points generate stalemate, preventing any practical reforms being implemented. Concentrating a range of functions in a central agency allows activities to be integrated and coordinated within the framework of a single organization, facilitating "joined-up" governance and consistent standards and procedures nationwide. The potential advantage of this hierarchical organization is a streamlined and coordinated administrative process regulating all major aspects of electoral governance, with the central EMB directly reporting to a cabinet minister who is, in turn, accountable to members of parliament and thus, ultimately, the general electorate. Permanent staff employed in the civil service and local authorities can be deployed to run elections, bringing a wealth of professional experience, specialized expertise, organizational structures, and technical resources to the process.

Elections are complex large-scale processes to manage, especially in the challenging conditions of large, developing societies, weak states, and post-conflict societies, where it is essential for public officials to have the managerial, organizational, and professional capacity to deploy and handle a wide range of human, technological, security, logistical, procurement, and financial resources over successive contests. As the IFES guide emphasizes: "It *is imperative that an election is professionally and independently administered. That it is planned and executed in a timely fashion, and the entire process enjoys the greatest possible levels of transparency, integrity and credibility*."[33] Without this capacity, even simple irregularities and human errors such as the mechanical breakdown of voting machines, threats against citizens in several local polling places, or inaccuracies and incomplete voter registers, can damage confidence in the credibility of the process and mobilize legal challenges or mass protests, so that the performance of electoral governance fails.

In addition, responsibility for specialized dimensions of electoral governance requires coordination across a complex range of other administrative agencies within the public sector, including the judiciary and courts accountable for dispute resolution and adjudication, agencies regulating campaign broadcasting and political finance, the security forces and the police, as well as organizations in civil society, notably political parties, the independent media, and election-watch NGOs. Moreover, devolving responsibility for electoral administration to local and regional agencies can generate disparities in citizens' rights within a country, for example, through registration procedures, the ability to cast an advance ballot, the hours of polling, or the requirements for voter id.[34]

Power Sharing Disperses Resources and Is Less Efficient

Centralized structures of electoral governance may also prove the most effective and efficient managerial arrangement under certain conditions, especially in long established democracies, and in stable and secure Western states, which have accumulated deep reservoirs of social trust and tolerance, an extended history of repeated elections, and effective channels of parliamentary accountability checking the executive, where losing parties in any one contest are relatively confident of their capacity to be returned to office on subsequent occasions. In this context, in many Western democracies, although there can always be questions raised about specific electoral irregularities and flaws, the basic fairness and impartiality of electoral authorities and processes are rarely seriously disputed. There is widespread trust in electoral procedures in established democracies such as Sweden and Norway, even where contests are managed by permanent public-sector employees working within a central government ministry, and administered by provincial and local authorities. Routine disputes about specific procedures or particular irregularities about voting procedures and electoral results can be resolved where losing parties and candidates file legal petitions requesting a recount and the courts resolve disputes impartially.

In this regard, the degree of party polarization that has spread in the United States ever since an army of lawyers descended upon the Florida debacle in 2000 remains exceptional, despite the fact that signs of a milder contagion of mistrust appear to be spreading to several other Anglo-American democracies, exemplified by passage of the Fair Votes Act in Canada and growing contention about alleged voter fraud in the UK.[35]

III: Evidence

The debate concerning the claimed virtues of power sharing deserves fresh examination against the available evidence for several reasons. In particular, the core concept of power sharing has not been applied systematically in the previous literature as a general conceptual framework to analyze diverse forms and agencies of electoral governance. Indeed, despite growing interest in the international community, beyond the study of electoral *systems*, until the last decade, remarkably little systematic empirical research by scholars has compared and analyzed many detailed aspects of electoral governance around the globe.[36] There is, however, a growing literature comparing the organizational structure and responsibilities of independent EMBs.[37] Similarly, outside of extensive body of literature on the role of money and politics in the United States, and case studies of states in Western Europe, only recently have studies of campaign finance started to compare regulatory agencies around the globe.[38] The available body of national case studies, and cross-national reports published by organizations such as IFES and International IDEA, indicates that considerable diversity exists in the roles, powers, and structures of all these administrative bodies, even among Western democracies, as well as differences in the multiple ways in which elections can be organized and run.[39] There are many varieties of power-sharing electoral governance, and it remains unclear which are most effective, as well as whether agencies are capable of overcoming the constraints arising from structural conditions in inhospitable environments and the neglect of the international community. If claims about the positive effects of power-sharing constitutions are correct, then it would be plausible to expect that standards of electoral integrity should be significantly strengthened by these arrangements. Thus we can test whether electoral integrity (measured by the summary PEI Index and its eleven dimensions) is significantly higher in countries with proportional representation electoral systems, strong legislatures capable of checking the executive, an independent judiciary, federalism decentralizing decision making, and freedom of the press.

To analyze the evidence, this study uses regression in the first model in Table 5.1 to analyze the effects of four types of political institutions (comparing the type of electoral system, the strength of parliament, the independence of the judiciary, and freedom of the press) on contemporary levels of electoral integrity, measured by the PEI Index. The type of electoral system for the lower house of parliament is classified from the International IDEA database into three basic types; majoritarian/plurality (coded 1), mixed (coded 2), and proportional representation (coded 3). The powers of parliament have been carefully monitored and classified in a worldwide comparison by Fish and Kroenig (2009).[40] The Parliamentary Powers Index assesses the strength of the national legislature. The index, based on thirty-two underlying dummy variables, gauges the legislature's sway of the executive, its institutional autonomy, its authority in specific areas, and its institutional capacity. The variable ranges from 0 (least powerful) to 1 (most powerful). The overall score is calculated by summing the number of powers that the national legislature possesses and dividing it by 32. For example, a country with a national legislature that possesses sixteen of the thirty-two parliamentary powers has a PPI of .50. Fish has argued that a strong parliament is a powerful predictor of democratization and, by extension, this should also display a similar relationship with electoral integrity.[41] There are debates about the underlying concept of judicial independence and also many de facto and de jure measures.[42] The independent judiciary measure in this study is from Henisz's (2000) coding. It is a dummy variable coded "1" if there is an independent judiciary.[43] Finally, the measure of freedom of the press uses Freedom House's estimates, which are computed by adding four component ratings: laws and regulations, political pressures and controls, economic influences, and repressive actions. The scale ranges from 0 (most free) to 100 (least free). The index is measured using the average score from 2001 to 2011.[44] Unfortunately, the analysis remains restricted, since the expert survey of PEI, which started in mid-2012, has not yet established longitudinal data where repeated elections are observed in many countries. Therefore, it is important to emphasize that there are difficulties in inferring the direction of causality when interpreting the results of the analysis of cross-national data. Thus, social conditions such as physical geography, the distribution of natural resources, and levels of economic development can be treated as long-term or invariable factors that are likely to influence the quality of contemporary elections. The constitutional arrangements in any state are also likely to shape the context of any electoral contest. Nevertheless, the quality of elections is also plausibly linked to many major institutions; for example, more competitive elections are likely to produce multiparty parliaments and stronger opposition parties, which can scrutinize the actions and policies of the governing party. All the institutional variables are measured in years lagged prior to the year of the PEI survey, but this can only be regarded as a partial control on endogeneity. Two models are employed to avoid problems of multicollinearity. In Model 1 (with parliamentary powers) and Model 2 (with the remaining institutional variables), multivariate regression controls for the key structural and international factors that previous chapters established as important predictors of electoral integrity.

Table 5.1 confirms the power-sharing thesis: *electoral integrity is usually greater in states with proportional representation electoral systems, strong parliaments, and press freedom.* Each of these factors shows strong and significant relationships. Moreover, all these institutional variables remain significantly

TABLE 5.1. *Political institutions and electoral integrity*

	Model 1		Model 2	
	B	S.E.	B	S.E.
INSTITUTIONS				
Type of electoral system (1 = Maj, 2 = Mixed, 3 = PR)			1.55*	.834
Parliamentary Powers	15.0*	6.75		
Independent judiciary			−1.55	2.13
Press freedom			.267***	.039
STRUCTURAL AND INTERNATIONAL CONTROLS				
Wealth (Sqrt per capita GDP ppp)	.074***	.021	.062***	.017
Natural resources (Rents as % GDP)	−1.05	.556	−.669	.435
Index of political globalization	.037	.054	.097*	.038
Regional electoral integrity	.250	.174	.002	.140
Constant	32.6		35.8	
Adjusted R^2	.542		.705	
N. countries	85		91	

Notes: OLS Regression analysis where the PEI Index is the dependent variable in eighty-five countries. All models used tolerance tests to check that they were free of problems of multicollinearity. See the technical appendix for more details about all the selected indices. ** Correlation is significant at the 0.01 level (2-tailed). * Correlation is significant at the 0.05 level (2-tailed).

Sources: Electoral Integrity Index: Electoral Integrity Project. 2014 (PEI-2.8); *Other indices from the Quality of Government Cross-National Dataset*, http://www.qog.pol.gu.se/data/.

related to electoral integrity, even after controlling for the key variables of wealth and natural resources as structural conditions, and the political globalization index and regional levels of electoral integrity, which previous chapters have established as important predictors of integrity. The primary exception concerns the measure of the independence of the judiciary, which is not significantly related to electoral integrity. The models explain considerable variance in levels of electoral integrity (Model 1 R^2 = .542 and Model 2 R^2 = .705).

As illustrated in Figure 5.1, press freedom proves a particularly powerful predictor; the greater the degree of media independence, such as in Norway, the Republic of Korea, and Slovakia, the higher the level of electoral integrity. By contrast, suppression of independent journalism in countries such as Zimbabwe, Belarus, and Equatorial Guinea is associated with worse quality elections. The independent media can serve multiple functions during any election through reporting on the performance of incumbents, providing a platform for debate among candidates, allowing parties to communicate their messages to the electorate, reporting on campaign developments, informing citizens on how to exercise their rights, monitoring the electoral process, including election-day proceedings, and reporting the results to the public. Normative theories of the public sphere suggest that the core roles of the news media are to serve as watchdogs guarding the public interest, as agenda setters

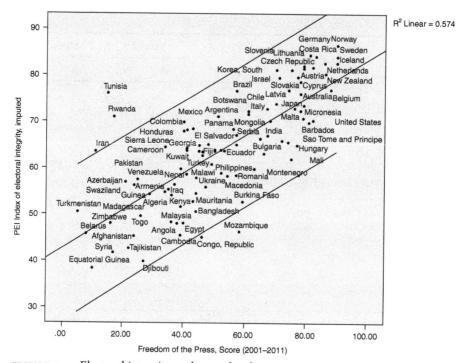

R² Linear = 0.574

FIGURE 5.1. Electoral integrity and press freedom.

Sources: Freedom of the Press, 2001–11, Freedom House; PEI Index Electoral Integrity Project. 2014.

highlighting pervasive problems, and as gatekeepers reporting a plurality of viewpoints.[45] The observed association linking press freedom with electoral integrity could plausibly run through how well journalists fulfill all these roles and responsibilities. Thus, the pattern lends support to previous studies suggesting that in countries such as the Philippines, Mexico, and Russia, independent media have been a powerful watchdog and agenda setter, safeguarding against electoral malpractice, informing the public, and mobilizing pressures for reform, through highlighting acts such as ballot rigging, voter fraud, and campaign finance scandals.[46] The news media also serve a positive function for the quality of elections, where reports strengthen the transparency of the electoral process, revealing any malpractice that occurs. By contrast, lack of a free press silences critics and makes it difficult or dangerous for reporters to highlight abuses of power by the ruling elites, for example in countries such as Syria, Turkmenistan, North Korea, and Eritrea, ranked lowest worldwide in the Reporters without Borders 2014 Press Freedom Index, where broadcasters remain under the thumb of the state. In general, the gatekeeping role of the free press is even more direct during the election campaign, in cases where journalists report the campaign and the results evenhandedly, fairly, and objectively,

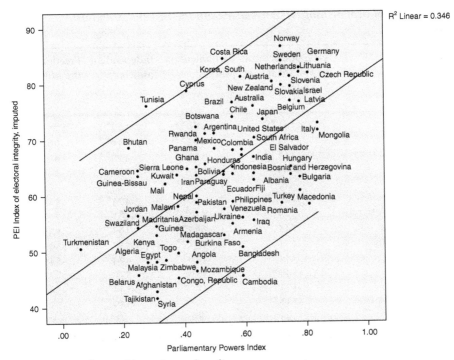

FIGURE 5.2. Electoral integrity and parliamentary powers.
Sources: Parliamentary Powers, Fish- Kroenig 2009; PEI Index Electoral Integrity Project. 2014.

including through the balance of news coverage devoted to the government and opposition parties, the fair allocation of free or paid airtime available to candidates and parties, and providing public access to pluralistic sources of information. Media watch organizations and international observers routinely monitor reporting during election campaigns, for example to document how much broadcasting time and print coverage was devoted to incumbents and challengers, whether journalists faced any obstacles or censorship, and whether any media outlets faced interference from authorities.[47] The role of social media in election campaigns is also receiving growing attention, although far more complex to monitor systematically by observers.

The oversight role of parliaments, and their capacity to check abuses of executive power and exert horizontal accountability, is also associated with greater electoral integrity, as shown by the scatterplot in Figure 5.2, although legislative strength is a weaker predictor than media freedom. Once more, countries such as Germany, the Czech Republic, and Lithuania are rated highly on both dimensions. This lends additional support to previous work emphasizing the general impact of stronger legislatures on the democratization process.[48] Especially where the judiciary and constitutional courts remain

TABLE 5.2. *Political institutions correlated with the PEI Index and its components*

Indices	Type of electoral system (Maj = 1, Mixed = 2, PR = 3)	Parliamentary powers	Independent judiciary	Freedom of the press
PEI index	.361**	.588**	.584**	.758**
Electoral laws	.334**	.467**	.346**	.665**
Electoral procedures	.353**	.522**	.499**	.693**
Voting district boundaries	.225*	.297**	.192	.346**
Voter registration	.346**	.460**	.475**	.526**
Party & candidate reg.	.325**	.538**	.487**	.718**
Media coverage	.145	.285**	.281**	.529**
Campaign finance	.275**	.441**	.553**	.505**
Voting process	.234*	.420**	.484**	.546**
Vote count	.340**	.556**	.510**	.677**
Results	.221*	.420**	.541**	.565**
Electoral authorities	.318**	.538**	.520**	.733**
# countries	94	86	93	97

Notes: **Correlation is significant at the 0.01 level (2-tailed). *Correlation is significant at the 0.05 level (2-tailed).

Sources: PEI Index Electoral Integrity Project. 2014. *The expert survey of Perceptions of Electoral Integrity*, (PEI-2.8); *Institutional indicators from the Quality of Government Cross-National Dataset*, http://www.qog.pol.gu.se/data/.

poorly institutionalized and under the control of executive appointees, the legislature provides the primary check on the chief executive. Their role can be expected to be particularly important in any revisions to electoral laws, although strong legislatures where the predominant party also controls the executive can also prove problematic if they reform laws purely in their own interests.

To go further, however, we can also explore how far political institutions are related not just to the summary PEI Index but also to each of its eleven dimensions. Table 5.2 shows the simple correlations (without controls) between the institutional indices and the PEI components, demonstrating that the relationships are remarkably consistent across each aspect, including the independence of the judiciary, with a few exceptions. Freedom of the media can be observed to be particularly powerfully correlated with the process of party and candidate registration, the vote count, the role of electoral authorities, and the quality of electoral laws.

To look further into the impact of the type of electoral system, Figure 5.3 describes the mean scores on the PEI Index and its eleven dimensions compared with the type of electoral system used for the lower house of parliament, classified from International IDEA, without any controls. As expected by advocates

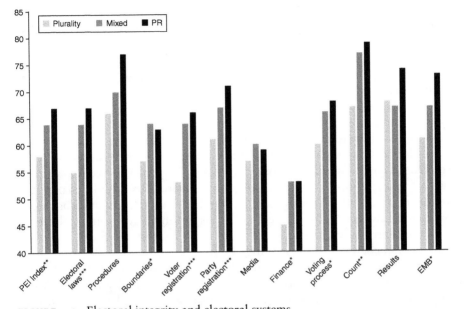

FIGURE 5.3. Electoral integrity and electoral systems.

Notes: The mean scores on the 100-point PEI Index and its dimensions by type of electoral system, where a higher score represents greater integrity. The significance of the mean differences was estimated by ANOVA. Significance * = .05, ** = .01, *** = .001.

Sources: Type of electoral system, International IDEA; PEI Index Electoral Integrity Project. 2014.

of power-sharing institutions, the PEI Index, is significantly higher under proportional representation electoral systems, with a nine-point gap over the mean PEI Index compared with plurality/majority systems. Moreover, a similar significant advantage for PR systems is evident across nine of the eleven subcomponents, especially in electoral procedures and the role of EMBs. Plurality SMDs are also significantly associated with less integrity for electoral district boundaries than electoral systems based on multimember constituencies.

IV: Conclusions

Therefore, arguments drawing upon classical liberalism and consociational democracy emphasize that institutions dispersing powers and responsibilities for electoral governance vertically and horizontally among different branches, levels, and agencies of government provide checks and balances that help prevent potential abuses by any single actor (including incumbent power holders). By generating multiple stakeholders, power-sharing constitutions are also believed to strengthen trust in the fairness, impartiality, and credibility of electoral process, even among losing candidates and parties. Finally, by heightening the incentives and opportunities for attempting ballot box fraud, the risks of malpractice by candidates are thought to be greater in single member district plurality electoral systems, where even one vote can make the difference between success and failure.

These are common arguments, although systematic evidence supporting these claims remains surprisingly limited in previous research. At the same time, however, there is certainly room for debate, since power-sharing arrangements may also have several potential *dis*advantages for electoral governance, for example if excessive fragmentation of responsibilities and roles across multiple agencies hinders the implementation of effective procedural reforms, prevents clear channels of public accountability and timely responsiveness for any problems that arise, disperses scarce managerial resources too thinly, maximizes potential entry points for corruption, and undermines uniform and consistent standards for citizens across all localities. If responsibility for running elections lies in one central government department, however, this can focus expertise, resources, and channels of accountability.

The evidence presented in this chapter provides considerable support for the advantages of several institutions that are at the heart of any power-sharing constitutional arrangements. Hence, proportional electoral systems, strong parliaments, and freedom of the press each serve to safeguard the integrity of the electoral process, providing checks on manipulation and malfeasance at different stages of the electoral cycle. The importance of these findings is that institutional reforms, such as initiatives strengthening the capacity and powers of legislators and independent media, are more amenable to programmatic intervention, unlike structural conditions such as levels of societal modernization and economic development, which usually evolve slowly over decades or even centuries, the blight of the resource curse, or how far societies are linked into global networks of international trade and communications. But the implementation of detailed registration and voting procedures, and the process of regulating and managing the conduct of elections, is the responsibility of a range of administrative agencies, so the next chapter turns to exploring the role, structure, and autonomy of these bodies.

6

Electoral Management

The explanations for flawed and failed contests considered so far emphasize the wider contextual environment, far removed from conducting any specific elections. An additional plausible argument focuses more directly on the structure, capacity, and ethos of the electoral authorities charged with administering elections. These are the front-line agencies embedded within the broader societal, international, and constitutional settings for electoral governance. Ideally, for contests to meet global norms electoral officials should ensure that they deliver public services meeting international standards.[1] Unfortunately, too often contests appear to fall foul of simple human errors, technical malfunctions, and logistical failures. Problems occur where polling stations run out of ballot papers. Poorly trained poll workers are unfamiliar with procedures. Dead people are listed on voter registers. Other legitimate citizens are turned away. Electronic voting machines break. Indelible ink washes off fingers. Ballot boxes have broken seals. Officials fail to check voter identification. Long lines delay closure. Electoral legitimacy can be damaged by accidental maladministration, and indeed official incompetence may facilitate intentional acts of partisan fraud and manipulation. Moreover, if administrative flaws arise on polling day, there are often minimal opportunities to correct them in a timely fashion, potentially damaging confidence in the electoral process and authorities.

Most attention to these sorts of problems has focused upon elections held in weak states, poorer developing societies, and contests held after regime transitions, but malpractice is by no means limited to these contexts. The ballot, voting machine, and counting problems emerging during the 2000 Bush v. Gore presidential election in the United States, and subsequent administrative reforms, motivated scholars to engage in this field.[2] Occasional incidents occur elsewhere, even in mature democracies with highly professional, experienced, and well-resourced electoral authorities. During the September 2013

Senate elections, for example, the Australian Election Commission lost 1,370 votes during a recount, generating the need for a complete rerun in Western Australia.[3] In Britain, the May 2014 local and European elections triggered police investigations concerning more than fifty cases of alleged fraud following complaints about "ghost" voters, multiple voting, and other flaws.[4] In the 2011 Canadian federal election, in several ridings automatic "robocalls" attempted to misdirect electors about the location of polling places.[5] In Switzerland, the world's oldest democracy, in 2011 one in ten referendum ballots were lost or shredded by cantons, whether intentionally or due to sloppiness, preventing a recount.[6] In elections to the German Bundestag, after 1990, rising number of petitions appealing against the results are an indication of growing suspicion by the electorate.[7]

Among all mature democracies, the nuts and bolts of American contests seem notoriously vulnerable to incompetence and simple human errors arising from the extreme decentralization and partisanship of electoral administration processes.[8] This is illustrated by (unintentionally) flawed ballot design in Florida, wait times of six hours or more to cast a ballot in Ohio, inaccurate state and local voter registers, insufficiently trained local poll workers, or the breakdown of voting machines in New York – all problems documented by the bipartisan Presidential Commission on Election Administration established by President Obama.[9] Standards are uneven; the Pew Center's 2012 Election Performance Index suggests that states such as North Dakota, Minnesota, and Wisconsin performed well against a range of quality indicators combining voting convenience and integrity, but others demonstrated more problems, including California, Oklahoma, and Mississippi.[10] During the 2014 midterm elections, a range of problems was reported on polling day, some trivial, others more serious, although whether arising from incompetence and maladministration or intentional dirty tricks remains to be determined. At least eighteen state election websites experienced disruptions on election day, preventing voters from using the sites to locate polling places and ballot information.[11] Elsewhere, people were turned away from Hartford Connecticut polling places that did not open on time since they had not received polling lists. The Chicago Board of Election Commissioners reported that more than 2,000 election judges did not turn up at their polling stations after receiving erroneous information from "robocalls." In Virginia, a State Department of Elections spokesman said that thirty-two electronic voting machines at twenty-five polling places experienced problems. In Virginia and North Caroline there were also claimed cases of electronic polling machine which recorded a vote for the democratic candidate when the screen was touched to cast a vote for the Republican.[12] The state-wide voter-registration system crashed in Texas so that poll workers were unable to confirm voter eligibility, forcing many to complete provisional ballots.[13] Meanwhile, new state laws requiring electors to present photo identification were reported to sow the seeds of confusion in several places such as Texas, Georgia, and North Carolina.[14]

In the light of these sorts of problems, this chapter focuses upon several conditions that are widely believed to strengthen electoral administration, including *organizational structure* (the establishment of EMBs) as independent administrative agencies that are legally separate from the executive branch), *functional capacity* (the degree of government effectiveness), and the *administrative ethos* (the predominant culture in the public sector).[15] Part I outlines reasons why each of these factors is thought to be important and what is known about these issues from previous research. The first explanation suggests that elections work better where electoral authorities are established as institutions that are formally separate administrative agencies operating at arms-length from government, to insulate them from executive meddling, rather than being embedded as units staffed by civil servants within existing government departments and local authorities. The second emphasizes functional effectiveness and how far the public sector has the skills, experience, powers, and resources to manage to deliver public goods and services, including, by extension, how far electoral authorities have sufficient technical expertise, trained and competent officials, consistent procedural guidelines and rules, sufficient planning time, and adequate budgets. The final account suggests that elections are more likely to meet international standards where an impartial and professional *administrative ethos* predominates among officials within the public sector, setting expectations about what is acceptable within the organization, with norms of unbiased service in the public interest predominating over a culture corrupted by patronage politics, partisanship, and clientelistic practices. Structure, functional capacity, and culture can be understood logically as separate explanations or conceptualized as related components in a nested model, where general levels of functional effectiveness and the predominant ethos within the public sector set the broader context within which electoral authorities operate. While the previous literature has focused most attention upon analyzing the consequences of the structural organization of electoral authorities on public confidence and trust in these bodies, the impact of each of these factors on the actual quality of electoral integrity has not been clearly established.

The first part of this chapter outlines the arguments. To test several propositions arising from these theories, Part II describes the evidence and operationalizes the key independent variables. Cross-national indicators are used to compare both governance effectiveness and the predominant bureaucratic ethos within each nation, drawing upon assessments by the World Bank Institute, the International Country Risk Group, and the Quality of Government institute.[16] To monitor the formal independence of electoral authorities (their *de jure* autonomy from executive control), three main types of organizational structure are distinguished: Governmental, Agency, and Mixed models, drawing on the ACE Project Electoral Knowledge Network and the International IDEA database to document their underlying features and to classify countries.[17] To analyze the impact of these factors on the *de facto* performance of elections, as in previous chapters, the study utilizes the PEI expert survey, including the overall summary PEI Index and several specific PEI indicators evaluating the performance of the electoral authorities, including their impartiality, managerial competence, and transparency. Part III tests whether the bureaucratic culture, functional effectiveness, and the de jure institutional autonomy of electoral management agencies do indeed predict electoral performance, as theorized. Fully specified models control for the range of other structural, international, and constitutional conditions established as important for integrity in previous chapters. The conclusion considers the main findings and their broader implications.

The main findings suggest, as expected, that electoral integrity is usually stronger in states characterized by effective governments with the capacity to deliver high quality public services as well as in states where the ethos of public administration is regarded as impartial and professional, serving the public interest while avoiding patronage politics and clientelism. By contrast to the established wisdom prevalent in electoral management guidelines and the advice issued by the international community, however, the study could detect no evidence supporting the claim that the quality of elections depends on the de jure legal structural independence of electoral authorities established as agencies separate from government. Thus, the impact of state capacity and informal norms in the bureaucratic culture seem to outweigh formal organizational structures.

I: Theoretical Claims

The roles and responsibilities of the central authorities tasked with managing elections vary substantially around the world. These organizations are often called EMBs, although this language can prove misleading if it is taken to imply that a single nation-wide organization has the authority to administer and regulate multiple dimensions of electoral contests. Typically, the central electoral agency at nation level is charged with implementing a wide range of tasks, which may include issuing detailed administrative guidelines and codes governing: the conduct of staff, candidates, political parties, and agents; validating and registering the nomination of political parties and candidates for elected office; determining qualifications and maintaining electoral registration databases; regulating procedures and facilities for polling; monitoring the vote tabulation process and compiling nation-wide results; and authorizing the official declaration of the vote and seat distribution. The central EMBs may be authorized with a broader mandate, including multiple additional responsibilities. Alternatively, several functions may be delegated to a range of specialized independent administrative and regulatory agencies, such as boundary commissions responsible for delimitation, regulatory bodies tasked with registering political parties and monitoring campaign finance, broadcasting authorities allocating any party political broadcasts, and courts and tribunals resolving electoral complaints and disputes.[18] Unitary and federal states also vary around the world in the decentralization of powers to officials responsible for administering elections at provincial, municipal, and district levels.

How should the performance of electoral authorities be evaluated? Officials should ideally meet several general guiding principles and values that are common in public-sector management, and that are thought to ensure legitimate and credible processes and outcomes meeting international standards. International IDEA's Handbook suggests that these principles include: de facto *independence* from undue interference in their activities from the executive branch or partisan forces; *integrity*, so that the process is free of fraud and corruption; *transparency*, to build trust in the accuracy and honesty of the process; *efficiency*, so that services are delivered effectively, equitably, and within budget; *impartiality*, so that officials are not biased toward any single contestant; and *professionalism*, so that staff have the training, expertise, and resources to manage tasks well.[19] Similar principles are echoed in many of the practical guidelines designed to strengthen electoral administration. For example, as an IFES report emphasizes: "*An effective planning process ensures that all electoral operations take place successfully, in a timely manner and are conducted in compliance with regulations. Electoral materials must have the right specifications, be in the right place, in the right quantity and at the right time. Electoral officials must be properly trained and fully aware of their functions and duties. All candidates must be registered according to existing legal provisions and timelines. It is through the effective management of all these processes and procedures that voters on Election Day are allowed to exercise their right to vote without legal, administrative, logistical or security impediments of any kind.*"[20] The Venice Commission for the Council of Europe also endorses similar norms: "Electoral Commissions (ECs) should be set up as independent, permanent and multi-tiered bodies; EC members should be appointed by different institutions, not to be recallable (except for certain specified disciplinary reasons) and receive standardized training in elections management; and EC procedures should be clear and efficient, allowing for inclusive discussions and effective decisions at the same time."[21]

Reflecting these values, there is widespread agreement that elections should be administered fairly and efficiently by an impartial body.[22] Voter registers should be accurate, up to date, and comprehensive. Participation in political procedures should be inclusive for all sectors of society, including engaging underrepresented groups such as young people, women, and minorities. Polling should be accessible and convenient for citizens, with special balloting facilities for those with limited mobility, including institutionalized populations, the homebound, and the disabled. Balloting should be secure and free of fraud, vote rigging, or any mechanical errors. The vote tabulation should be honest, accurate, and transparent, followed by the timely announcement of the results. Voting should be universal, equal, free, secret and with direct suffrage. Processes and outcomes should be widely regarded as legitimate and just by losers as well as winners. It is challenging to meet these performance standards – and often many more.

While the desirability of these general goals is widely agreed in the official guidelines issued by agencies in the international community, it is tricky to assess how far the performance of electoral authorities actually meets these standards. Optimal performance may also require some trade-offs among these values, for example the need for institutional autonomy of senior officials, to protect decisions from undue external pressures and to avoid partisan favoritism, has to be balanced against the need for the accountability of public bodies, to ensure that administrators use public resources in an appropriate manner. Moreover, debate continues about the most appropriate institutional designs to achieve these performance standards. The most comprehensive studies comparing the structure and organization of EMBs has been produced by international agencies, notably IFES, International IDEA, the ACE Project, and regional organizations such as the Asia Foundation, the Council of Europe, OAS, and OSCE. In particular, International IDEA's *Handbook of Electoral Management Design*, and the accompanying ACE Project Electoral Knowledge Network online database, provide the most comprehensive worldwide classification of the formal organization of electoral authorities.[23] Systematic comparative evidence comparing de jure institutional independence with de facto performance still remains limited, however, and most studies evaluating the role of these bodies have focused upon analyzing performance indicators in single nation studies[24] and also in selected descriptive "best practice" cases.[25] A decade ago, Pastor noted that the unglamorous side of electoral administration had been largely relegated to a dusty and obscure corner of public administration.[26] This is no longer true, as a growing body of academic research has started to throw light on the structure, powers, and functions of electoral authorities within specific regions, although it remains the case that systematic comparative research on EMBs remains underdeveloped and undertheorized.[27]

Types of Formal Institutional Design

The organizational structures of EMBs vary worldwide, and the most important differences are illustrated schematically in Figure 6.1. The most common classification of EMBs was first developed by Lopez-Pintor.[28] This typology was subsequently refined further in the comprehensive worldwide study produced by International IDEA. The conventional framework distinguishes three types of formal institutional structures which have been termed "Governmental," "Mixed," and "Independent" models. Unfortunately, the original choice of terms, which has been widely adopted in the literature, can confuse the *de jure* formal–legal independence of any body and its *de facto* autonomy from undue external interference, a matter that remains to be determined in the light of the empirical evidence. De jure or formal executive independence refers to the constitutional and legal instruments that govern the electoral authorities, and how far these allow the authorities to make decisions without external interference

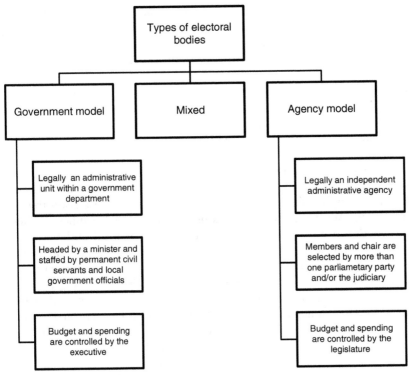

FIGURE 6.1. Types of EMBs.

or constraints from outside actors. De facto or actual executive independence, by contrast, refers to how far in practice electoral authorities make their decisions without external interference or constraints. Hence in this book, to avoid the risks of this potential conceptual slippage, the term '*Agency model*' is used to imply that the organization is established constitutionally or legally to operate at arm's length from the executive branch.

Government Model

In many established democracies, electoral administration was traditionally handled by local and national government officials, with courts handling any disputes. The central authorities responsible for managing elections were typically located in the Ministry of Interior, Ministry of Justice, Home Office, or equivalent department of state. This arrangement persists today in several European states, such as the Swedish Electoral Authority, the German Ministry of Interior, the Swiss Federal Chancellery, and the Norwegian Ministry for Local Government and Regional Development. In these states, the civil service has a general reputation for professional neutrality and impartiality. This system was originally used to manage elections post-independence in many former colonies, such as in Nigeria, Sierra Leone, and Uganda, although there has been an increasing tendency toward transferring these responsibilities to independent administrative agencies.[29] Among all countries worldwide, International IDEA estimates that around one quarter continues to use the Governmental model for running elections.[30]

In this model, a unit located within a central government department is responsible for administering elections, staffed by permanent civil servants and headed by a cabinet minister who is directly accountable to the legislature, and thus indirectly to the electorate. The Governmental model exists in those countries "where elections are organized and managed by the executive branch through a ministry (such as the Ministry of the Interior) and/or through local authorities. Where EMBs under the Governmental model exist at national level, they are led by a minister or civil servant and they are answerable to a cabinet minister. With very few exceptions they have no "members." Their budget falls within a government ministry and/or under local authorities."[31] This model persists in several European countries, as described in detail in the French case study in the previous chapter.[32] The day-to-day administration of elections, such as maintaining voter registries, organizing balloting, running polling places, and counting ballots, is devolved to government authorities at provincial, state, municipal, and constituency levels. The national parliament retains the primary prerogative of law making, establishing the statutory framework of electoral regulations, with regional and local officials responsible for the detailed application and implementation of these procedures in each locality, and the courts interpreting the laws and adjudicating disputes.

There are many important variations in these arrangements across countries, however, especially in degree of centralization and local decentralization, reflecting long-standing contrasts between unitary and federal states. In countries such as France, considerable power over elections is concentrated in the governing party and the core executive in central government, with other branches of government exercising a minor role. In other states, such as Sweden, multiparty parliaments exercise strong checks over the decisions of the executive, and the courts and the office of the ombudsman provide further safeguards in rule adjudication and dispute resolution. The United States, in particular, remains exceptional, compared with most other long-standing democracies, in its high degree of partisanship and decentralization. As described in the previous chapter, American elections follow the Governmental model, with state and local officials primarily responsible for administering elections, and heavy reliance on the partisan appointment of local officials who supervise volunteer part-time poll workers. Traditionally, due to constitutional requirements, the US federal government's role in elections has been strictly limited, although this role has expanded somewhat in recent years with attempts to improve standards amid growing concern arising about the uneven performance of local and state electoral bodies, leading to the 2002 Help America Vote Act and establishment of the bipartisan US Election Assistance Commission.[33]

One potential advantage of the Governmental model is that electoral authorities can call upon the existing resources of the public sector to run elections, including commonly deploying the permanent pool of skilled, experienced, and trained full-time employees at national and local authority levels to administer contests. Electoral authorities can also use the existing technological and communication infrastructure of national and local governments, reducing overhead costs and the duplication of services. In democratic states, the model also provides a clear chain of accountability for any errors that arise. Local government staff are supervised by national electoral officials who are, in turn, accountable to a government minister and thus ultimately subject to parliamentary oversight and the general electorate.

At the same time, however, the main danger is that where electoral administration is the responsibility of civil servants working in central ministries or local authorities, and thus subject to executive control, the process is thought vulnerable to either the actual or the perceived abuse of power and the risk of manipulation to benefit the interests of the governing party or parties. This is particularly dangerous in states with predominant parties, fragmented opposition parties, and weak parliamentary and judicial oversight of the executive. Electoral officials need to be impartial and independent of government or other external influences from political parties, special interests, or the military if the process and results are to be trusted as credible, transparent, and fair. What works in Sweden, Belgium, and Denmark may therefore be far from appropriate in, say, the Prime Minister's Office in Singapore, the Ministry of Interior in Syria, or the Election Council in Vietnam, all of which also have a Governmental model of electoral administration.

Agency Model

Recent years have seen several post-industrial countries adopting new public-sector management reforms where several government functions are transferred from central department of state to specific administrative and regulatory agencies in the public sector.[34] This structure has long been common in the United States. In several Anglo-American countries, including New Zealand, the United Kingdom, and Australia, in recent decades the tendency has been to establish more specialized organizations, as well as decentralizing decision making and administration from the center toward the periphery, thereby fragmenting responsibility for public services that used to be the province of large bureaucratic ministries. Similar trends have been observed in Canada, France, and the Netherlands, although they are thought to be less marked in Belgium, Finland, Germany, and Sweden.[35] Independent regulatory and administrative agencies have been established in the public sector to provide delegated authority over many policy areas, such as environmental protection, food safety, pharmaceuticals, and telecoms. It is widely believed that this separation of specialized agencies from direct government control avoids political interference and potential conflicts of interest, as well as being more efficient, and thus strengthens the delivery of goods and services in the public interest.[36]

Reflecting this development, many countries transferred responsibilities for election management from government departments to legally independent administrative agencies, with chief executives composed of experts or partisan members, which operate at arm's length from the executive. The names of these bodies vary in different countries, and they are often called "Electoral Commissions," "Electoral Tribunals," "Electoral Boards," "Electoral Courts," "Departments of Elections," "Election Institutes," "Election Councils," and so on, known generically as EMBs.[37] Agency models of electoral administration create "arms-length" separation from the government through the mechanism of establishing de jure formal–legal independence. The Agency model has often been established to run the first elections following regime transitions, such as the National Election Commission in Poland, the Independent Election Commission in South Africa, and the Central Election Bureau in Romania. The model has also become increasingly popular among established democracies; for example, through agencies such as the Australian Electoral Commission (since 1984), and the UK Electoral Commission (since 2000). This type of arrangement is described by International IDEA as those where elections are organized and managed by an EMB that is institutionally independent and autonomous from the executive branch of government, and that has and manages its own budget. Under the Independent Model, an EMB is not accountable to a government ministry or a department. It may be accountable to the legislature, the judiciary, or the head of state. EMBs under the Independent Model may enjoy varying degrees of financial autonomy and accountability, as well as varying levels of performance accountability. They are composed of members from outside the permanent civil service.[38]

The organizational structure, legal mandate, and administrative functions of electoral agencies vary substantially from one country to another, however, as does the de facto autonomy of these agencies, according to their constitutional and legal status, their scope and mandate, provisions for the nomination, appointment, and removal of senior members, the capacity for external actors and other branches of government to overrule the agency's decisions and oversee its operations, and the body's financial independence. One major challenge facing analysts is therefore how best to distinguish formal from actual independence. The practice of how the law operates may differ sharply from the text on paper, not least given the Orwellian propensity of regimes to misappropriate positive terms in doublespeak. Thus, electoral authorities are categorized by International IDEA as formally "independent" in autocracies such as the Central Election Committee in Kazakhstan, the Electoral Commission in Zimbabwe, and the Elections and Boundary Commission in Swaziland, all states ranked poorly on the overall summary PEI Index of electoral integrity, as well as being given low rankings in expert evaluations of the fairness of electoral officials and the competence of election management. In Russia, the nominally independent Central Electoral Commission has been seen to be responsive to pressures from incumbent politicians.[39] Whether election agencies have sufficient resources and powers to manage contests effectively also varies around the world. In some transitional states, the international community has encouraged new regimes to establish formally independent election agencies. In subsequent elections, however, the government has allocated limited staffing, restricted powers, or inadequate budgets to these agencies, so that officials are unable to build capacity or fulfill their responsibilities.

Mixed Model
Finally, rather than falling neatly into just two categories, International IDEA also identifies a Mixed or Hybrid model of electoral management. In these "there are usually two component EMBs, and dual structures exist: a policy, monitoring or supervisory EMB that is independent of the executive branch of government (like an EMB under the Independent model) and an implementation EMB located within a department of state and/or local government (like an EMB under the Governmental model). Under the Mixed model, elections are organized by the component governmental EMB, with some level of oversight provided by the component independent EMB."[40] Mixed models exist in countries as diverse as Portugal, Sri Lanka, Argentina, Slovakia, and Japan.

In Spain, for example, several functions are reserved for the General Directorate of Internal Policy located within the Ministry of Interior, including coordinating electoral processes, deploying communications and information electoral technologies, maintaining the party register, and managing state grants for election expenses by political parties. Other government departments play a role, including the Ministry of Economy and Finance (which oversees the Electoral Census Office), the Ministry of Foreign Affairs and Cooperation (in all matters relating to the exercise of voting rights of Spanish citizens abroad), the Ministry of Defense facilitating voting by armed forces personnel, the State Society of Posts and Telegraphs (for voting by mail), as well as delegations and sub-delegations of the government and local councils. In addition, Election Boards at central, provincial, and local levels are agencies composed of experts from the judiciary and political parties who are responsible for ensuring the transparency and impartiality of the electoral process.[41]

The Distribution of Types of EMBs
Global estimates differ somewhat in the classifications and benchmarks used to distinguish types of EMBs.[42] The elections management database by the ACE Project/International IDEA provides the most comprehensive coverage, and this indicates that today most countries have an Agency model of electoral authorities that is legally separate from government (found in 131 countries out of 187 independent nation states worldwide, or 70%). Electoral authorities are located within a government department in about a fifth of all countries

worldwide (33 countries or 18%), while the remainder of states (23 countries or 12%) have Mixed systems.

Several subcomponents concerning the size, composition, and membership tenure of senior officials in central or national electoral agencies are also classified in the ACE Project/International IDEA database. One concerns the varied rules and qualifications for nomination and appointment of senior electoral officials. According to the ACE Project/International IDEA database, the small group of senior managers at the top of the agency is nominated by the legislature in around one third of countries worldwide, while the executive nominates these officials in around one quarter of countries, with the remainder having mixed procedures. The ACE Project/International IDEA database also suggests that expertise is the most common basis for nomination and appointment of senior officials, such as legal, academic, or judicial qualifications, the criterion used in two-thirds of countries. By contrast a third of countries use mixed qualification criteria, and a few countries (6%) select officials based on their partisanship alone.

The Role of Administrative Agencies in Electoral Integrity

Why might the type of organizational structure and legal autonomy explain the role of electoral authorities in flawed or failed elections? The first argument, reflecting classical liberal assumptions about the limited role for the state, suggests that the de jure legal independence, understood in terms of the formal organizational structure of EMBs, is critical for integrity. Formal–legal independence is thought to strengthen actual independence. The claimed advantages of the Agency model is that by insulating electoral officials from outside pressures, this helps to curb any potential conflict of interest, partisan meddling, and the abuse of power by external forces, especially where it is suspected that the electoral arbitrator is biased toward incumbent politicians, political parties, the governing party, or powerful elites. In tightly fought and close contests, it is believed that electoral agencies are more likely to serve (and to be seen by all parties to serve) as impartial and fair umpires when regulating procedures, running elections, managing the count, announcing the final results, investigating misconduct, and adjudicating complaints. Thus International IDEA advises: "The EMB must be able to operate free of interference, simply because any allegation of manipulation, perception of bias, or alleged interference will have a direct impact not only on the credibility of the body in charge but on the entire election process."[43] By delegating responsibility for electoral administration to independent agencies, politicians agree to abide by the rules, strengthening the credibility of the electoral process.[44] This argument echoes many of the liberal claims about the virtues of constitutional checks and balances in the main branches of government discussed in the previous chapter. The importance of independence is a prevalent perspective within the international community; for example, a recent report for Elections Canada emphasizes: "Most election officers and scholars regard independence as the single most crucial test of the soundness of electoral governance arrangements."[45] The major risks of concentrating responsibilities within a single central governmental depart-ment unit is that this body is more easily manipulated by the party or parties controlling the executive, for example if the outcome of a contest threatens the power of incumbent elites. This risk is heightened if other institutional checks and balances remain weak, such as the oversight role of parliament and the judiciary. Conflicts of interest can also occur where EMBs are responsible for both administering elections and also for monitoring complaints and disputes, which may be directed against electoral officials. Given the risks, most interna-tional agencies do not advocate this model.

At the same time, however, regulatory policies and administrative procedures may be less coherent if decision making is dispersed across multiple indepen-dent national agencies, weakening coordinated or "joined-up" governance, for example if separate specialist bodies are established for the regulation of cam-paign broadcasting, the allocation of political finance, party registration, and boundary delimitation. With the decentralization of decision making to local authorities, basic procedures, such as the hours polling stations are open, or the qualifications and application processes to be included on the electoral reg-ister, can vary from one locality to another and thus citizens' fundamental vot-ing rights will not be consistently applied across all jurisdictions. Some poorly resourced local agencies that have suddenly to ramp up efforts to run contests at periodic intervals, may lack the professional experience, permanent person-nel, and technical machinery to manage these tasks well. Decentralization giv-ing more discretion to local electoral officials also expands the number of entry points and thus the potential risks of corruption and malfeasance. If prob-lems arise, it remains more difficult to establish "where the buck stops" among multiple agencies with overlapping functions, weakening accountability. For example, even if both Democrats and Republicans agree that there should not be excessively long lines at polling stations, it remains difficult to implement straightforward solutions in the United States, such as those suggested by the Presidential Commission, due to the dispersed authorities of the state and local bodies running elections.[46]

By contrast, a potential advantage of the more centralized Governmental model is a streamlined and coordinated administrative process regulating all major aspects of electoral governance, with the EMB directly reporting to a minister who is, in turn, accountable directly to parliament. The professional expertise, organizational structures, and technical resources of staff employed in the civil service and in local authorities can be deployed to manage periodic elections, avoiding duplication. This arrangement may work particularly well in many long-established democracies such as Sweden, where the public-sector bureaucracy is widely regarded as impartial and professional, there is strong parliamentary accountability, and multiple constitutional checks and balances exist in the constitution. National elections are somewhat akin to large-scale military operations, where a hierarchical command-and-control organization and rule-based top-down form of decision making are both potentially well suited to coordinate strategic mechanical operations. Electoral policies and procedures can be uniformly and consistently applied by the central agency across multiple local jurisdictions. If any problems occur, the hierarchical chain of bureaucratic authority and political accountability is clearly established. Any procedural reforms that are necessary to strengthen elections, such as revisions to the electoral register or amendments to identification requirements, can be rolled out relatively straightforwardly across the whole country.

Moreover the links between the formal–legal structure and the actual independence of the body are complex to establish and they need to be demonstrated. Studies have attributed violent protests by opposition parties to perceptions that the election commission was biased toward the ruling party, such as in Nigeria in 2007, Ethiopia in 2005, and Kenya in 2007, despite the nominal structural independence of these agencies.[47] In the 2011 presidential election in Belarus, for example, the Central Election Commission was a legally independent twelve-member permanent agency based outside of the Ministry of Justice, but half the members were appointed by the president and the remainder by the ruling party predominating in the legislature. At lower levels, as well, most officials in local precincts (93%) were nominated by pro-government organizations.[48]

Most empirical research has drawn on surveys to examine whether the type of electoral institutions shape citizens confidence in elections. Scholars comparing public opinion in Latin America have reported that the formal independence of these bodies from political control strengthens citizens' confidence and trust in the fairness of the electoral process: "Professional and independent EMBs free from partisan influence and government control provide a much greater chance of successful elections, particularly relative to those EMBs dominated by a single party."[49] Several similar studies have also compared the structure and competence of electoral commissions in sub-Saharan Africa.[50] Hence Kerr found that Africans expressed more confidence in elections when EMBs performed effectively (measured in eighteen countries in sub-Saharan Africa by expert evaluation of EMB capacity and actual autonomy). At the same time, the importance of formal autonomy for public trust remains a matter for debate, since a study by Birch based on the Comparative Study of Electoral Systems found that the de jure autonomy of EMBs was unrelated to public confidence in electoral processes.[51]

What remains to be determined is whether the de jure autonomy of electoral authorities improves the actual quality of elections, not just public confidence. De jure formal autonomy can be measured by institutional indicators from the ACR Project/International IDEA database such as the procedures and terms used for the nomination, appointment and dismissal of senior officials, executive or legislative control over the agency's budget, and whether electoral officials are nominated based on their partisanship or expertise.[52] Indeed, in a comparative study, Birch found that the type of independent or governmental models of electoral administration (classified by International IDEA) had no significant impact on electoral malpractice.[53]

Functional Effectiveness and State Capacity

Another common argument assumes that, in practice, functional effectiveness and state capacity are probably critical for the quality of electoral governance. I have argued in previous work that the quality of governance, combined with institutions of democratic accountability, are both vitally important for determining whether administrative agencies respond competently to public needs when managing the delivery of goods and services.[54] The emphasis on building state capacity in developing societies and emerging economies is hardly new, as it is echoed in the work of seminal thinkers from Samuel Huntington to Francis Fukuyama.[55] It also reflects the contemporary emphasis on "good governance" by the Bretton Woods financial institutions. Since the mid-1990s, the augmented Washington Consensus has emphasized the importance of establishing rule of law as a precondition for an effective development, including access to justice, an independent judiciary, and professionally trained security forces. Similarly, the World Bank has emphasized the importance of developing integrity, transparency, and lack of corruption in the public sector, to ensure that aid improves public goods and services and thus reaches poor people, rather than ending up in the pockets of political and economic elites. Democracy has sometimes been regarded as one necessary component of "good" governance, among others, but it is preferable to treat democracy and governance as conceptually separate and distinct phenomenon.[56]

The importance of functional effectiveness and state capacity are illustrated by electoral problems that arise from happenstance and accident, or lack of administrative capacity and technical experience. A clear example comes from experience of Kenyan general elections. The 2007 contest ended in inter-communal riots and widespread bloodshed. In an effort to avoid repeating this debacle, in planning for the 2013 contest, the election commission adopted high-tech voter-registration and vote-count processes. Despite investing around $120 million on equipment, problems of late procurement and deployment meant that electronic voter-identification laptops with digital scanners ran out of power and had to be abandoned half way through polling day, only around one in ten polling stations was able to transmit the ballot results to headquarters electronically, while the electronic results-reporting system experienced a software glitch and it was also abandoned a day and a half into the count.[57] The problems were not obviously intentional or strategic; instead human error and the adoption of technical solutions that could not be supported can be blamed. The complex operation of training and deploying thousands of local officials, and the technical and human resources required for organizing effective elections, is a major challenge even for long-standing EMBs, let alone for officials attempting to run contests following humanitarian crises, such as disruptive conditions in the aftermath of the 2010 earthquake in Haiti, or in new-born independent states such as Timor-Leste, as part of the peace-building process, such as in the Democratic Republic of Congo in 2006, Nepal in 2008, or Afghanistan in 2004, and in countries experiencing regime transitions, such as following the Arab uprisings in Tunisia, Libya, and Egypt.[58]

As documented in previous chapters, the international community has invested heavily in providing technical assistance for elections and building the capacity of EMBs so that they become more professional, effective, impartial, and independent.[59] Nation-wide elections are highly complex, costly, and large-scale events, requiring long-term strategic planning, while raising politically sensitive logistical and administrative issues. Almost no contests are implemented flawlessly due to the enormous demands elections often make on managerial, technical, legal, human, and financial resources. Per capita costs are substantial in elections held as part of peace-keeping initiatives; for example, in 2004 an estimated US$190 million was spent by the Afghan electoral authorities (more than $20 per elector) on direct costs, without taking account of the additional indirect expenses for security, civic education, and electoral observation.[60] Moreover, where problems occur during the campaign or on polling day, there is often minimal time for any corrective actions to be taken, derailing the best-laid strategic plans and risk assessments. Given the complexities and the scale of the resources required to manage such events successfully – involving perhaps the greatest nation-wide mobilization outside of war-time – flawless contests are hard to organize, even in long-established democracies. Thus the effectiveness and competence of officials working in electoral agencies should have a major impact on the quality of contests in any country, especially in developing societies.

Administrative Culture

Finally, the predominant ethos and culture of the public sector may also be expected to influence administrative processes and performance. The administrative culture refers to the norms and values shaping beliefs about appropriate standards of behavior, and thus how public servants should work.[61] Along with the broader constitutional context, these norms can shape how organizations structures operate and thus explain how the Agency model may have very different outcomes in, say, South Africa and Kazakhstan. The importance of an impartial administrative culture is recognized by the Venice Commission Code of Conduct, which suggests that where this tradition is missing, then independent electoral commissions need to be established at all levels.[62] In general, well-functioning bureaucratic states are characterized by a public-sector culture that prioritizes a range of values such as impartiality, effectiveness, legality, efficiency, transparency, and integrity. Where officials working in EMBs also reflect these general values and cultural norms, then the management of elections can be expected to serve the public interest, for example by treating all candidates and parties impartially and equitably. By contrast, in administrative cultures where patronage politics, clientelistic practices, and corruption predominate, electoral authorities are more likely to prove biased and partisan, reducing trust in the process and outcome.[63] Under clientelism, public officials are more likely to favor particular incumbents in exchange for direct payments or continued access to state resources, such as employment, goods, or services. Linkages can be direct or sustained over a longer period by webs of obligation and reciprocity, for example where ruling parties reappoint senior electoral commissioners or judges in courts of appeal who fail to investigate official electoral complaints, or who regularly overturn opposition petitions.

Although clientelism is commonly assumed to encourage malpractice, systematic evidence testing this thesis has not been clearly demonstrated, in part due to the limited evidence that has been available in the past measuring this phenomenon. In the previous literature, Evans and Rauch provided a pioneering study assessing bureaucratic governance and analyzing the general links between the quality of bureaucratic governance and economic growth. The authors concluded that in the countries under comparison, state bureaucracies characterized by meritocratic recruitment and rewarding career ladders generated higher rates of economic growth. More recently, Bo Rothstein has examined the impact of the Quality of Government, conceptualized in terms of the concept of impartiality, on several diverse variables including institutional trust, economic growth, corruption, welfare outcomes, and life satisfaction.[64] In previous work I demonstrated that the quality of bureaucratic governance (measured by the ICRG) influenced how far states delivered peace, prosperity, and welfare.[65] Chapter 3 also demonstrated that electoral integrity is worse in rentier states where the economy is heavily dependent upon the natural resources of oil and gas, as well as in societies which the public sees as highly corrupt. Following a similar logic, from the available evidence we can test whether the predominant bureaucratic culture – more specifically indicators of professionalism and impartiality in public administration – predict levels of electoral integrity.

II: Classification and Evidence

Several broad measures of functional effectiveness and the predominant bureaucratic ethos are available in cross-national data, and these can be employed to monitor the quality of public administration in any country, providing an indirect proxy to compare the capacity and ethos of the EMBs. Use of these indicators can throw light on the proposition, in particular, that electoral integrity (measured by the PEI Index and by expert evaluations of the performance of electoral authorities) is strengthened in states where a professional and impartial bureaucratic ethos prevails in the public sector, and by contrast is undermined in states where clientelism and patronage politics prevails.

Measuring the Predominant Bureaucratic Culture

The first pioneering comparative study of the quality of bureaucratic governance was developed by Evans and Rauch, based on expert assessments of meritocratic recruitment and predictable career ladders in the public sector. The survey gathered data during the early-1990s in around three dozen middle- and low-income countries.[66] Another measure assessing bureaucratic governance is the World Bank's Resource Allocation Index, which estimates the contemporary quality of public administration, based on their annual Country Policy and Institutional Assessment exercise, but unfortunately evidence is only available for a limited number of developing countries.

For this chapter, the predominant bureaucratic culture and ethos in the public sector in each country is measured by using the Quality of Governance Institute's expert survey measuring dimensions of the culture of public administration including levels of professionalization and impartiality in 135 countries around the world.[67] The general purpose of the QoG survey is to measure the structure and behavior of the public sector across countries. The survey covers a variety of topics that are seen as relevant to the structure and functioning of the public administration according to the literature, but where quantitative indicators are unavailable for a large number of countries, such as meritocratic recruitment, internal promotion and career stability, salaries, impartiality, effectiveness/efficiency, and bureaucratic representation. The QoG impartiality composite index seeks to measure how far government employees implement laws and policies through favoritism, for example responding to kickbacks or personal clientelistic contacts, or whether they act fairly and impartially.[68] The professionalism index seeks to measure how far public-sector employees are recruited based on meritocratic qualifications and career experience, or whether political and personal connections are important.

For additional robustness checks, similar models are run using the Political Risk Service's Group (PRSG) International Country Risk Guide. The PRSG's *Quality of Government* index combines three components: bureaucratic quality, corruption, and law and order.[69] *Bureaucratic Quality* measures how far the country's public sector is characterized by (i) regular processes of meritocratic recruitment and career advancement, (ii) independence from political pressures, and (iii) the ability to provide continuous administrative services during government changes.[70] *Corruption* in the regime is measured by actual or potential corruption from excessive patronage, nepotism, and secret party funding, as well as demands for special payments or bribes in the financial transaction with public-sector employees. Lastly, *Law and Order* is assessed by the strength and impartiality of the legal system, including how far there is popular observance of the law or if the law is routinely ignored without sanction. This data set covers more than one hundred nation states over time, with observations based on expert assessments since 1984. The PRSG indicators have been widely used in the previous research literature.[71] Thus the conceptual framework and the core components underlying the PRSG's Quality of Government index closely mirror the distinction between patronage and bureaucratic cultures of governance.

Measuring Government Effectiveness and Functional Capacity

Unfortunately, we lack standardized cross-national data that would allow direct comparison of the functional capacity of EMBs to deliver effective elections, such as their budgets, staffing, or training. What we can compare, however, are general measures of the quality of the civil service and public services provided by governments, as an indirect proxy for the capacity of EMBs. To assess state functional capacities, this study draws upon the World Bank Institute "good" governance indices developed by Kaufmann, Kraay, and Mastruzzi as proxy indicators of the quality of the public sector and government effectiveness. These measures, available from 1996 to 2013, provide comprehensive worldwide geographic coverage.[72] The World Bank Institute composite indices, derived from multiple sources, are designed to measure six dimensions of good governance: "government effectiveness," "political stability," "rule of law," "voice and accountability," "regulatory quality," and "control of corruption."[73] Of these, "government effectiveness" is the most relevant proxy indicator to assess the general capacity of the public-sector bureaucracy, including staff employed at central, regional, and local levels by the electoral authorities. This concept is understood by the WBI as follows: "Government effectiveness captures perceptions of the quality of public services, the quality of the civil service and the degree of its independence from political pressures, the quality of policy formulation and implementation, and the credibility of the government's commitment to such policies."[74] This measure is therefore a suitable proxy to gauge the functional effectiveness of electoral bodies, based on the assumption that public servants in these organizations operate similarly to other administrative agencies and government departments.

III: The Links with Electoral Integrity

So what are the links between the selected measures of the de factor structural independence of the electoral body, the bureaucratic ethos, government effectiveness, and the PEI indicators of perceptions of electoral integrity? Table 6.1 shows the regression models where the first model enters the Governmental and Agency types of electoral management body, with Mixed models as the default category.

The results suggest that, despite the widespread assumption that governmental models raise risks of undue political interference and the appearance of partisan bias, the *formal organizational structure of EMBs is not a significant predictor of levels of electoral integrity*. This echoes earlier work by Birch and by Hartlyn et al, who were also unable to detect any link between models of formal EMB independence and electoral malpractice.[75] Figure 6.3

TABLE 6.1 *Electoral authorities and electoral integrity*

	Model 1 Type EMB		Model 2 Government effectiveness		Model 3 Impartial bureaucracy		Model 4 Professional bureaucracy	
	B	S.E.	B	S.E.	B	S.E.	B	S.E.
Electoral authorities								
IDEA government model of EMB	-.677	2.57	1.277	2.39	-3.00	3.59	-3.28	3.40
IDEA agency model of EMB	1.33	2.02	1.26	1.91	-.788	2.89	-.556	2.74
WBI government effectiveness			5.19***	1.05				
QoG bureaucratic culture: impartiality					6.80***	2.57		
QoG bureaucratic culture: professionalism							3.88**	1.40
Institutional controls								
Type of electoral system (1 = Maj, 2 = Mixed, 3 = PR)	1.52	.841	1.62*	.801	2.76*	1.24	3.44*	1.31
Independent judiciary	1.67	2.15						
Press freedom	.265***	.040	.206***	.041			.105	2.81
Structural and international controls								
Wealth (Sqrt per capita GDP ppp)	.070***	.018						
Natural resources (Rents as % GDP)	-.721	.445	-.402	.422	-1.17*	.576	-1.35*	.606
Index of political globalization	.095*	.038	.059	.038	.037	.055	.035	.061
Regional electoral integrity	.011	.142	.043	.130	.431*	.181	.603**	.189
Constant	60.7		64.2		31.6		3.49	
Adjusted R^2	.701		.730		.555		.626	
# countries	91		91		64		64	

Notes: OLS Regression analysis where the PEI Index is the dependent variable. Models used tolerance tests to check that they were free of problems of multicollinearity, a process which involved dropping some control variables. See the Technical Appendix for more details about all the selected indices. *Sources:* PEI Index Electoral Integrity Project. 2014 (PEI-2.8); *Other indices from the Quality of Government Cross-National Dataset*, http://www.qog.pol.gu.se/data/. **Correlation is significant at the 0.01 level (2-tailed). *Correlation is significant at the 0.05 level (2-tailed).

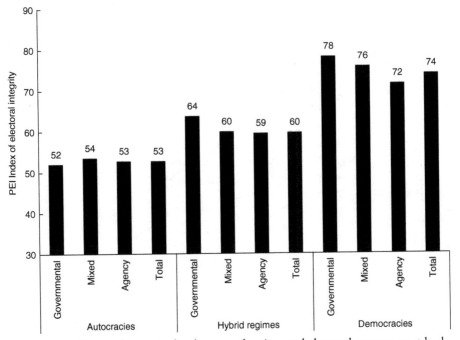

FIGURE 6.2. Electoral integrity by the type of regime and electoral management body. *Note*: The type of regime is classified from Freedom House. Not free = Autocracies, Semi-free = Hybrid regimes; Free = Democracies. The type of EMB is classified by International IDEA. N. 97 countries.

further confirms these observations by comparing the PEI Index broken down by the type of regime and the type of EMB model. It is apparent that the level of electoral integrity is relatively low in the autocracies, irrespective of the type of EMB in use. In both hybrid regimes and democracies, however, the Governmental model slightly outperforms the Agency model.

Several Reasons Could Help to Explain this Counterintuitive Observation

One explanation could be that autonomous administrative agencies may also have several weaknesses, especially if they lack access to the organizational resources, permanent professional staff, and the technical capacities that are available to a dedicated electoral unit embedded within a major department of state.

Alternatively, de jure independence on paper may not produce de facto autonomy; in Orwellian speak, many autocracies have quickly learned to tack the label "independent" onto the name of electoral authorities as a convenient façade, irrespective of how far politicians overrule the agency's decisions, such as by sacking or failing to reappoint an outgoing chief executive. As illustrated

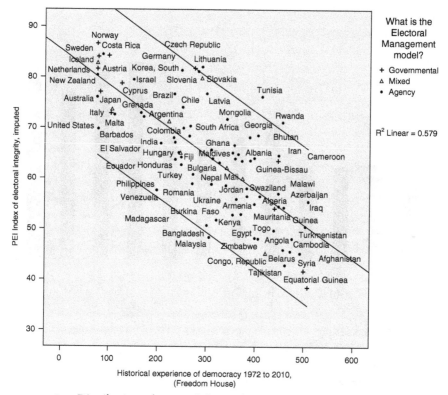

FIGURE 6.3. Distribution of types of electoral management bodies.
Sources: PEI Index Electoral Integrity Project. 2014. *The expert survey of Perceptions of Electoral Integrity*, (PEI-2.8). N. 97.

in Figures 6.2, 6.3, and 6.4, International IDEA classifies a hodge-podge of regimes as having the Governmental model, ranging from established democracies with a long tradition of an impartial and trusted civil service, such as Sweden, Norway, Germany, and Austria, on the one hand, to long-standing autocracies where ruling elites blatantly restrict political competition and violate human rights, exemplified by North Korea, Iran, Cuba, and Equatorial Guinea, on the other. International IDEA also categorizes EMBs as independent in Togo, Cambodia, and Belarus. Any classification which lumps together such disparate regimes raises questions of face validity. The appearance of independence may well be convenient window-dressing disguising agencies in the pocket of the ruling party and powerful elites. Unfortunately, this explanation remains to be investigated since we lack reliable cross-national evidence comparing the scope and capacities of electoral authorities, an issue requiring further research.

Finally, the explanation may be a path-dependent historical legacy. As parliamentary elections spread in Europe, states traditionally administered

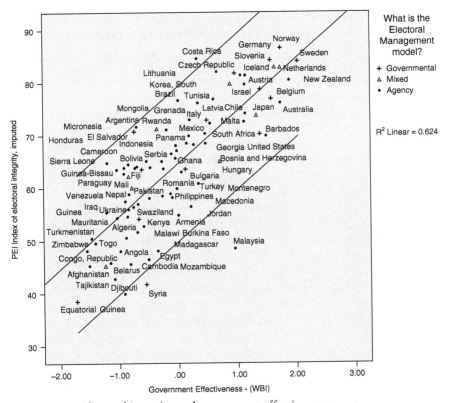

FIGURE 6.4. Electoral integrity and government effectiveness.
Sources: PEI Index Electoral Integrity Project. 2014. *The expert survey of Perceptions of Electoral Integrity*, (PEI-2.8). N. 97.

contests through the existing machinery of state, and government departments at national, provincial, and local levels continue to exercise these responsibilities in many established democracies today, for example in Denmark, the United States, and Germany (see Figure 6.4). By contrast, regimes that have transitioned from autocracy more recently during the third wave era, such as Lithuania, Chile, and Latvia, and that also face greater challenges in establishing trust in the impartiality of the electoral authorities, are likely to have faced greater domestic and international pressures to adopt independent EMBs. Figure 6.3 illustrates how the stock of democracy (the historical experience of democracy during the third wave era) compares with the distribution of types of EMBs and levels of integrity, showing how many of the long-established democracies persist with the Governmental model. It can also be observed that the Agency model is widely distributed and it includes many states where integrity is problematic, such as Togo, Zimbabwe, and Malaysia. Although this study is unable to nail down the exact reason, given data limitations, overall the findings suggest good reasons to be skeptical about the assumption that de facto autonomy from political interference necessarily follows from the formal organizational structure of the electoral body.

On the other hand, the regression analysis in Model 2 confirms that the WBI indicator monitoring government effectiveness and state capacity in delivering general public goods and services is a powerful proxy predictor of the integrity of elections as well, even with controls. Figure 6.4 illustrates the underlying pattern in more detail. Thus, countries with public services that generally work well are also likely to have efficient and professionally run contests that minimize problems arising from malfeasance, maladministration, and technical failures. This finding is hardly surprising, given that the overwhelming majority of national, state, and local officials running elections on a day-to-day basis in most countries is drawn from employment in the public sector, supplemented by a smaller number of partisan officials, temporary poll workers, and part-time staff. Where the cadre of public administrators in local government is well-trained, professional, technically skilled, and competent, then this expands the pool of staff who can also be deployed to help run elections. Indeed, Model 2 suggests that once government effectiveness is entered into the equation, then several other control factors drop out as insignificant, with the exception of press freedom and the type of electoral system, which remain significant. Thus, many of the relationships observed earlier may contribute toward electoral integrity more generally through strengthening government effectiveness and state capacity.

What about the bureaucratic ethos? This is closely associated with government effectiveness, and indeed qualities such as professionalism and impartiality in public administration help to explain why governments work well. Separate regression models need to be run to avoid problems of multicollinearity. It should be noted that the number of cases under comparison also drops in these models, due to the coverage in the QoG survey, making it hazardous to compare the results directly across all four models. Models 3 and 4 in Table 6.1 demonstrate that both impartiality and professionalism are important qualities in explaining electoral integrity, remaining significant predictors once several controls are introduced. The models suggest *that the professionalism and impartiality of the public sector, and the overall effectiveness of the public sector, are all strongly associated with better quality elections.* The quality of state governance predicts the delivery of a wide range of other public goods and services, ranging from schooling and health care to transportation and economic growth.[76] In the same way, state capacity with an impartial and professional public sector also serves to ensure effectively run elections that avoid technical malfunctions and human errors. Classical liberalism often emphasizes a mistrust of the state, given the dangers of the abuse of powers by rulers, and therefore the need for checks and balances upon the executive. We have already observed that electoral integrity is indeed higher in countries with political institutions that divide power among branches of government and that ensure

TABLE 6.2. *Electoral authorities correlated with the PEI Index and its components*

Indices	Type of EMB	WBI government effectiveness	QoG bureaucratic impartiality	QoG bureaucratic professionalism
PEI Index	−.256*	.787**	.630**	.392**
Electoral laws	−.064	.528**	.303*	.254*
Electoral procedures	−.187	.723**	.603**	.345**
Voting district boundaries	−.074	.381**	.161	.074
Voter registration	−.308**	.644**	.453**	.261*
Party & candidate reg.	−.112	.664**	.502**	.311*
Media coverage	−.210*	.495**	.352**	.309*
Campaign finance	−.287**	.647**	.522**	.369**
Voting process	−.209*	.635**	.488**	.258*
Vote count	−.162	.715**	.467**	.231
Results	−.296**	.649**	.608**	.308*
Electoral authorities	−.170	.735**	.569**	.390**
# Countries	96	97	65	65

Notes: **Correlation is significant at the 0.01 level (2-tailed). *Correlation is significant at the 0.05 level (2-tailed).

Sources: PEI Index Electoral Integrity Project. 2014. *The expert survey of Perceptions of Electoral Integrity, (PEI-2.8); Other indicators from the Quality of Government Cross-National Dataset,* http://www.qog.pol.gu.se/data/.

transparency from the independent media. Nevertheless, a professional and impartial bureaucracy is also critical for making elections work. For further robustness checks, subsequent models were also run using the PRSG's *Quality of Government* index, which combines measures of bureaucratic quality, corruption, and law and order. The results of these models (not displayed) replicate in all the essentials the same results as Models 3 and 4 in Table 6.1, suggesting that the findings are robust and not dependent on the choice of indicators and data sources.

To explore the evidence in more detail, Table 6.2 looks at how far the indicators of electoral authorities are associated with PEI evaluations of each of the stages of the electoral cycle. The type of EMB is coded from low (Governmental = 1) to high (Agency = 3). The simple correlations, without controls, suggest that, contrary to assumptions pervasive within the international community, in fact de facto autonomous administrative electoral agencies are associated with significantly *poorer* quality elections across half the expert evaluations. The range of possible reasons has already been discussed, relating to factors such as the gap between de facto and de jure independence, as well as selection effects for which types of regimes have adopted Agency models of election management. Government effectiveness in each country is consistently linked with better election quality across all steps in the cycle – but especially evaluations of the electoral authorities. Bureaucratic impartiality is also significantly related to almost all stages in the election, while bureaucratic professionalism is significant for four stages out of eleven.

IV: Conclusions

The performance of electoral officials varies around the world. This matters for many reasons; evidence suggests that widespread public doubts about the fairness of the voting process and the impartiality of the authorities serves to undermine turnout, fuel contentious protests, and erode confidence in political parties, parliaments and governments.[77] Maladministration in established democracies is a matter of concern, requiring legal or procedural reforms, but occasional incidents are unlikely to have a lasting impact on the reservoir of electoral legitimacy in these states unless mistakes are repeated over successive contests. The potential consequences of even minor technical irregularities, such as out-of-date electoral registers, a handful of missing ballots, or late-opening polling places, are likely to be far more damaging for perceptions of electoral integrity by sowing the seeds of suspicion in deeply divided societies with a recent history of conflict and instability, such as in Thailand, Afghanistan, and Nigeria. Moreover, administrative errors and incompetence, such as slipshod ballot box security or inaccurate counts, also mean that intentional cases of fraud and manipulation may become more common.

In seeking to explain electoral integrity, most attention has focused upon the legal autonomy of EMBs. It is argued that formal separation of powers and responsibilities limits the abuse of power and builds trust in an impartial electoral process and results. Alternatively in Governmental models, the chief executives responsible for elections are senior public servants located within a government department that is part of the core executive, such as within the Ministry of Interior. Core managerial and regulatory tasks are carried out by permanent civil servants in a department headed by a cabinet minister accountable to parliament, with administrative responsibilities for day-to-day operations delegated to staff in regional and local government. The potential advantages are a clearer chain of accountability and more coordinated and uniform administrative processes. Or there may be a Mixed model, combining elements of both types of organization.

The evidence in this chapter suggests that much of the focus in the literature overemphasizes the importance of the formal–legal structure of election authorities rather than examining state capacity and the informal norms that shape the professionalism and impartiality of public servants in bureaucratic cultures. The quality of elections is influenced by the general effectiveness of governments – monitored by factors such as the quality of the civil service and public services, the independence of public-sector agencies from political pressures, and the quality of policy formulation and implementation. Where public administration is based upon a cadre of well-trained, experienced, and competent officials, then electoral authorities can call on these resources to manage effective and efficient contests. Where these qualities are lacking, however, so that the public sector is undermined by partisan politics, clientelistic favors, and corrupt practices, then the quality of electoral management is likely to suffer along with the broader delivery of public goods and services. The challenge for reformers is therefore to consider not just how to establish the legal structure, powers, and mandates of election agencies on paper, but how to transform the informal culture of public administration to make elections work more effectively, without malpractice and maladministration. Elections are flawed, just as other public services suffer, where officials struggle with limited organizational capacity, poor technical expertise, inexperienced and poorly paid temporary staff, and/or inadequate financial resources. The next chapter goes on to consider the implications that follow for what the international community and domestic reforms can do to improve the quality of elections and thereby strengthen the legitimacy of elections.

PART III

CONCLUSIONS

7

Conclusions: Lessons for Strengthening Electoral Integrity

This chapter draws together the main lessons learned from the evidence examined in this book, as well as outlining a range of strategic interventions that could help to strengthen electoral integrity. There is no single "one size fits all" solution to the problems that have been described, but nevertheless there are some remedies that could be attempted in every case under comparison. What remains to be determined – which is the task confronting the final volume in this planned trilogy – is the effectiveness of each of these measures and thus which types of reforms should be prioritized on the policy agenda.

I: Understanding Why Elections Fail

Damaging consequences arise from malpractices such as gerrymandering and malapportionment of district boundaries, lack of a level playing field in money and media access during the campaign, or stuffing ballot boxes and vote buying on polling day. The previous volume in this series demonstrated that such practices violate basic political rights and fundamental freedoms, weaken the accountability of elected officials, erode public faith in the electoral process, and catalyze street protests, social conflict, and regime instability.[1] Several mainstream schools of thought have long dominated the extensive literature seeking to explain processes of democratization, and these arguments can be extended and applied to understanding electoral flaws and failures. Thus structural, international and institutional theories are reviewed and tested against the empirical evidence in this study, in the attempt to generate a more comprehensive theoretical framework that has the capacity to account for the complex phenomena of electoral integrity and malpractice.

The oldest tradition in political sociology, based upon modernization theories, emphasizes the constraints arising from fixed structural conditions that have long been thought to lie at the heart of processes of democratization.

This approach focuses upon the challenges of holding elections meeting international standards in some of the world's ethnically divided societies with years of civil war, in developing countries with inequality, poverty, and illiteracy, and in oil-rich rentier states afflicted by the "resource curse." Risks of contentious elections held under these conditions can undermine confidence in the fairness and impartiality of electoral authorities, as well as damaging citizen's faith in democracy.[2] International factors provide an alternative perspective, stressing the impact of external observer missions, the provision of technical assistance and aid by the international community and bilateral donors, and the diffusion of global norms through cosmopolitan communications encouraging states to observe universal human rights. The role of political institutions is the final plausible theory considered in this book, highlighting the desirability of constitutional designs based on power-sharing principles, providing safeguards protecting against executive manipulation of the rules of the electoral game, as well as the importance of the structure, culture, and capacities of EMBs. Electoral authorities established as independent administrative agencies, in particular, are widely believed to reassure political parties, especially the losing side, about the overall fairness and impartiality of electoral procedures and authorities, while simultaneously limiting the capacity of the governing parties to meddle in the process in attempts to strengthen their electoral advantage.

Each of these arguments deserves systematic scrutiny. The results of the empirical evidence analyzed in this book provide some support for the conventional wisdom – while throwing doubt on several other claims.

Structural Conditions

The sociological perspective has long been regarded as one of the most plausible explanations for processes of democratization – as well as the underlying societal conditions in which elections either fail or flourish. This approach typically focuses on a range of fixed conditions, including each society's wealth and income (and thus indicators of economic growth, human development, and social inequality), as well as the role of physical geography (the size and location of a state), inherited colonial legacies, patterns of ethnic heterogeneity, deep-seated cultural attitudes and values, and the distribution of natural resources. Conditions in each society are regarded from the modernization perspective as largely static, or else as phenomena like human development and political culture, which evolve at a glacial pace over successive decades or even centuries. The first propositions in the book's core model, illustrated in Figure 1.3, suggest that fixed structural conditions should exert direct effects upon levels of electoral integrity (H[1]) as well as having indirect effects (H[3]) via constitutional power sharing and the agencies of electoral governance. Thus, the book theorizes that all things being equal elections are likely to be well managed in more affluent societies, characterized by extensive access to modern communication and information technologies, dense transportation networks, widespread literacy, education and use of the media, and a workforce of well-trained professional managers engaged in public-sector governance.

Economic explanations emphasize that wealth matters for democracy and for the quality of elections; not surprisingly, the empirical evidence in this study confirms the first hypothesis: richer economies usually have better quality elections, according to the PEI Index. Chapter 3 demonstrated that wealth was consistently directly associated with greater electoral integrity, irrespective of the range of structural controls employed in successive models. This process was observed to function primarily through a stepped shift, however, rather than a linear process of progressive development. In other words, once countries reached a minimal threshold of economic development (around $15,000 per capita GDP in ppp), then elections usually met international standards. Among poorer countries falling below this threshold, however, elections are riskier operations and malpractices tend to become more common. Moreover, the impact of wealth continues to prove a significant predictor of the quality of elections across all the successive multivariate models presented in subsequent chapters that employ a wide range of international and institutional controls. This finding has not been demonstrated before in previous studies, although it is hardly unexpected given the extensive research literature over more than six decades linking economic development and democracy.

Exactly why these contrasts in electoral quality arise between rich and poor societies, however, remains a matter of interpretation. On the one hand, a sociological explanation in line with the classic Lipset argument suggests that more affluent societies expand the size of the moderate middle classes, generate civic associations, labor unions, and professional organizational networks serving as a buffer between citizens and the state, strengthen access to information through literacy, schooling, and mass media, encourage cultural values of trust and tolerance long associated with democracy, and reduce the extremes of rich and poor common in agrarian societies. This is the direct route depicted schematically in H^1. On the other hand, institutional theories, examined in later chapters, suggest that more affluent nations also have the resources – including human, financial and technical – that strengthen the capacity of public-sector management and facilitates elections meeting international standards. This is the indirect route. The close links observed between levels of economic development and measures of government effectiveness lend credibility to the latter interpretation.

Moreover, among constraints, the book confirms that countries with an abundance of natural resources (measured by per capita oil and gas revenues as a percentage of GDP) usually experience problems with the quality of their elections, as well as with broader processes of democratization. This pattern was found to persist despite controlling for many other related factors, notably the types of religious culture in Muslim majority countries. Thus, for Arab states, the effect of oil seems to trump the type of faith. Nevertheless, this remains a probabilistic statement, not an inevitable destiny, which helps to explain the quality of contests in Equatorial Guinea and Turkmenistan despite some obvious outliers such as Norway. Natural resources and oil-dependent economies often generate rentier states that benefit rich elites but where there are stark socioeconomic inequalities, lack of investment in human capital and basic welfare services, an economy built on the labor of migrant workers and expatriate visitors without citizenship rights or employment protection, and the patronage politics of crony state capitalism.[3] The contrasts in the PEI Index observed between contests held in Kuwait and Equatorial Guinea, however, suggest that even oil-rich authoritarian states can still improve the quality of their elections. The effects of natural resources persisted in subsequent chapters with international controls, although the coefficients became insignificant or inconsistent once institutional controls were included in multivariate models.

Finally, contests in states closer to the equator, and elections in countries with a predominant Orthodox or Muslim culture, were also often riskier propositions. By contrast, the historical experience of democracy and autocracy in a country during recent decades, or the "stock of democracy" was important for the contemporary quality of elections – with democratic institutions and cultures consolidated over successive contests. Consolidation means than even where specific irregularities occur – the Florida fiasco – the reservoir of trust and confidence that institutions gradually accumulate over time is sufficient to overcome these problems through regular democratic channels for the adjudication of disputes, including the courts and legal reforms, rather than through direct actions that destabilize the electoral process, such as violent protests or opposition boycotts. Thus, the first few elections held after the initial transition from autocracy and in the early stages of democratization are indeed risky. Yet in some favorable circumstances, emerging economies where citizens have lived for decades under authoritarian one-party states or military dictatorships, such as Slovakia, Lithuania, and Chile, can still develop effective electoral processes meeting international standards within a relatively short period. On the other hand, many other fixed conditions often assumed to constrain the quality of elections around the world failed to predict contemporary patterns of electoral integrity – including the physical size of countries, colonial legacies, and ethnic fractionalization.

International Forces

Domestic conditions are often regarded as primary, but international factors are also likely to shape the quality of elections, with direct effects on electoral integrity as well as indirect effects upon the constitutional arrangements depicted schematically in Figure 1.3. Chapter 4 presented the evidence concerning the influence on electoral integrity of three sets of international factors: cosmopolitan communications, where information about global norms flows across national borders; the provision of technical assistance and development aid for capacity building; and the role of electoral observer missions. The evidence in this chapter confirms that globalization does indeed have an impact on electoral integrity, as predicted, with cosmopolitan societies most likely to hold contests that meet international standards. By strengthening the flow of international information across national borders, through ties of trade interdependence, communication flows, and membership of multilateral organizations, this process spreads global norms and international standards of electoral integrity.[4]

For similar reasons, the general quality of elections in a particular world region also influences electoral integrity within specific countries. The positive effects of this process are most easily exemplified by the explicit democratic conditions stipulated by the EU before states are accepted for membership. States aspiring to join the EU, such as the Czech Republic and Poland, had a major incentive to meet these requirements and thereby gain access to economic and social benefits from an open market. But once granted membership, this carrot disappeared, hence political backsliding in Hungary and an indifferent electoral performance in several Balkan states. Regional effects are also not always beneficial and negative effects can also be observed, notably illustrated by Russia's hegemonic role in destabilizing elections in Eastern Ukraine. Once globalization and regional effects are entered into the models, the earlier structural factors of economic development and natural resources continue to play a significant role.

Finally, although election aid and electoral observers are two of the most commonly used instruments designed to strengthen elections, the cross-national evidence compared in this book was unable to establish a significant link at aggregate level between these interventions and the contemporary quality of elections around the world. This does not mean that there were no effects, however, and a cautious and agnostic conclusion is the most appropriate interpretation, reflecting the Scottish verdict of "not proven." One reason concerns the role of selection effects in determining which elections receive the most attention from the development community. The effect of specific interventions and programs is also best evaluated by methods such as before-and-after studies, within country state-level comparisons, natural or field experiments, qualitative interviews or social surveys, or by process-tracing case studies, rather than by the broad-brush approach of macrolevel statistical analysis taken at one point of time. The next volume in this trilogy will evaluate specific programs in far more detail using these types of techniques to get a firmer grip on the evidence. The core findings about international forces therefore echo previous studies about the role of cosmopolitan communications and regional organizations in the democratization process.[5] The conclusions extend the logic to demonstrate similar effects at work strengthening electoral integrity, although failing to establish equivalent evidence concerning the role of international electoral observers or development aid.

Institutions

Alternative explanations lie in research on comparative political institutions that focuses upon the constitutional design, especially the powers and capacities of the core agencies for electoral administration, and the incentives and constraints that arise from these arrangements. The constitution in any state provides the broadest context for electoral governance. This includes, in particular, types of electoral system, as well as the role and powers of national parliaments, the capacity and independence of the courts and judiciary, and freedom of the mass media. Each of these institutions can provide critical checks and balances, countering the potential abuse of power of the executive as well as strengthening transparency and accountability. The structure and responsibilities of electoral authorities – commonly known as EMBs – are the core administrative agencies implementing policies, but their roles and responsibilities are embedded within this wider institutional environment. Hence, constitutional power-sharing arrangements are expected to have both direct and indirect effects on electoral integrity, as depicted in the core schematic model in Figure 1.3.

Arguments drawing upon classical liberalism and consociational democracy emphasize that the dispersal of powers and responsibilities for electoral governance both vertically and horizontally among different branches, levels, and agencies of government provides checks and balances that help prevent potential abuses by any single actor (including governing parties). By generating multiple stakeholders, power-sharing constitutions are also believed to strengthen trust in the fairness, impartiality, and credibility of electoral process, even among losing candidates and parties, building acceptance of the rules of the game. Finally, by heightening the incentives and opportunities for attempting ballot box fraud, the risks of malpractice by candidates are thought to be greatest in single member district plurality electoral systems, where even a single vote can make the difference between success and failure.

These are common arguments, although systematic and convincing proof supporting these claims remains limited in previous research. At the same time, however, there is certainly room for debate, since power-sharing arrangements may also have several potential *dis*advantages for electoral governance. For example, they may lead to excessive fragmentation of responsibilities and roles across multiple agencies that hinders the implementation of effective procedural reforms, prevents clear channels of public accountability and timely responsiveness for any problems which arise, disperses scarce managerial resources too thinly, maximizes potential entry points for corruption, and undermines uniform and consistent standards for citizens across all localities. The problems documented in US states and localities can exemplify many of these issues. By contrast, if responsibility for supervising elections and monitoring performance standards is centralized within a single government department, with local authorities responsible for day-to-day implementation, this can strengthen the pool of expertise, available resources, and clear channels of hierarchical accountability.

The evidence presented in this book provides considerable support confirming the direct advantages of power-sharing constitutional arrangements. Hence

Chapter 6 demonstrated that three institutions – proportional representation electoral systems, strong and effective parliaments, and freedom of the press – each serve to safeguard the integrity of the electoral process. The most plausible reasons for this relationship, we suggest, are that these institutions provide checks on manipulation and malfeasance by the executive branch, expand disclosure and transparency, and strengthen oversight and accountability. This enhances our understanding based on many previous studies examining the general virtuous of power-sharing arrangements for processes of democratization.[6] Moreover, institutional reforms, such as initiatives strengthening the capacity and powers of legislators and the judiciary, or training for journalists and broadcasters, are more amenable to programmatic intervention than attempts to alter structural conditions that usually evolve slowly over decades or even centuries, such as levels of societal modernization and economic development, the blight of the resource curse, or how far societies are linked into global networks of international trade and communications. At the same time, the independent judiciary, which was expected to play an important role in electoral dispute resolution and the prevention of illicit acts of voter fraud, did not emerge as significant, according to the indicators.

The implementation of detailed electoral procedures, and the process of managing the conduct of elections, is the responsibility of a range of administrative agencies. The book has examined the organizational structure of types of electoral authorities, as well as general patterns of government effectiveness, and the cultural ethos of public administration, to evaluate whether these factors also strengthen electoral performance. In seeking to explain this phenomenon, most attention in the previous research literature has focused upon the legal independence of EMBs. It is often assumed that formal separation of powers, through establishing a separate autonomous administrative agency responsible for managing elections, has the virtue of limiting executive meddling and building trust in the impartiality of the electoral process. This is usually assumed to be more effective than Governmental models, where the chief executives responsible for elections are senior public servants located within a government department that is part of the core executive, such as a unit within the Ministry of Interior. Core managerial and regulatory tasks are carried out by permanent civil servants in a department headed by a cabinet minister accountable to parliament, with administrative responsibilities for day-to-day operations delegated to staff in regional and local government. Many studies emphasize the potential dangers in the Government model, including the risks of executive manipulation of the rules of the game and lack of legislative oversight or public transparency, yet it may also have several potential advantages through establishing a clearer chain of accountability and providing more coordinated and uniform administrative processes. Alternatively, countries may adopt a mixed model, combining elements of both types of organization.

The results of the analysis in Chapter 6 lead to the conclusion that much of the focus in the literature overemphasizes the importance of the *formal*–legal structure of election authorities, and instead more attention should be paid to the issues of state capacity and the *informal* cultural norms that shape the behavior of public servants. The evidence indicates that how well electoral procedures work is influenced by the general effectiveness of the state – monitored by factors such as the quality of the civil service and public services, the independence of public-sector agencies from political pressures, and the professional quality of policy formulation and implementation. Where public administration has a cadre of well-trained, experienced, and competent officials, operating in a professional and impartial culture, then electoral authorities can call on these resources to manage effective and efficient contests. Where these qualities are lacking, however, so that the public sector is undermined by incompetence, partisanship, favoritism, and corruption, then electoral management suffers.

Thus Chapter 6, pulling together all the major findings, demonstrated the book's overall conclusions: in general countries are most likely to demonstrate electoral integrity if they combine state capacity (allowing electoral officials to deliver effective public services) with the broader institutional checks on the process derived from power-sharing arrangements. This includes PR electoral systems (and thus multiparty legislatures and coalition cabinet governments), strong legislatures (and thus parliamentary oversight counterbalancing the executive branch), as well as freedom of the press (to ensure transparency and detect any cases of electoral malfeasance). Electoral officials succeed best where they have the capacity to deliver public services effectively while being constrained from overextending their powers by a broader institutional context ensuring accountability, transparency, and responsiveness. In general, developed postindustrial societies are most likely to have the resources to invest in professional public administration as well as being closely integrated into networks of global communications and regional organizations. In other words, it is no accident that the states observed to rank highest in electoral integrity include long-standing democracies and affluent societies with this mix of characteristics, exemplified by Norway, Sweden, the Netherlands, and Austria, as well as younger third wave democracies and emerging economies, such as Lithuania, the Czech Republic, and Slovenia. No single factor could hope to be the magic bullet to explain why elections fail – or succeed. But a blend of favorable social characteristics, international conditions, and institutional structures make elections far more likely to meet international standards.

II: Reforms to Strengthen Electoral Integrity

Building upon these insights, what reforms would help to strengthen electoral integrity? As the previous volume argued, several steps could be taken that could address malpractice and improve the quality of elections. These range from improving monitoring by gathering better performance evaluation and needs-assessment evidence, to providing technical assistance expanding the functional capacity of electoral authorities, addressing constitutional and legal reforms, strengthening oversight and accountability, as well as expanding the scope of international agreements raising electoral standards. Based on the currently available body of evaluation research, however, it remains difficult to establish with any confidence which of these should be recommended as effective initiatives for strengthening electoral integrity in diverse contexts and, rather than any "off the peg" solutions, policies need to be carefully tailored to meet the specific needs and challenges of each contest.

Monitoring Performance Indicators

One important step to improve our understanding of these matters would be to collect additional evidence to compare observed contrasts in the work of election authorities. In-depth case studies, using techniques such as interviews with senior officials and also representative surveys of middle management staff, poll workers, and ordinary citizens help to throw light on the performance of electoral authorities in particular countries and regions, as well as being useful for building broader theoretical insights that could then be examined through other techniques. Yet it remains difficult to generalize cross-nationally from these methods.

An additional tool arises from systematic evidence-based performance indicators that have been implemented by several electoral authorities in countries at the forefront of the new public-sector management movement, including the United States and the United Kingdom.[6] Management by results recommends using performance indices, both qualitative and quantitative, which should be closely matched to strategic organizational goals. The aim is to monitor and report how effectively core objectives are achieved both by individual managers and collectively by organizational units[7] Information gathered from similar standardized measures could ideally be collected by specific EMBs, using a harmonized template. The results could then be collected and further standardized by relevant agencies within the international community, such as by the Global Elections Organization (GEO) and the Association of European Election Officials, to assess the performance, responsibilities, cultural ethos and functional capacities of electoral authorities in different countries and world regions. Indicators should ideally touch upon multiple dimensions of performance to address a range of questions where little reliable information is currently available. For example, how many staff are employed as permanent electoral officials in the central and regional offices, and in local polling stations, measured as a ratio of the size of the electorate? Are senior officials well-trained, qualified professionals, and permanent staff seasoned over successive contests, or are they relatively new to the work, recruited for each specific contest? Are there standardized and transparent procedures with formal legal rules to ensure equal access across all polling places, or do more ad hoc practices prevail in different areas? What is the size of the budget allocated for running elections, and is this sufficient for the task and responsibilities of the agency? Do local polling workers have sufficient skills in deploying (and fixing) new electronic technologies, such as biometric registration programs and electronic voting machines? If administrative errors occur, are there clear channels of accountability, and mechanisms for organization learning to correct mistakes?

An alternative indicator of state capacity and performance efficiency would monitor the total cost of government spending upon elections (on a per capita basis), throughout the electoral cycle, an approach that is useful to identify priorities for development aid. United Nations Development Programme (UNDP) published a pioneering report comparing the cost of elections in 2006, but far more research needs to be conducted to generate more reliable and comprehensive estimates.[8] The International Monetary Fund already compiles general and central government revenues and outlays by major function, such as spending on the military or education, based on standardized data from National Accounts.[9] Unfortunately, these data are not disaggregated in sufficiently granular detail to facilitate monitoring spending on electoral activities.

At the same time, it cannot be assumed that the cost on elections is indicative of state capacity or government efficiency. Indeed, expenditure could also be inversely related to electoral quality; the greatest flow of international development aid and the most expensive contests have typically been observed to occur during the first transitional election following a major regime change, which is therefore also the riskiest period for running these contests.[10] Costs usually decline over successive elections – especially the substantial investment in maintaining security, training staff, and purchasing equipment, as elections become institutionalized and EMBs gradually build sustainable capacity. Information about behavioral and financial performance indicators could ideally be gathered by electoral management bodies in conjunction with experts in public administration and national statistical offices and then standardized by the international community to allow the structure, capacity, and functions of electoral bodies to be compared on a consistent basis. Ultimately, this process could be written into the standard operating procedures for electoral authorities, providing reliable metrics for election commissioners to monitor the performance of regional units, local managers, and the front-line troops.

Evaluating the Effectiveness of Capacity Building and Technical Assistance

Another major set of initiatives, which could also usefully be expanded, has sought to evaluate programs designed to strengthen the capacity of EMBs and local electoral officials. Many multilateral agencies and bilateral donors have sought to strengthen the work of EMBs. This includes technical assistance provided by the International Institute for Democracy and Electoral Assistance (IDEA), the International Foundation for Election Systems (IFES), the National Democratic Institute for International Affairs (NDI), UNDP, and the Carter

Center, in partnership with regional organizations such as the European Union, the Organization for Security and Cooperation in Europe, the Council of Europe, the Organization of American States, bilateral partners such as USAID and the Swedish International Development Cooperation Agency (SIDA), and local stakeholders.[11] Elections are large-scale, complex, and sensitive operations and EMBS need the logistical capacity: to develop strategic and operational plans; to assess election costs and prepare budgets; to improve voter registration processes; to implement procurement plans; to manage the vote count; and to handle any complaints and disputes. International agencies, regional organizations and bilateral donors have also worked with local stakeholders to strengthen political parties and the independent media, to address judicial dispute resolution mechanisms, to increase the participation of women, young people, and minorities, and to improve civic education.

Within the United Nations, the Electoral Assistance Division (EAD), located within the Secretary General's Department of Political Affairs, monitors needs assessment to evaluate whether the UN should respond to state requests for assistance and provide countries with technical advice for holding elections. This division is deeply involved in postconflict peace-building activities and it was even briefly under UN Department of Peacekeeping Operations supervision before moving to the Department of Political Affairs. Since 1991, more than one hundred countries have requested and received UN assistance with holding referendums, plebiscites, and elections. The division works closely with the UNDP, which provides the "boots on the ground." UNDP has stepped up its technical assistance to strengthening electoral processes and management during the last decade, as did many regional agencies, multilateral organizations, and NGOs. UNDP has identified ten main entry points, which currently guide how the organization provides electoral assistance: electoral system reform, strengthening electoral administration, building sustainable electoral processes, mobilization and coordination of resources, civic and voter education, electoral dispute resolution, support to domestic observation, working with political parties, media strengthening and increasing women's participation. UNDP provides both event- and process-driven support during the electoral cycle. During the last decade, the UNDP alone has invested from US$1.2 to $1.5 billion (US) every year to programs strengthening democratic governance in 130 developing countries worldwide, out of a total UNDP annual budget of around $5 billion. In total, UNDP has assisted 83 countries with elections with expenditures of approximately $2.2 billion between 1999 and 2011.[12] The total cost fluctuates a lot annually, however, with the highest spending during years of large-scale international efforts to support postconflict elections, such as in Afghanistan, Sudan, Nigeria, and Burundi. In the context of electoral assistance, the largest UNDP focus area has been upon strengthening electoral administration, accounting for approximately one quarter of the total effort. Initiatives by UNDP included launching the Global Programme for Electoral Cycle Support (GPEC) in 2009, designed to help countries improve their electoral laws, processes, and institutions and to enhance the participation of women in electoral processes.[13]

Thus, capacity development has been perhaps the most common mainstream attempt to strengthen institutional capacity. Technical assistance has been provided most commonly in areas such as electoral administration and planning, review of electoral laws and regulations, electoral dispute resolution, boundary delimitation, voter registration, election budgeting, logistics, procurement of election materials, use of technologies, training of election officials, voter and civic education, voting and counting operations, election security, and coordination of international donor assistance.

This activity has usually been assessed by organizations and bilateral donors within the international community by qualitative case-study methods, based on observation and interviews with a range of local stakeholders.[14] Nevertheless, it would be useful to supplement these methods with more systematic studies using rigorous evaluation methods across a wide range of programs, activities, agencies, and contexts. In particular, capacity building initiatives are well designed to be assessed through randomized control experiments, where the type of training, content, and level are randomly distributed across treatment groups to monitor the most effective programs. Experiments are becoming an increasingly common approach in political science, behavioral economics, and developmental policy studies – especially to make more rigorous causal inferences about the effectiveness of alternative interventions, such as different ways of implementing programs on schooling, health, or poverty alleviation, as well as alternative ways of casting a ballot, sources of campaign information, or civic mobilization efforts.[15] Randomization is the rigorous "gold" standard for making causal inferences using varied research designs and techniques through lab, survey, field, and natural experiments. Experimental designs have been employed in many aspects of governance and development.[16] Evidence-based independent evaluations are recognized by many donor agencies in the development community, notably USAID and the UK Department of International Development, as important to ensure that results are achieved, to shape funding expenditure and strategic program priorities, and to improve performance effectiveness and organizational learning. Extending this approach to evaluate capacity building programs for electoral management conducted by some of the major international agencies would provide invaluable information helping to assess the most effective learning strategies and training methods. It is also critical for evaluation reports to move beyond narrowly technocratic criteria and specific interventions, such as the use of international observers in polling places, so as to consider the broader political and institutional environment.

In addition, several sequential steps in the implementation process can be used in policy evaluations, distinguishing short-term policy outputs, medium-term outcomes, and long-term impacts. It is most straightforward to observe policy outputs, such as the establishment of new administrative procedures or guidelines designed to implement new laws, for example concerning poll worker training, voter registration procedures, or expanded balloting facilities. It is far more difficult to pin down the outcomes of such procedural revisions, such as whether the formal guidelines are observed in practice, whether training improves performance, or whether registration procedures have unintended consequences. It is even more challenging to establish the diffuse societal impacts flowing from programmatic interventions and public policies, however, and thus whether new regulations achieve their ultimate goals by strengthening democratic governance, as proponents hope. In terms of "what works," as with any other policy assessment, this clearly depends upon the normative standards and objectives of reformers, the benchmarks and indices used to monitor change, and the time-period that is compared, for example whether evaluating short-term outputs or long-term consequences. One of the main challenges of policy evaluation methods is to go beyond describing short-term outputs toward assessing whether initiatives help produce sustainable developmental goals and cumulative public goods.

Assessing Constitutional and Legal Procedural Reforms

Another set of issues concerns assessing reforms introduced to strengthen the constitutional and legal framework of electoral procedures. As part of its role in providing technical assistance for EMBs, agencies in the international community, including International IDEA, IFES, the OAS, and the ACE project, have sought to compare practices and legal regulations of electoral administration, campaign finance, and campaign broadcasting in countries around the world. 18 Constitutions also contain important clauses regulating the conduct and management of elections. A large research agenda is required to compare the constitutional and legal frameworks governing each of these areas and determining the most appropriate regulations that meet international standards.[17]

In response to these challenges, a growing body of applied policy analysis has developed to study the framework for electoral law and administration, drawing upon comparative political science, legal studies, and public-sector management. Work has focused upon the institutional framework surrounding election rules, including the design and reform of constitutions, electoral laws and procedural regulations; the role, independence, and powers of EMBs; the capacity, skills, and training of election officials; legal voter registration and polling requirements; the regulation of campaign finance and broadcasting; the provision of balloting facilities; the establishment of complaints and dispute resolution mechanisms; and the deployment of new voting technologies, including online polling.

In particular, ever since the Florida controversy in the 2000 race, and the polarization of issues of voter registration and flaws in voting technologies, interest in electoral administration has grown among American scholars.[18] New research has evaluated the effects of moving from localized to state-coordinated voter registers, the introduction of new electronic voting machines replacing mechanical models, and the use of convenience voting such as early in-person voting, voting by mail, absentee voting, electronic voting, and voting by fax and election-day registration. While work in the United States has focused on the effects of these reforms on differential patterns of turnout, far less is known about their general impact on campaigns, costs, fraud, security, and party support, especially across countries.[19] Thus, further research that compares the distribution of such voting facilities across countries, and experimental analysis evaluating the varied impacts of such reforms, would also greatly expand understanding of these issues.

Strengthening Accountability and Oversight

When establishing effective processes of electoral management and the legal framework, it is insufficient to promote transparency and effective regulations unless attention is also given to issues of accountability and oversight. Most work on transparency has focused on the role of international observer missions – but far less is known cross-nationally about domestic election-watch organizations, including the deployment of new social media such as crowdsourcing. Further research should establish which elections are observed by domestic agencies, what role they play, and whether the judgments of domestic watch organizations largely coincide and thereby reinforce international missions – or whether these assessments diverge. In addition, both parliaments and the courts can play an important potential role in the electoral process, although little systematic research has explored the process of parliamentary oversight of electoral authorities and the judicial role in dispute resolution mechanisms. Yet this is a critical issue, since far too many contentious elections have ended with the major protagonists at loggerheads, parties bitterly disputing the results, and conflict spilling over onto the streets.[20] Cries of fraud are commonplace, especially among losers in tight winner-take-all presidential races. Protests have recently contested the outcome in places as diverse as Kabul, Karachi, Kuala Lumpur, and Caracas. Accusations of vote rigging, corruption, and stolen elections are particularly common in cultures stamped by a long history of past malpractice, undermining public confidence in the process, associated with Mexican practices of vote buying by the PRI, overwhelming pro-government coverage in the Russian airways, and outbreaks of inter-communal violence in Nigeria. These disputes can have serious consequences both for social conflict and for regime stability. Further research therefore needs to establish what forms of legislative oversight ensure that electoral authorities meet international standards and what resolution mechanisms, including the judiciary and courts, are most effective to resolve any disputes occurring during or immediately after elections.

Expanding the Scope of International Conventions

The primary challenge in many countries is to incorporate fundamental principles and global norms of electoral integrity into domestic laws, as well as expanding the scope of international and regional treaties as core pillars of human rights. The role of the United Nations in promoting human rights is nothing new, but the end of the Cold War era in the early 1990s witnessed a decisive shift in the priority given to strengthening democratic governance. The General Assembly underscored the United Nation's active support for representative democracy by passing a resolution on 21 February 1991 declaring that "periodic and genuine elections" are a "crucial factor in the effective enjoyment ... of a wide range of other human rights." A series of similar resolutions have been passed periodically by the General Assembly over the years.[21] The United Nations is committed to strengthening human rights and elections. Article 21 in the 1948 Universal Declaration of Human Rights declares that "the will of the people shall be the basis of the authority of government; this will be expressed in periodic and genuine elections which shall be by universal and equal suffrage and shall be held by secret vote or by equivalent free voting procedures" guaranteeing everyone "the right to take part in the government of his country, directly or through freely chosen representatives."[22] These principles have been elaborated and endorsed in many subsequent international treaties and instruments, notably the International Covenant on Civil and Political Rights, and the International Covenant on Economic, Social and Cultural Rights, which entered into force in 1976.[23] The General Assembly underscored the United Nation's active support for representative democracy on 21 February 1991 by passing a resolution declaring that "periodic and genuine elections" are a "crucial factor in the effective enjoyment ... of a wide range of other human rights." A series of similar resolutions has been passed periodically by the General Assembly over the years.[24]

Therefore, the core principles of electoral integrity have been long endorsed by the international community, but unless the standards of elections reflect these principles, by eliminating common malpractice and enforcing human rights, contests will fail to strengthen democracy and reduce conflict. Unfortunately, too often international conventions are not yet fully integrated into domestic laws, so that official endorsement of treaties by governments has not been translated into practice. Therefore, there is a substantial role for human rights organizations, such as local and international branches of Human Rights Watch and Amnesty International, to monitor compliance with existing conventions.

Equally importantly, there are many significant components of electoral rights, including the role of campaign finance and campaign communications, that are still not covered by any international treaty, even though multilateral organizations are laying the foundations for a broader agreement.[25] This indicates a major opportunity for human rights bodies, NGOs, and regional organizations to advance debate and develop a broad global consensus about the most appropriate standards and principles for regulating money and media during election campaigns, thereby expanding electoral rights.

Therefore, this book has established with greater certainty some of the core drivers of why elections are flawed or fail. Yet the results also generate many important further questions, which go beyond the scope of this volume, concerning the range of options available on this policy agenda, in particular which of these types of interventions are the most effective in strengthening electoral integrity – and which are less worthwhile. It is to these issues that the next volume turns when bringing systematic evidence to bear enabling us to evaluate what is to be done.

Technical Appendix

The Perceptions of Electoral Integrity Expert Rolling Survey

To supplement existing sources of evidence, the PEI expert survey, launched by the Electoral Integrity Project, aims to provide a comprehensive, systematic, and consistent way to monitor and compare the quality of elections worldwide. The study draws on evaluations of electoral integrity provided by a range of independent election experts. This appendix summarizes the project and the research design.

The Electoral Integrity Project

The project involves a team of scholars, including research staff, visiting fellows, and postgraduate interns, based at Harvard University's Kennedy School of Government and the University of Sydney, as well as an international Advisory Board and global networks of colleagues meeting at a series of events and workshops. The six-year research project has been generously funded by the award of the Kathleen Fitzpatrick Australian Laureate from the Australian Research Council. Supplementary support for specific events has been provided by several other sponsors, including the Weatherhead Center for International Affairs, the Roy and Lila Ash Center for Democratic Governance and Innovation, and the Australian Studies Committee at Harvard University, as well as International IDEA, Global Integrity, the Sunlight Foundation, the Open Society Institute, and the Hewlett Foundation.

The Concept of Electoral Integrity

The concept of *"electoral integrity"* in this project refers to international standards and global norms governing the appropriate conduct of elections. These standards have been endorsed in a series of authoritative conventions, treaties, protocols, and guidelines by: agencies of the international community, notably by the decisions of the UN General Assembly; by regional bodies such as the Organization for Security and Cooperation in Europe (OSCE), the Organization of American States (OAS), and the African Union (AU); and by member states of the UN. Following endorsement, these standards apply universally to all countries. The notion of an electoral cycle can be conceptualized as the series of sequential steps illustrated in Figure 1.1. The international community has adopted the electoral cycle approach by recognizing that it is inadequate to parachute observers in to scrutinize only the end processes of balloting, vote count, and results if there is not also a longer-term assessment of each contest.

Measuring Electoral Integrity

To operationalize this conceptual framework, the survey asks experts to evaluate elections using forty-nine indicators, grouped into eleven categories reflecting the whole electoral cycle. The items are listed in Table 2.2. Using a comprehensive instrument, experts assess whether each national parliamentary and presidential contest meets international standards during the preelection period, the campaign, polling day, and its aftermath. The overall PEI Index is constructed by summing the forty-nine separate indicators for each election and for each country. The PEI Index is standardized to 100 points. Election scores are ranked and subdivided by thirds into contests with high, moderate, and low levels of electoral integrity. Similar 100-point standardized indices are constructed for each of the eleven components of the electoral cycle.

Election Coverage

The PEI-2.8 release of the data set used in this study has collected the expert evaluations for almost all national parliamentary and presidential elections held in ninety-seven independent nation-states (with a population of more than 100,000) from 1 July 2012 to 31 December 2014.[1] In cases of simultaneous legislative and executive elections, the survey monitored the latter. In countries using second ballot (run-off) majoritarian electoral systems, the survey assessed the final contest.

Experts

The survey design and questionnaire was developed in consultation with Professor Jorgen Elklit (Aarhus University) and Professor Andrew Reynolds (University of North Carolina, Chapel Hill). The method of pooling expert knowledge has been used for years for measuring complex issues, such as to assess the risks of building nuclear plants, levels of corruption, and processes of democratization.

Around forty domestic and international experts were consulted on each election, with requests to participate sent on a rolling basis within a month of the end of polling day using a database including over 9,000 experts. The survey results in PEI-2.8 are drawn from the views of 1,251 election experts, producing an overall mean response rate of 28%.

An *expert* is defined as a political (or other social) scientist who has written about, or who has other demonstrated knowledge of, the electoral process in a particular country. Specifically, demonstrated knowledge is defined by the following criteria: (1) membership of a relevant research group, professional network, or organized section of such a group; (2) existing publications on electoral or other country-specific topics in books, academic journals, or conference papers; (3) employment at a university or college as a teacher. Occasionally other social scientists – from law, sociology, or, to a lesser degree, economics, anthropology, mathematics, or statistics – were also used. The selection sought a roughly 50:50 balance between international and domestic experts, the latter defined by location or citizenship.

Reliability Tests

The data have been tested and found to demonstrate high levels of internal reliability (consistency among experts), external reliability (when compared with equivalent independent indicators), and legitimacy (when expert judgments are compared with public assessments).[2]

Time Period

The release of the data set (PEI_2.8) in this study includes 113 national parliamentary and presidential elections held in ninety-seven countries from 1 July 2012 to 31 December 2014. The rolling survey will continue to cover national elections held each year, gradually broadening the comparison worldwide.

PEI Index Construction

The electoral integrity items in the survey were recoded, where a higher score consistently represents a more positive evaluation. Missing data were estimated based on multiple imputation of chained equations in groups composed of the eleven sub-dimensions. The PEI Index is then an additive function of the forty-nine imputed variables, standardized to 100 points. Subindices of the eleven subdimensions in the electoral cycle are summations of the imputed individual variables, also standardized for comparison.

Confidence Intervals

When interpreting the results, it should be noted that modest differences in the PEI Index are unlikely to be statistically significant at reasonable confidence intervals. It is more useful to focus on the range of indicators across the cycle and more substantial differences between elections or between countries. Confidence intervals were constructed for the summary PEI Index based on the number of experts who responded for each election and country.

Data Availability

All data and the codebook are available for download at: http://thedata .harvard.edu/dvn/dv/PEI. Data can be examined at the level of each country, each election, or individual experts. Analysis can be conducted for the summary PEI Index, the eleven components, or the forty-nine individual indicators. Those preferring alternative conceptualizations of the quality of elections are free to reaggregate the indicators and thereby create alternative measures. The PEI-2 Codebook provides detailed descriptions of all variables and imputation procedures. The project also publishes an annual *Yearbook of Elections*, which provides more detailed descriptions of the contests and results.

All other details about the project are available at www.electoralinte grityproject.com

Notes

1. Introduction: Why Do Elections Fail?

1 Pippa Norris, Richard Frank, and Ferran Martinez i Coma. 2015. "Contentious elections: From votes to violence." In *Contentious Elections: From Ballots to Barricades*, eds. Pippa Norris, Richard Frank, and Ferran Martinez i Coma. New York: Routledge.

2 Pippa Norris. 2014. *Why Electoral Integrity Matters*. New York: Cambridge University Press; Pippa Norris, Richard W. Frank, and Ferran Martinez i Coma, eds. 2014. *Advancing Electoral Integrity*. Oxford: Oxford University Press.

3 Pippa Norris, Richard Frank, and Ferran Martinez i Coma. 2014. *Contentious Elections: From Ballots to Barricades*. New York: Routledge.

4 There are many mechanisms of political and electoral accountability. See Mark N. Franklin, Stuart Soroka, and Christopher Wlezien. 2014. "Elections." In *The Oxford Handbook Public Accountability*, eds. Mark Bovens, Robert E. Goodin, and Thomas Schillemans. New York: Oxford University Press.

5 See also Pippa Norris. 2014. "The new research agenda studying electoral integrity." In special issue of *Electoral Studies*. 32(4): 563–75; Pippa Norris, Richard W. Frank, and Ferran Martinez i Coma, eds. 2014. *Advancing Electoral Integrity*. Oxford: Oxford University Press.

6 Domenico Tuccinardi, ed. 2014. *International Obligations for Elections: Guidelines for Legal Frameworks*. International IDEA: Stockholm; Carter Center. 2014. *Elections Obligations and Standards Database: A Carter Center Manual*. The Carter Center: Atlanta, Georgia. http://www.cartercenter.org/des-search/des/Introduction.aspx.

7 Avery Davis-Roberts and David J. Carroll. 2010. "Using international law to assess elections." *Democratization*. 17(3): 416–41; David J. Carroll and Avery Davis-Roberts. 2013. "The Carter Center and election observation: An obligations-based approach for assessing elections." *Election Law Journal*. 12(1): 87–93.

8 Eric Posner. 2014. *The Twilight of Human Rights Law*. New York: Oxford University Press.

9   Beth Simmons. 2009. *Mobilizing for Human Rights: International Law in Domestic Politics.* New York: Cambridge University Press, p. 125.

10 Pippa Norris. 2011. *Democratic Deficit: Critical Citizens Revisited.* New York: Cambridge University Press.

11 For these variations, see Louis Massicotte, Andre Blais, and Antoine Yoshinaka. 2004. *Establishing the Rules of the Game.* Toronto: University of Toronto Press, chapter 3.

12 Domenico Tuccinardi, ed. 2014. *International Obligations for Elections: Guidelines for Legal Frameworks.* Stockholm: International IDEA.

13 European Commission for Democracy through Law (Venice Commission). October 2002. *Code of good practice in electoral matters: guidelines and explanatory report.* Venice Commission: Venice. http://www.venice.coe.int/webforms/documents/CDL-AD(2002)023rev-e.aspx

14 Organization for Security and Cooperation in Europe. 2010. *Election Observation Handbook.* Warsaw: OSCE/ODIHR, 6th ed.

15 European Commission. 2007. *Compendium of International Standards for Elections.* European Commission: Brussels: EC/NEEDS, 2nd ed.

16 See Domenico Tuccinardi, ed. 2014. *International Obligations for Elections: Guidelines for Legal Frameworks.* Stockholm: International IDEA, Table II.1, p. 14.

17 For a discussion about the diffusion of global norms, see Martha Finnemore and Kathryn Sikkink. 1998. "International norm dynamics and political change." *International Organization.* 52(4): 887–917.

18 Mona Lena Krook. 2009. *Quotas for Women in Politics: Gender and Candidate Selection Reform Worldwide.* New York: Oxford University Press.

19 See, for example, Pippa Norris and Andrea Abel van Es. 2016. *Checkbook Elections? Political Finance in Comparative Perspective.* Magnus Öhman and Hani Zainulbhai. 2011. *Political Finance Regulation: The Global Experience.* Washington, DC: IFES. http://www.ifes.org/files/Political_Finance_Regulation_The_Global_Experience.pdf

20 Jørgen Elklit and Palle Svensson. 1997. "What makes elections free and fair?" *Journal of Democracy.* 8(3): 32–46; Jørgen Elklit and Andrew Reynolds. 2005 "A framework for the systematic study of election quality." *Democratization.* 12 (2): 147–62.

21 Louis Massicotte, Andre Blais, and Antoine Yoshinaka. 2004. *Establishing the Rules of the Game.* Toronto: University of Toronto Press.

22 Pippa Norris and Andrea Abel van Es. 2016. *Checkbook Elections? Political Finance in Comparative Perspective.*

23 Sarah Birch. 2012. *Electoral Malpractice.* Oxford: Oxford University Press.

24 David J. Carroll and Avery Davis-Roberts. 2013. "The Carter Center and election observation: An obligations-based approach for assessing elections." *Election Law Journal.* 12(1): 87–93; Domenico Tuccinardi, ed. 2014. *International Obligations for Elections: Guidelines for Legal Frameworks.* Stockholm: International IDEA.

25 Thomas Carothers. 2002. "The end of the transition paradigm." *Journal of Democracy.* 13: 5–21; Larry Diamond. 2002. "Thinking about hybrid regimes." *Journal of Democracy.* 13(2): 21–35; Steven Levitsky and Lucan Way. 2010. *Competitive Authoritarianism: Hybrid Regimes after the Cold War.* New York: Cambridge University Press.

26 See, for example, Fabrice Edouard Lehoucq and Iván Molina Jiménez. 2002. *Stuffing the Ballot Box: Fraud, Electoral Reform, and Democratization in Costa Rica*. New York: Cambridge University Press; Beatriz Magaloni. 2006. *Voting for Autocracy: Hegemonic Party Survival and Its Demise in Mexico*. Cambridge: Cambridge University Press; Andreas Schedler, ed. 2006. *Electoral Authoritarianism: The Dynamics of Unfree Competition*. Boulder and London: Lynne Rienner; Jason Brownlee. 2007. *Authoritarianism in an Age of Democratization*. New York: Cambridge University Press; Valerie J. Bunce and Sharon L. Wolchik. 2011. *Defeating Authoritarian Leaders in Post-Communist Countries*. New York: Cambridge University Press; Steven Levitsky and Lucan Way. 2010. *Competitive Authoritarianism: Hybrid Regimes after the Cold War*, New York: Cambridge University Press; Andreas Schedler. 2012. *The Politics of Uncertainty Sustaining and Subverting Electoral Authoritarianism*. CIDE: Mexico City; Alberto Simpser. 2013. *Why Parties and Governments Manipulate Elections: Theory, Practice and Implications*. New York: Cambridge University Press.

27 Susan D. Hyde. 2011. *The Pseudo-Democrat's Dilemma*. Ithaca: Cornell University Press; Judith Kelley. 2012. *Monitoring Democracy: When International Election Observation Works and Why It Often Fails*. Princeton, NJ: Princeton University Press; Daniella Donno. 2013. *Defending Democratic Norms*. New York: Oxford University Press.

28 See, for example, Bruce E. Cain, Todd Donovan, and C.J. Tolbert. 2008. *Democracy in the States: Experimentation in Election Reform*. Washington DC: Brookings Institution Press; Brian L. Fife, 2010. *Reforming the Electoral Process in America*. Santa Barbara, CA: Praeger; Michael J. Hanmer, 2009. *Discount Voting: Voter Registration Reforms and Their Effects*. New York: Cambridge University Press; Martha Kropf and David C. Kimball. 2011. *Helping America Vote: The Limits of Election Reform*. New York: Routledge; R. Michael Alvarez, Lonna Atkeson, and Thad E. Hall, eds. 2012. *Confirming Elections: Creating Confidence and Integrity through Election Auditing*. New York: Palgrave Macmillan; Barry C. Burden and Charles Stewart III, eds. 2014. *The Measure of American Elections*. New York: Cambridge University Press; R. Michael Alvarez and Bernard Grofman. 2014. *Election Administration in the United States*. New York: Cambridge University Press.

29 Pippa Norris. 2012. *Making Democratic Governance Work*. New York: Cambridge University Press.

30 Andreas Schedler. 2002. "The menu of manipulation." *Journal of Democracy*. 13(2): 36–50.

31 Organization for Security and Cooperation in Europe. 2007. *Handbook for Long-Term Election Observers: Beyond Election Day Observation*. Warsaw: OSCE/ODIHR.

32 http://www.idea.int/publications/15_years_supporting_democracy/a_continous_cycle.cfm

33 See Pippa Norris, Richard W. Frank, and Ferran Martinez i Coma, eds. 2014. *Advancing Electoral Integrity*. Oxford: Oxford University Press.

34 The combined Freedom House/Polity V measure of democratization created by Jan Teorell is derived from the Quality of Government data set. http://www.qog.pol.gu.se/

35   See, for example, the overview of the literature discussed in Jan Teorell. 2010. *Determinants of Democratization.* New York: Cambridge University Press.

36   See, for example, the political map illustrated by http://www.freedomhouse.org/report-types/freedom-world

37   Seymour Martin Lipset. 1959. "Some social requisites of democracy: Economic development and political legitimacy." *American Political Science Review.* 53: 69–105. See also Seymour Martin Lipset. 1960. *Political Man: The Social Basis of Politics.* New York: Doubleday; Seymour Martin Lipset, Kyoung-Ryung Seong, and John Charles Torres. 1993. "A comparative analysis of the social requisites of democracy." *International Social Science Journal.* 45(2): 154–75; Seymour Martin Lipset and Jason M. Lakin. 2004. *The Democratic Century.* Oklahoma: The University of Oklahoma Press.

38   Robert W. Jackman. 1973. "On the relation of economic development and democratic performance." *American Journal of Political Science.* 17: 611–21; Kenneth A. Bollen. 1979. "Political democracy and the timing of development." *American Sociological Review.* 44: 572–87; Kenneth A. Bollen. 1983. "World system position, dependency and democracy: The cross-national evidence." *American Sociological Review.* 48: 468–79; Kenneth A. Bollen and Robert W. Jackman. 1985. "Political democracy and the size distribution of income." *American Sociological Review.* 50: 438–58; Gregory C. Brunk, Gregory A. Caldeira, and Michael S. Lewis-Beck. 1987. "Capitalism, socialism, and democracy: An empirical inquiry." *European Journal of Political Research.* 15: 459–70; Evelyne Huber, Dietrich Rueschmeyer, and John D. Stephens. 1993. "The impact of economic development on democracy." *Journal of Economic Perspectives.* 7 (3): 71–85. Ross E. Burkhart and Michael S. Lewis-Beck. 1994. "Comparative democracy: The economic development thesis." *American Political Science Review.* 88: 903–10; John F. Helliwell. 1994. "Empirical linkages between democracy and economic growth." *British Journal of Political Science.* 24 (2): 225–48; Tatu Vanhanen. 1997. *Prospects for Democracy: A Study of 172 Countries.* New York: Routledge; Robert J. Barro. 1999. "Determinants of democracy." *Journal of Political Economy.* 107(6): 158–83; Adam Przeworski, Michael E. Alvarez, Jose Antonio Cheibub, and Fernando Limongi. 2000. *Democracy and Development: Political Institutions and Well-Being in the World, 1950–1990.* New York: Cambridge University Press.

39   For a useful summary, see, for example, the discussion in Jan Teorell. 2010. *Determinants of Democratization.* New York: Cambridge University Press.

40   Seymour Martin Lipset. 1959. "Some social requisites of democracy: Economic development and political legitimacy." *American Political Science Review.* 53: 69–105; Manus I. Midlarsky, ed. 1997. *Inequality, Democracy and Economic Development.* Cambridge: Cambridge University Press; Carloes Boix. 2003. *Democracy and Redistribution.* Cambridge: Cambridge University Press; Daron Acemoglu and James A. Robinson. 2006. *Economic Origins of Dictatorship and Democracy.* New York: Cambridge University Press.

41   Samuel P. Huntington, 1991. *The Third Wave: Democratization in the Late Twentieth Century.* Norman: University of Oklahoma Press

42   Michael L. Ross. 2013. *The Oil Curse: How Petroleum Wealth Shapes the Development of Nations.* Princeton, NJ: Princeton University Press.

43 Robert A. Dahl. 1971. *Polyarchy: Participation and Opposition.* New Haven, CT: Yale University Press.

44 Ronald Inglehart and Christopher Welzel. 2005. *Modernization, Cultural Change, and Democracy: The Human Development Sequence.* New York: Cambridge University Press.

45 Donald Horowitz. 1985. *Ethnic Groups in Conflict.* Berkeley: University of California Press.

46 Michael Ross. 2012. *The Oil Curse.* Princeton, NJ: Princeton University Press.

47 For a discussion, see Carolien van Ham. 2013. "Why do elections fail? Explaining election integrity in third and fourth wave regimes." Paper presented at the Annual Conference of the American Political Science Association, 28–31 August 2013, Chicago.

48 Daniella Donno. 2013. *Defending Democratic Norms.* New York: Oxford University Press.

49 For a review of some of these initiatives, see Thomas Carothers. 1999. *Aiding Democracy Abroad.* Washington DC: Carnegie Endowment for International Peace; Jean Grugel. 1999. *Democracy without Borders: Transnationalisation and Conditionality in New Democracies.* London: Routledge; Michael Cox, G. John Ikenberry, and Takashi Inoguchi, eds. 2000. *American Democracy Promotion: Impulses, Strategies, and Impacts.* New York: Oxford University Press; Peter Burnell, ed. 2000. *Democracy Assistance: International Co-Operation for Democratization.* London: Frank Cass; Jon C. Pevehouse. 2002. "With a little help from my friends? Regional organizations and the consolidation of democracy." *American Journal of Political Science.* 46 (3): 611–26; Jon C. Pevehouse. 2002. "Democracy from the outside-in? International organizations and democratization." *International Organization.* 56 (3): 515+; Jon C. Pevehouse. 2004. *Democracy from Above: Regional Organizations and Democratization.* New York: Cambridge University Press; Carnegie Endowment for International Peace. *Critical Mission: Essays on Democracy Promotion.* Washington DC; Andrew F. Cooper and Thomas Legler. 2007. *Intervention Without Intervening? The OAS Defense and Promotion of Democracy in the Americas.* New York: Palgrave Macmillan; Peter Burnell. 2011. *Promoting Democracy Abroad: Policy and Performance.* New Brunswick, NJ: Transaction Publishers.

50 UNDP. 2012. *Evaluation of UNDP Contribution to Strengthening Electoral Systems and Processes.* New York: UNDP.

51 See, for example, James Manor. 2007. *Aid That Works: Successful Development in Fragile States.* Washington DC: The World Bank; Ted Piccone and Richard Youngs, eds. 2006. *Strategies for Democratic Change: Assessing the Global Response.* Washington DC: Democracy Coalition Project; Thomas Carothers. 1999. *Aiding Democracy Abroad.* Washington DC: Carnegie Endowment for International Peace; Jean Grugel. 1999. *Democracy without Borders: Transnationalisation and Conditionality in New Democracies.* London: Routledge; Peter Burnell, ed. 2000. *Democracy Assistance: International Co-Operation for Democratization.* London: Frank Cass; Thad Dunning. 2012. *Natural Experiments in the Social Sciences.* New York: Cambridge University Press.

52 Nahomi Ichino and Matthias Schuendeln. 2012. "Deterring or displacing electoral irregularities? Spillover effects of observers in a randomized field experiment in Ghana." *Journal of Politics.* 74(1): 292–307.

53 Ursula E. Daxecker and Gerald Schneider. 2014. "Electoral monitoring." In *Advancing Electoral Integrity*, eds. Pippa Norris, Richard W. Frank, and Ferran Martinez i Coma. New York: Oxford University Press.

54 Marina Ottoway and Teresa Chung. 1999. "Towards a new paradigm." *Journal of Democracy*. 10(4).

55 Jonathan Fisher. 2013. "The limits – and limiters – of external influence: Donors, the Ugandan Electoral Commission and the 2011 elections." *Journal of Eastern African Studies*. 7(3): 471–91.

56 The new government led by General Abdel Fatah al-Sisi engaged in a brutal crackdown on the political opposition, including killing thousands of demonstrators, jailing thousands of Muslim Brotherhood supporters, and prosecuting civil society activists and journalists to stifle dissent. Egyptian courts sentenced over 1,200 people to death. By continuing to give more than US$650 million aid to General Sisi's military government, the state department prioritized maintaining Egyptian relations over values respecting the rule of law and the peaceful electoral process. See Human Rights First. April 10, 2014. "U.S. Policy Toward Egypt Should Advance Human Rights." http://www.humanrightsfirst.org/press-release/us-policy-toward-egypt-should-advance-human-rights

57 Ryan Jablonski. 2013. "How aid targets votes: The impact of electoral incentives on foreign aid distribution." *World Politics*. 66(02): 293–330.

58 See, for example, Susan D. Hyde. 2011. *The Pseudo-Democrat's Dilemma*. Ithaca: Cornell University Press; Sarah Birch. 2012. *Electoral Malpractice*. Oxford: Oxford University Press; Judith Kelley. 2012. *Monitoring Democracy: When International Election Observation Works and Why it Often Fails*. Princeton, NJ: Princeton University Press; Daniella Donno. 2013. *Defending Democratic Norms*. New York: Oxford University Press; Nahomi Ichino and Matthias Schuendeln. 2012. "Deterring or displacing electoral irregularities? Spillover effects of observers in a randomized field experiment in Ghana." *Journal of Politics*. 74(1): 292–307.

59 Jonathan Hartlyn, Jennifer McCoy, and Thomas Mustillo. 2008. "Electoral governance matters: Explaining the quality of elections in contemporary Latin America." *Comparative Political Studies*. 41: 73–98.

60 For a discussion, see Jonathan Hartlyn, Jennifer McCoy, and Thomas Mustillo. 2008. "Electoral governance matters: Explaining the quality of elections in contemporary Latin America." *Comparative Political Studies*. 41: 73–98.

61 George Tsebelis. *Veto Players: How Political Institutions Work*. Princeton, NJ: Princeton University Press.

62 Arend Lijphart. 2012. *Patterns of Democracy*. New Haven: Yale University Press, 2nd edition. For a review of the extensive literature, see Rudy B. Andweg. 2000. "Consociational democracy." *Annual Review of Politics*. 3:509–36. For the development of alternative versions of this concept, see Gerhard Lehmbruch. 1967. *Proporzdemokratie. Politisches System und politische Kultur in der Schweiz und Osterreich*. Tubingen: Mohr; Jurg Steiner. 1974. *Amicable Agreement versus Majority Rule: Conflict Resolution in Switzerland*. Chapel Hill: University of North Carolina Press; Hans Daalder. 1974. "The consociational democracy theme." *World Politics*. 26: 604–21; Kenneth McRae, ed. 1974. *Consociational Democracy: Conflict Accommodation in Segmented Societies*. Toronto: McClelland

and Stewart; Klaus Armingeon. 2002. "The effects of negotiation democracy: A comparative analysis." *European Journal of Political Research.* 41: 81; Arend Lijphart. 2002. "Negotiation democracy versus consensus democracy: Parallel conclusions and recommendations." *European Journal of Political Research.* 41 (1): 107–13; Wolf Linder and Andre Baechtiger. 2005. "What drives democratization in Asia and Africa?" *European Journal of Political Research.* 44: 861–80. For an early and influential critique, see Brian Barry.1975. "Review article: Political accommodation and consociational democracy." *British Journal of Political Science.* 5(4): 194.

63 For a similar distinction between structure, function and culture, see K. Lalenis, M. de Jong, and V. Mamadouh, eds. 2002. *The Theory and Practice of Institutional Transplantation.* Dordrecht: Kluwer; Christopher Pollitt and Gerrt Bouckaart. 2004. *Public Management Reform: A Comparative Analysis.* Oxford: Oxford University Press.

64 See, for example, Daniel C. Hallin and Paolo Mancini. 2004. *Comparing Media Systems.* New York: Cambridge University Press; Open Society Institute. 2005. *Television Across Europe: Regulation, Policy, and Independence.* Budapest: OSI; Frank Esser and Thomas Janitzsch, eds. 2012. *The Handbook of Comparative Communication Research.* London: Routledge; European Broadcasting Union. 2014. *Legal focus: EBU principles for election coverage in new and developing democracies.* Brussels: EBU. European Broadcasting Union. 2014. *Legal focus: EBU principles for election coverage in new and developing democracies.* Brussels: EBU.

65 Reginald Austin and Maja Tjernstrom, eds. 2003. *Funding of Political Parties and Election Campaigns.* Stockholm: International IDEA, Table 1, pp. 185–8.

66 Jesús Orozco-Henríquez, ed. 2010. *Electoral Justice: The International IDEA Handbook.* Stockholm: International IDEA.

67 Sarah Birch. 2011. *Electoral Malpractice.* Oxford: Oxford University Press, pp. 122–3.

68 Robert A. Pastor, 1999. "The role of electoral administration in democratic transitions." *Democratization.* 6(4):1–27; Shaheen Mozaffar and Andreas Schedler. 2002. "The comparative study of electoral governance: Introduction." *International Political Science Review.* 23(1): 5–27.

69 Rafael López-Pintor. 2000. *Electoral Management Bodies as Institutions of Governance,* New York: United Nations Development Programme; Alan Wall, Andrew Ellis, Ayman Ayoub, Carl W. Dundas, Joram Rukambe, and Sara Staino. 2006. *Electoral Management Design: The International IDEA Handbook.* Sweden: International IDEA; Ismaila M. Fall, Mathias Hounkpe, Adele L. Jinadu, and Pascal Kambale, eds. 2011. *Election Management Bodies in West Africa: A Comparative Study of the Contribution of Electoral Commissions to the Strengthening of Democracy.* Johannesburg: Open Society Initiative for West Africa.

70 UNDP. 2012. *Evaluation of UNDP Contribution to Strengthening Electoral Systems and Processes.* New York: UNDP.

71 Christian Opitz, Hanne Fjelde, and Kristine Hoglund. 2013. "Including peace: the influence of electoral management bodies on electoral violence." *Journal of Eastern African Studies.* 7(4): 713–31.

72 Sarah Birch. 2008. "Electoral institutions and popular confidence in electoral processes: a cross-national analysis." *Electoral Studies.* 27 (2): 305–20. See also

Andrew James Klassen. 2014. "Perceptions of electoral fairness." Unpublished PhD thesis. Canberra: Australian National University; Jonathan Hartlyn, Jennifer McCoy, and Thomas Mustillo. 2008. "Electoral governance matters: Explaining the quality of elections in contemporary Latin America." *Comparative Political Studies.* 41: 73–98; Guillermo Rosas. 2010. "Trust in elections and the institutional design of electoral authorities: Evidence from Latin America." *Electoral Studies.* 29: 74–90; Antonio Ugues, Jr. 2014. "Electoral management in Central America." In *Advancing Electoral Integrity*, eds. Pippa Norris, Richard W. Frank, and Ferran Martinez i Coma. New York: Oxford University Press.

73 Robert A. Pastor. 1999. "A brief history of electoral commissions." In *The Self-Restraining State: Power and Accountability in New Democracies*, eds. Andreas Schedler, Larry Diamond, and Marc F. Plattner. Boulder, CO: Lynne Rienner, pp. 75–82; Robert A. Pastor. 1999. "The role of electoral administration in democratic transitions." *Democratization.* 6(4):1–27; Shaheen Mozaffar and Andreas Schedler. 2002. "The comparative study of electoral governance: Introduction." *International Political Science Review.* 23(1): 5–27; Mamoudou Gazibo. 2006. "The forging of institutional autonomy: A comparative study of Electoral Management Commissions in Africa." *Canadian Journal of Political Science.* 39(3): 611–33; Sarah Birch. 2008. "Electoral institutions and popular confidence in electoral processes." *Electoral Studies.* 27: 305–20; Emmanuel Debrah. 2011. "Measuring governance institutions' success in Ghana: The case of the Electoral Commission, 1993–2008." *African Studies.* 70(1): 25–45; Alexander B. Makulilo. 2009. "Independent Electoral Commission in Tanzania: A false debate?" *Representation.* 45 (4):435–53; Nicholas Kerr. "Popular perceptions of free and fair elections in Sub-Saharan Africa." In *Advancing Electoral Integrity*, eds. Pippa Norris, Richard W. Frank, and Ferran Martinez i Coma. Oxford: Oxford University Press; Badala Tachilisa Balule. 2008. "Election management bodies in the SADC region: An appraisal of the independence of Botswana's independent electoral commission." *South African Journal on Human Rights.* 24: 104–22; Nicholas Kerr. 2014. "Public perceptions of election quality in Africa: A cross-national analysis." In *Advancing Electoral Integrity*, eds. Pippa Norris, Richard Frank, and Ferran Martinez i Coma. New York: Oxford University Press.

2. Evidence

1 Steven Levitsky and Lucan Way. 2010. *Competitive Authoritarianism: Hybrid Regimes after the Cold War.* New York: Cambridge University Press.

2 Pippa Norris, Richard W. Frank, and Ferran Martinez i Coma. 2015. "Contentious elections: From ballots to barricades." In *Contentious Elections*, eds. Pippa Norris, Richard W. Frank, and Ferran Martinez i Coma. New York: Routledge; Emily Beaulieu. 2014. *Electoral Protests and Democracy in the Developing World.* New York: Cambridge University Press.

3 Estimates are derived from Susan D. Hyde and Nikolay Marinov. *Codebook for National Elections across Democracy and Autocracy (NELDA)* 3rd release, 10 November 2011. See also estimates by Scott Straus and Charles Taylor. 2012. "Democratization and electoral violence in Sub-Saharan Africa, 1990–2008." In

Voting in Fear: Electoral Violence in Sub-Saharan Africa, ed. Dorina Bekoe. United States Institute of Peace: Washington, DC. Straus and Taylor also compiled the African Electoral Violence Dataset 1990–2008.

4 Paul Collier. 2009. *Wars, Guns and Votes: Democracy in Dangerous Places.* New York: HarperCollins; Roland Paris. 2004. *At War's End: Building Peace after Civil Conflict.* Cambridge: Cambridge University Press; Michael W. Doyle and Nicholas Sambanis. 2006. *Making War and Building Peace.* Princeton, NJ: Princeton University Press; Roland Paris and Timothy D. Sisk, eds. 2009. *The Dilemmas of Statebuilding.* Oxford: Routledge; The Global Commission on Elections, Democracy and Security. 2012. *Deepening Democracy: A Strategy for improving the Integrity of Elections Worldwide.* Sweden: IDEA.

5 Lorraine Carol Minnite. 2010. *The Myth of Voter Fraud.* Ithaca: Cornell University Press; Richard L. Hasen. 2012. *The Voting Wars: From Florida 2000 to the Next Election Meltdown.* New Haven: Yale University Press; Tova Andrea Wang. 2012. *The Politics of Voter Suppression: Defending and Expanding Americans' Right to Vote.* Ithaca: Cornell University Press.

6 US opinion polls show that many believe that fraud at the ballot box is a widespread problem; for example, in May 2014 a Marquette Law School poll of the Wisconsin electorate found that more than one-third of Republicans shared the belief that "voter impersonation affects a thousand or more votes" in each Wisconsin election, compared with one-fifth of Democrats. https://law.marquette.edu/poll/2014/05/21/new-marquette-law-school-poll-finds-wisconsin-governors-race-tied/ See Emily Beaulieu. 2014. "From Voter ID to Party ID: How Political parties affect perceptions of election fraud in the U.S." *Electoral Studies.* 35: 24–32.

7 See, for example, the database on state-level voter identification laws and subsequent court decisions compiled by the National Conference of State Legislatures at http://www.ncsl.org/research/elections-and-campaigns/voter-id.aspx.

8 Robert F. Bauer, Benjamin L. Ginsberg, et al. 2014. *The American Voting Experience: Report and Recommendations of the Presidential Commission on Election Administration.* Washington DC. For more details, see https://www.supportthevoter.gov/

9 Michael Pal, *Canadian Election Administration on Trial: The 'Robocalls' case and the Opitz decision.* Paper presented at EIP/MEDW workshop prior to the IPSA World Congress, Montreal, July 18, 2014. For more details, see also http://www.democracy.arts.ubc.ca/fairelectionsact/

10 See UK Electoral Commission. 2014. *Electoral Fraud in the UK: Final Report and Recommendations.* London: UK Electoral Commission.

11 http://www2.ohchr.org/english/law/ccpr.htm

12 http://www.cartercenter.org/des-search/des/Default.aspx

13 John Hardin Young. 2009. *International Election Principles: Democracy and the Rule of Law.* Chicago: American Bar Association.

14 Michael R. Alvarez, Thad Hall, and Susan Hyde, eds. 2008. *Election Fraud.* Washington DC: Brookings Institution Press; Sarah Birch. 2011. *Electoral Malpractice.* Oxford: Oxford University Press.

15 Susan D. Hyde. 2011. *The Pseudo-Democrat's Dilemma.* Ithaca: Cornell University Press; Sarah Birch. 2012. *Electoral Malpractice.* Oxford: Oxford University

Press; Judith Kelley. 2012. *Monitoring Democracy: When International Election Observation Works and Why It Often Fails.* Princeton, NJ: Princeton University Press.

16 Thomas Carothers. 2002. "The end of the transition paradigm." *Journal of Democracy.* 13: 5–21; Fareed Zakaria. 1997. "The rise of illiberal democracy." *Foreign Affairs.* 76(6): 22–41; Larry Diamond. 2002. "Thinking about hybrid regimes." *Journal of Democracy.* 13(2): 21–35; Steven Levitsky and Lucan A. Way. 2002. "The rise of competitive authoritarianism." *Journal of Democracy.* 13(2): 51–65; Andreas Schedler, ed. 2006. *Electoral Authoritarianism: The Dynamics of Unfree Competition.* Boulder; Lynne Rienner, Steven Levitsky, and Lucan A. Way. 2010. *Competitive Authoritarianism: Hybrid Regimes after the Cold War.* New York: Cambridge University Press.

17 Pippa Norris. Norris. 2014. *Why Electoral Integrity Matters.* New York: Cambridge University Press.

18 Eric C. Bjornlund. 2004. *Beyond Free and Fair: Monitoring Elections and Building Democracy.* Washington DC: Woodrow Wilson Center Press; Susan D. Hyde. 2011. *The Pseudo-Democrat's Dilemma.* Ithaca, NY: Cornell University Press; Judith Kelley. 2012. *Monitoring Democracy: When International Election Observation Works and Why it Often Fails.* Princeton, NJ: Princeton University Press.

19 United Nations. 2005. *Declaration of Principles for International Election Observation and Code of Conduct for International Elections Observers.* New York: United Nations. http://www.cartercenter.com/documents/2231.pdf

20 Susan D. Hyde and Nikolay Marinov. 2011. *Codebook for National Elections across Democracy and Autocracy (NELDA).* 3rd release, 10 November 2011; Judith Kelley. Quality of Elections data. http://sites.duke.edu/kelley/data/.

21 Judith Kelley. 2012. *The Good, the Bad, and the Ugly: Rethinking Election Monitoring.* Stockholm: International IDEA.

22 OSCE/ODIHR, *Republic of Azerbaijan Presidential Elections 9 October 2013 Election Observation Mission Final Report.* (Warsaw: OSCE/ODIHR, 24 December 2013).

23 http://www.assembly.coe.int/nw/xml/News/News-View-EN.asp?newsid=4699&lang=2&cat=31

24 Ursula Daexler and Gerald Schneider. 2014. "Electoral monitoring." In *Advancing Electoral Integrity*, eds. Pippa Norris, Richard W. Frank, and Ferran Martinez i Coma. New York: Oxford University Press.

25 Christopher J. Fariss. 2014. "Respect for human rights has improved over time: Modeling the changing standard of accountability." *American Political Science Review.* 108: 297–318.

26 Thomas E. Patterson and Wolfgang Donsbach. 1996. "News decisions: Journalists as partisan actors." *Political Communication.* 13(4): 455–68.

27 Pippa Norris. 2000. *A Virtuous Circle.* New York: Cambridge University Press; Pamela Shoemaker and Akiba A. Cohen. 2006. *News around the World.* New York: Routledge.

28 William A. Hachten. 1996. *The World News Prism.* 4th ed. Ames, Iowa: Iowa University Press.

29 I. Wallerstein. 1974. *The Modern World-System.* New York: Academic Press; Elad Segev and M. Blondheim, 2013. "America's global standing according to

popular news sites from around the world." *Political Communication*. 30(1): 139–61; Pippa Norris and Ronald Inglehart. 2009. *Cosmopolitan Communications*. New York: Cambridge University Press; Elad Segev, Tamir Sheafer, and Shaul R. Shenhav. 2013. "Is the world getting flatter? A new method for examining structural trends in the news." *Journal of the American Society for Information Science and Technology*. 64(12): 2537–47.

30 Catie Snow Bailard and Steven Livingston. 2014. "Crowdsourcing accountability in a Nigerian election." *Journal of Information Technology & Politics*. 11(4): 346–67; John Paul Lederach. 2012. "Crowdsourcing during post-election violence in Kenya." In *The Technology of Nonviolence: Social Media and Violence Prevention*. Joseph G. Bock, ed. Cambridge, MA: MIT Press; Max Bader. 2013. "Crowdsourcing election monitoring in the 2011–2012 Russian elections." *East European Politics*. 29(4): 521–35.

31 See Pippa Norris. 2014. "Does the world agree about standards of electoral integrity? Evidence for the diffusion of global norms," Special issue of *Electoral Studies*. 32(4): 576–88.

32 For more details of the sixth wave World Values Survey, including access to the codebook and data, see www.worldvaluessurvey.org

33 Pippa Norris. 2014. *Why Electoral Integrity Matters*. NY: Cambridge University Press. Ch 5: 91–110.

34 Michael Pal. 2014. *"Canadian Election Administration on Trial: The 'Robocalls' case and the Opitz decision."* Paper presented at EIP/MEDW workshop prior to the IPSA World Congress, Montreal 18 July 2014.

35 UK Electoral Commission. 2014. *Electoral Fraud in the UK: Final Report and Recommendations*. London: UK Electoral Commission.

36 Robert F. Bauer, et al, 2014. *The American Voting Experience: Report and Recommendations of the Presidential Commission on Election Administration*. Washington DC. For more details, see www.supportthevoter.gov.

37 See, for example, Mikhail Myagkov, Peter C. Ordeshook, and Dimitri Shakin. 2009. *The Forensics of Election Fraud: Russia and Ukraine*. New York: Cambridge University Press; Christian Breunig and Achim Goerres. 2011. "Searching for electoral irregularities in an established democracy: Applying Benford's Law tests to Bundestag elections in Unified Germany." *Electoral Studies*. 30(3): 534–45; Gonzalo Castaneda. 2011. "Benford's law and its applicability in the forensic analysis of electoral results." *Politica Y Gobierno*. 18(2): 297–329; Luis Pericchi and David Torres. 2011. "Quick anomaly detection by the Newcomb-Benford Law, with applications to electoral processes data from the USA, Puerto Rico and Venezuela." *Statistical Science*. 26(4): 502–16; Walter R. Mebane, Jr. 2012. "Comment on 'Benford's Law' and the detection of election fraud." *Political Analysis*. 19(3): 269–72; Bernd Beber and Alexandra Scacco. 2012. "What the numbers say: a digit-based test for election fraud." *Political Analysis*. 20(2): 211–34; Raul Jimenez and Manuel Hidalgo. 2014. "Forensic analysis of Venezuelan elections during the Chavez Presidency." *Plos One*. 9(6): 20–9.

38 Fabrice Edouard Lehoucq and Iván Molina Jiménez. 2002. *Stuffing the Ballot Box: Fraud, Electoral Reform, and Democratization in Costa Rica*. New York: Cambridge University Press.

39 Lorraine Carol Minnite. 2010. *The Myth of Voter Fraud*. Ithaca: Cornell University Press; R. Michael Alvarez and Frederick J. Boehmke. 2008. "Correlates of

fraud: Studying state election fraud allegations." In R. Michael Alvarez, Thad Hall and Susan Hyde, eds. *Election Fraud*. Washington DC: Brookings Institution Press.

40 See Justin Levitt. 2007. *The Truth about Voter Fraud*. Brennan Center for Justice at New York University School of Law. New York: Brennan Center. http:// brennan.3cdn.net/e20e4210db075b482b_wcm6ibohl.pdf.

41 See, for example, Susan D. Hyde. 2007. "Experimenting in democracy promotion: international observers and the 2004 presidential elections in Indonesia." *Perspectives on Politics*. 8(2): 511–27; Nahomi Ichino and Matthias Schuendeln. 2012. "Deterring or displacing electoral irregularities? Spillover effects of observers in a randomized field experiment in Ghana." *Journal of Politics*. 74(1): 292–307; Fredrik Sjoberg. 2012. "Making voters count: Evidence from field experiments about the efficacy of domestic election observation." Harriman Institute Working Paper 1.

42 Pippa Norris. 2004. "Will new technology boost turnout?" In *Electronic Voting and Democracy: A Comparative Analysis*, eds. Norbert Kersting, and Harald Baldersheim. London: Palgrave. 193–225.

43 Devra C. Moehler, 2010. "Democracy, governance, and randomized development assistance." *Annals of the American Academy of Political and Social Science*. 628: 30–46.

44 See, for example, the discussion in James N. Druckman, Donald P. Green, James H. Kuklinski, and Arthur Lupia, eds. 2011. *Cambridge Handbook of Experimental Political Science*. NY: Cambridge University Press; Rebecca B. Morton and Kenneth C. Williams. 2010. *Experimental Political Science and the Study of Causality: From Nature to the Lab*. NY: Cambridge University Press; Thad Dunning. 2012. *Natural Experiments in the Social Sciences*. NY: Cambridge University Press.

45 Transparency International Corruption Perception Index. http://www .transparency.org/research/cpi/overview

46 Todd Landman and Edzia Carvalho. 2010. *Measuring Human Rights*. London: Routledge.

47 See Geraldo L. Munck. 2009. *Measuring Democracy: A Bridge between Scholarship and Politics*. Baltimore: The Johns Hopkins Press.

48 Andreas Schedler. 2012. "Judgment and measurement in political science." *Perspectives on Politics*. 10(1): 21–36; Ferran Martinez i Coma and Richard W. Frank. 2014. "Expert judgments." Chapter 4 in *Advancing Electoral Integrity*, eds. Pippa Norris, Richard W. Frank, and Ferran Martinez i Coma. New York: Oxford University Press.

49 The Varieties of Democracy project, see https://v-dem.net/

50 Marco R. Steenbergen and Gary Marks. 2007. "Evaluating expert judgments." *European Journal of Political Research*. 46: 347–66.

51 Mary Meyer and Jane Booker. 2001. *Eliciting and Analyzing Expert Judgment: A Practical Guide*. Society for Industrial and Applied Mathematics.

52 See Pippa Norris, Jørgen Elklit, and Andrew Reynolds. 2014. "Methods and evidence." Chapter 3 in *Advancing Electoral Integrity*, eds. Pippa Norris, Richard W. Frank, and Ferran Martinez i Coma. New York: Oxford University Press.

53 Mary Meyer and Jane Booker. 2001. *Eliciting and Analyzing Expert Judgment: A Practical Guide*. Society for Industrial and Applied Mathematics.

54 This understanding of sequential steps is similar to the notions developed in Andreas Schedler. 2002. "The menu of manipulation." *Journal of Democracy*. 13(2): 36–50.

55 Pippa Norris and Andrea Abel van Es. 2016. *Checkbook Elections? Political Finance in Comparative Perspective.*

56 Pippa Norris. 2001. "US campaign 2000: Of pregnant chads, butterfly ballots and partisan vitriol." *Government and Opposition.* 36(1): 3–26; Jonathan N. Wand, Kenneth W. Shotts, Jasjeet S. Sekhon, Walter R. Mebane, Jr., Michael C. Herron, and Henry E. Brady. 2001. "The butterfly did it: The aberrant vote for Buchanan in Palm Beach County, Florida." *American Political Science Review.* 95(4): 793–810.

57 Pippa Norris, Ferran Martinez i Coma and Richard W. Frank. 2014. "Assessing the quality of elections." *Journal of Democracy.* 24(4): 124–35.

58 The Quality of Government data set. http://www.qog.pol.gu.se/

59 The Ace Project: http://aceproject.org/.

60 Similar issues confront the construction and use of indicators of democratization and human rights; see, for example, Geraldo L. Munck and Jay Verkuilen. 2002. "Conceptualizing and measuring democracy: Evaluating alternative indices." *Comparative Political Studies.* 35 (1): 5–34; Todd Landman and Edzia Carvalho. 2010. *Measuring Human Rights.* London: Routledge; Geraldo L. Munck. 2009. *Measuring Democracy: A Bridge between Scholarship and Politics.* Baltimore, MD: The Johns Hopkins Press.

61 Staffan Lindberg. 2006. *Democracy and Elections in Africa.* Baltimore, MD: The Johns Hopkins University Press.

62 Alberto Alesina and Enrico Spolaore. 2003. *The Size of Nations.* Cambridge, MA: MIT Press.

63 Susan D. Hyde and Nikolay Marinov. *Codebook for National Elections across Democracy and Autocracy (NELDA).* Nov. 10, 2011.

64 See Adam Przeworski, Michael E. Alvarez, Jose Antonio Cheibub, and Fernando Limongi. 2000. *Democracy and Development: Political Institutions and Well-Being in the World, 1950–1990.* New York: Cambridge University Press.

65 Sylvia Bishop and Anke Hoeffler. *Free and Fair Elections: A New Database.* Codebook. See http://www.csae.ox.ac.uk/datasets/free-fair-elections/default.html

66 Geraldo L. Munck. 2009. *Measuring Democracy: A Bridge between Scholarship and Politics.* Baltimore, MD: The Johns Hopkins Press.

67 See https://www.freedomhouse.org/report/freedom-world-2014/methodology#.VJyfgF4AKA

68 The democracy indicator in Polity IV is an additive eleven-point scale (0–10). The operational indicator of democracy is derived from coding the competitiveness of political participation (variable 2.6), the openness and competitiveness of executive recruitment (variables 2.3 and 2.2), and constraints on the chief executive (variable 2.4). Both competitiveness and openness are coded based on elections. See Monty G. Marshall, Ted Robert Gurr, and Keith Jaggers. 2014. *Polity IV Project: Political Regime Characteristics and Transitions, 1800–2013. Dataset Users' Manual.* University of Maryland, Center for Systemic Peace. http://www.systemicpeace.org/inscr/p4manualv2013.pdf. The correlation between the Polity IV democracy–autocracy scale and the PEI Electoral Integrity scale is moderately strong (R = .636**, p = .000, N = .88).

69 José Antonio Cheibub, Jennifer Gandhi, and James Raymond Vreeland. 2010. "Democracy and dictatorship revisited." *Public Choice.* 143(2-1): 67–101.

70 Carles Boix, Michael K. Miller, and Sebastian Rosato. 2013. "A complete dataset of political regimes, 1800–2007.'" *Comparative Political Studies.* 46(12): 1523–54.

71   Tracy Campbell. 2006. *Deliver the Vote: A History of Election Fraud, an American Political Tradition 1742–2004.* New York: Basic Books.

72   Alberto Simpser. 2013. *Why Governments and Parties Manipulate Elections.* New York: Cambridge University Press, p. 47.

73   Pippa Norris and Andrea Abel van Es. 2016. *Checkbook Elections? Political Finance in Comparative Perspective.*

74   Commission De L'Union Africaine. 2013. *Rapport De La Mission D'observation De L'Union Africaine Aux Elections Legislatives, Senatoriales Et Municipales Du 26 Mai 2013 En Republique De Guinee Equatoriale.* http://pa.au.int/en/sites/default/files/MOEAU%20Rapport%20Final%20Guinee%20Equatoriale%20%202013.pdf

75   Amnesty International. 1 October 2013. *"Equatorial Guinea: Continued institutional and key human rights concerns In Equatorial Guinea: Amnesty international submission to the UN Universal Periodic Review, May 2014.I"* http://www.amnesty.org/en/library/info/AFR24/013/2013/en

76   Sarah Birch. 2012. *Electoral Malpractice.* Oxford: Oxford University Press.

77   Clifton W. Sherrill. 2014. "Why Hassan Rouhani won Iran's 2013 presidential election." *Middle East Policy.* 21(2): 64–75.

78   After the election, the Electoral Commission announced that it would seek to address malapportionment by redrawing district boundaries. *The Malay Mail,* 26 December 2013. "In upcoming redelineation, EC seeks to balance unequal-sized election seats." http://www.themalaymailonline.com/malaysia/article/in-upcoming-redelineation-ec-seeks-to-balance-unequal-sized-election-seats

79   Brigitte Welsh. 2013. "Malaysia's elections: A step backward." *Journal of Democracy.* 24(4): 136–50.

80   Steven J. Rosenstone, Roy L. Behr, and Edward H. Lazarus. 1996. *Third Parties in America.* Princeton, NJ: Princeton University Press.

81   http://www.oas.org/es/sap/deco/moe/mexico2012/default.asp

82   Beatriz Magaloni. 2006. *Voting for Autocracy: Hegemonic Party Survival and Its Demise in Mexico.* Cambridge: Cambridge University Press.

83   Richard L. Hasen. 2012. *The Voting Wars: From Florida 2000 to the Next Election Meltdown.* New Haven: Yale University Press.

84   See, for example, Steven Levitsky and Lucan Way. 2010. *Competitive Authoritarianism: Hybrid Regimes after the Cold War.* New York: Cambridge University Press.

85   Jennifer Gandhi and Ellen Lust-Okar. 2009. "Elections under authoritarianism." *Annual Review of Political Science.* 12: 403–22; Alberto Simpser. 2013. *Why Governments and Parties Manipulate Elections: Theory, Practice and Implications.* New York: Cambridge University Press.

86   Pippa Norris, Richard W. Frank, and Ferran Martinez i Coma, eds. 2014. *Contentious Elections.* NY: Routledge.

87   See, for example, Susan D. Hyde. 2011. *The Pseudo-Democrat's Dilemma.* Ithaca: Cornell University Press; Sarah Birch. 2012. *Electoral Malpractice.* Oxford: Oxford University Press; Judith Kelley. 2012. *Monitoring Democracy: When International Election Observation Works and Why it Often Fails.* Princeton, NJ: Princeton University Press; Daniella Donno. 2013. *Defending Democratic Norms.* New York: Oxford University Press; Thomas Carothers. 2002. "The end of

the transition paradigm." *Journal of Democracy.* 13: 5–21; Pippa Norris, Richard W. Frank, and Ferran Martinez i Coma, eds. 2014. *Advancing Electoral Integrity.* New York: Oxford University Press.

88 Democratic capital is measured by the number of consecutive years from 1930 to 1995 that a country was democratic, as classified by Beck et al. (2001). The correlation with the contemporary PEI Index is strong and significant (R = .571** p = .000, N = .93).

89 Martin Bull and Gianfranco Pasquino. 2007. "A long quest in vain: Institutional reforms in Italy." *West European Politics* 30(4): 670–91; Gianfranco Baldini. 2011. "The different trajectories of Italian electoral reforms." *West European Politics* 34(3): 644–63.

90 Tova Andrea Wang. 2012. *The Politics of Voter Suppression: Defending and Expanding Americans' Right to Vote.* Ithaca: Cornell University Press.

91 Richard L. Hasen. 2012. *The Voting Wars: From Florida 2000 to the Next Election Meltdown.* New Haven: Yale University Press.

92 The Perceptions of Electoral Integrity (PEI) Index was strongly and significantly correlated with real per capita GDP (R = .590** p = .000, N = .96), for reasons discussed in the next chapter.

3. Structural Constraints

1 For a fascinating and detailed account, see Noah Coburn and Anna Larson. 2013. *Derailing Democracy in Afghanistan: Elections in an Unstable Political Landscape.* New York: Columbia University Press. See also UNDP. *Human Development Report 2013: The Rise of the South.* New York: UNDP. http://hdr.undp.org/sites/default/files/reports/14/hdr2013_en_complete.pdf

2 For a discussion, Sarah Birch. 2012. *Electoral Malpractice.* Oxford: Oxford University Press; Carolien van Ham. 2013. "Why do elections fail? Explaining election integrity in third and fourth wave regimes." Paper presented at the Annual Conference of the American Political Science Association, 28–31 August 2013, Chicago.

3 Seymour Martin Lipset. 1959. "Some social requisites of democracy: Economic development and political legitimacy." *American Political Science Review.* 53: 69–105. See also Seymour Martin Lipset. 1960. *Political Man: The Social Basis of Politics.* New York: Doubleday; Seymour Martin Lipset, Kyoung-Ryung Seong, and John Charles Torres. 1993. "A comparative analysis of the social requisites of democracy." *International Social Science Journal.* 45(2): 154–75; Seymour Martin Lipset and Jason M. Lakin. 2004. *The Democratic Century.* Oklahoma: The University of Oklahoma Press.

4 Seymour Martin Lipset. 1959. "Some social requisites of democracy: Economic development and political legitimacy." *American Political Science Review.* 53: 75.

5 Seymour Martin Lipset. 1959. "Some social requisites of democracy: Economic development and political legitimacy." *American Political Science Review.* 53: 75. The most recent statement of this relationship by Lipset and Lakin suggests that capitalist free-market economies produce multiple commodities which are critical for democracy, by creating more heterogeneous and diverse centers of wealth and power. This reduces the economic control of the state and provides the basis

for opposition organizations, they suggest, and the economic foundation for an active civil society. See Seymour Martin Lipset and Jason M. Lakin. 2004. *The Democratic Century*. Oklahoma: The University of Oklahoma Press. Chapter 5.

6 Dankwart Rustow. 1970. "Transitions to democracy." *Comparative Politics*. 2: 337–63.

7 J. Krieckhaus. 2004. "The regime debate revisited: A sensitivity analysis of democracy's economic effect." *British Journal of Political Science*. 34(4): 635–55.

8 Robert W. Jackman. 1973. "On the relation of economic development and democratic performance." *American Journal of Political Science*. 17: 611–21; Kenneth A. Bollen. 1979. "Political democracy and the timing of development." *American Sociological Review* 44: 572–87; Kenneth A. Bollen. 1983. "World system position, dependency and democracy: The cross-national evidence." *American Sociological Review*. 48: 468–79; Kenneth A. Bollen and Robert W. Jackman. 1985. "Political democracy and the size distribution of income." *American Sociological Review*. 50: 438–58; Gregory C. Brunk, Gregory A. Caldeira, and Michael S. Lewis-Beck. 1987. "Capitalism, socialism, and democracy: An empirical inquiry." *European Journal of Political Research*. 15: 459–70; Evelyne Huber, Dietrich Rueschmeyer, and John D. Stephens. 1993. "The impact of economic development on democracy." *Journal of Economic Perspectives*. 7(3): 71–85. Ross E. Burkhart and Michael S. Lewis-Beck. 1994. "Comparative democracy: The economic development thesis." *American Political Science Review*. 88: 903–10; John F. Helliwell. 1994. "Empirical linkages between democracy and economic growth." *British Journal of Political Science*. 24 (2): 225–48; Tatu Vanhanen. 1997. *Prospects for Democracy: A Study of 172 Countries*. New York: Routledge; Robert J. Barro. 1999. "Determinants of democracy." *Journal of Political Economy*. 107 (6): 158–83; Adam Przeworski, Michael E. Alvarez, Jose Antonio Cheibub, and Fernando Limongi. 2000. *Democracy and Development: Political Institutions and Well-Being in the World, 1950–1990*. New York: Cambridge University Press; Seymour Martin Lipset, Kyoung-Ryung Seong, and John Charles Torres. 1993. "A comparative analysis of the social requisites of democracy." *International Social Science Journal*. 45(2): 154–75; Seymour Martin Lipset and Jason M. Lakin. 2004. *The Democratic Century*. Oklahoma: The University of Oklahoma Press; Daron Acemoglu, Simon Johnson, and James A. Robinson. 2008. "Income and democracy." *American Economic Review*. 98(3): 808–42.

9 Adam Przeworski, Michael E. Alvarez, José Antonio Cheibub, and Fernando Limongi. 1996. "What makes democracies endure?" *Journal of Democracy*. 7:1 (January): 39–55; Adam Przeworski and F. Limongi. 1997. "Modernization: theories and facts." *World Politics*. 49:155–83; Adam Przeworski, Michael E. Alvarez, José Antonio Cheibub, and Fernando Limongi. 2000. *Democracy and Development: Political Institutions and Well-Being in the World, 1950–1990*. New York: Cambridge University Press.

10 Pippa Norris. 2008. *Driving Democracy: Do Power-sharing Institutions Work?* New York: Cambridge University Press, Chapter 4.

11 Robert Barro. 1999. "Determinants of democracy." *Journal of Political Economy*. 107(6): 158–193.

12 Pippa Norris. 2008. *Driving Democracy: Do Power-sharing Institutions Work?* New York: Cambridge University Press, p. 88.

13 Pippa Norris. 2014. *Why Electoral Integrity Matters.* New York: Cambridge University Press, Chapter 4.

14 B. Davidson. 1992. *The Black Man's Burden: Africa and the Curse of the Nation-State.* Random House, New York.

15 Robert A. Dahl. 1998. *On Democracy.* New Haven: Yale University Press.

16 Sarah Birch. 2011. *Electoral Malpractice.* Oxford: Oxford University Press.

17 See the Quality of Government Institute, www.qog.pol.gu.se

18 Kanchan Chandra. 2004. *Why Ethnic Parties Succeed: Patronage and Ethnic Headcounts in India.* Cambridge: Cambridge University Press; Daniel Posner. 2005. *Institutions and Ethnic Politics in Africa.* Cambridge: Cambridge University Press.

19 Pippa Norris and Ronald Inglehart. 2009. *Cosmopolitan Communications.* New York: Cambridge University Press.

20 Sarah Birch. 2011. *Electoral Malpractice.* Oxford: Oxford University Press, Tables 3.1 and 3.2.

21 Sarah Birch. 2011. *Electoral Malpractice.* Oxford: Oxford University Press. P. 65.

22 Lisa Chauvet and Paul Collier. 2009. "Elections and economic policy in developing countries." *Economic Policy.* 24(59), 509–50.

23 Adam Przeworski, Michael E. Alvarez, José Antonio Cheibub, and Fernando Limongi. 2000. *Democracy and Development: Political Institutions and Well-Being in the World, 1950–1990.* New York: Cambridge University Press.

24 Amartya Sen. 1999. *Development as Freedom.* New York: Anchor Books. The UNDP's Human Development Index (HDI) is a composite index that measures the average achievements in a country in three basic dimensions of human development: a long and healthy life, as measured by life expectancy at birth; knowledge, as measured by the adult literacy rate and the combined gross enrolment ratio for primary, secondary, and tertiary schools; and a decent standard of living, as measured by GDP per capita in purchasing power parity (PPP) US dollars.

25 See, for example, UNDP 2002. *Deepening Democracy in a Fragmented World: 2002 Human Development Report.* New York: UNDP as well as the 2014 UNDP data http://hdr.undp.org/en/content/table-1-human-development-index-and-its-components.

26 See, for example, Michael L. Ross. 2001. "Does oil hinder democracy?" *World Politics.* 53: 325–61; N. Jensen and L. Wantchekon. 2004. "Resource wealth and political regimes in Africa." *Comparative Political Studies.* 37, 816–41; Carles Boix 2003. *Democracy and Redistribution.* Cambridge: Cambridge University Press; M.L. Ross. 2004. "How do natural resources influence civil war? Evidence from thirteen cases." *International Organization.* 58 (1): 35–67; Stephen Haber and Victor Menaldo. 2011. "Do natural resources fuel authoritarianism? A reappraisal of the resource curse." *American Political Science Review.* 105(1): 1–26; Michael L. Ross. 2013. *The Oil Curse: How Petroleum Wealth Shapes the Development of Nations.* Princeton, NJ: Princeton University Press.

27 Paul Collier and Nicholas Sambanis, eds. 2005. *Understanding Civil War.* Washington DC: World Bank; M. Humphreys. 2005. "Natural resources, conflict, and conflict resolution – uncovering the mechanisms." *Journal of Conflict Resolution.* 49(4): 508–37; Richard Snyder. 2006. "Does lootable wealth breed disorder? A political economy of extraction framework." *Comparative Political Studies.* 39(8): 943–68.

28 Sarah Birch. 2011. *Electoral Malpractice.* Oxford: Oxford University Press. Pp. 64–5.

29 S. Anderson and P.M. Heywood. 2009. '"The politics of perception: Use and abuse of transparency international's approach to measuring corruption.'" *Political Studies,* 57(4), 746–67.

30 Prominent papers in this literature include Paulo Mauro. 1995. "Corruption and growth." *Quarterly Journal of Economics.* 110(3):681–712; Stephen Knack and Philip Keefer. 1995. "Institutions and economic performance: cross-country tests using alternative institutional measures." *Economics & Politics.* 7(3):207–27; Raphael LaPorta, Florencio Lopez-de-Silanes, Andrei Shleifer, and Robert Vishny. 1999. "The quality of government." *Journal of Law, Economics, and Organizations.* 15(1): 222–79. This literature is surveyed in detail in Rose-Ackerman (2004).

31 Alternative indices of corruption were tested and found to suffer from similar problems, such as the bribe payer's index and the World Bank Institution's Control of Corruption.

32 William Easterly and Ross Levine. 2003. "Tropics, germs, and crops: How endowments influence economic development." *Journal of Monetary Economic.* 50:3–39; Alberto Alesina and Enrico Spolaore. 2003. *The Size of Nations.* Cambridge, MA: MIT Press; Jan Teorell. 2010. *Determinants of Democratization: Explaining Regime Change in the World, 1972–2006.* New York: Cambridge University Press.

33 The Electoral Commission of India. http://eci.nic.in/eci_main1/the_setup.aspx; *The Times of India.* 18 Feb. 2014. "Polls to cost country Rs 3,500 crore this year."

34 See Daron Acemoglu, Simon Johnson, and James A. Robinson. 2002. "Reversal of fortune: Geography and institutions in the making of the modern income distribution.'" *The Quarterly Journal of Econometrics.* 118: 1231–94; Dani Rodrik, Arvind Subramanian, and Francesco Trebbi. 2004. '"Institutions rule: The primacy of institutions over geography and integration in economic development." *Journal of Economic Growth.* 9(2): 131–165.

35 William Easterly and Ross Levine. 2003. '"Tropics, germs, and crops: How endowments influence economic development.'" *Journal of Monetary Economic.* 50:3–39.

36 Alberto Alesina, Arnaud Devleeschauwer, William Easterly, Sergio Kurlat, and Romain Wacziarg. 2003. "Fractionalization." *The Journal of Economic Growth.* 8:155–94; Alberto Alesina, and Eliana La Ferrara. 2005. "Ethnic diversity and economic performance." *Journal of Economic Literature.* 43(3): 762–800; Stuart J. Kaufman. 2001. *Modern Hatreds: The Symbolic Politics of Ethnic War.* Ithaca: Cornell University Press; Paul Collier and Nicholas Sambanis, eds. 2005. *Understanding Civil War.* Washington DC: World Bank; Michael W. Doyle and Nicholas Sambanis. 2006. *Making War and Building Peace.* Princeton: Princeton University Press.

37 For an argument challenging the conventional wisdom that more ethnically or religiously diverse countries are more likely to experience significant civil violence, however, see James D. Fearon and David D. Laitin. 2003. "Ethnicity, insurgency, and civil war." *American Political Science Review.* 97(1): 75–90.

38 Jack Snyder. 2000. *From Voting to Violence: Democratization and Nationalist Conflict.* New York: W.W. Norton; Edward D. Mansfield and Jack Snyder. 2007. *Electing to Fight: Why Emerging Democracies go to War.* Cambridge, MA: MIT Press.

39 See, for example, Roland Paris. 2005. *At War's End: Building Peace after Civil Conflict.* New York: Cambridge University Press; Paul Collier and Nicholas Sambanis, eds. 2005. *Understanding Civil War.* Washington DC: World Bank; Michael W. Doyle and Nicholas Sambanis. 2006. *Making War and Building Peace.* Princeton: Princeton University Press; Chaim Kaufmann. 1996. "Possible and impossible solutions to ethnic civil wars." *International Security.* 20(4): 136–75.

40 Alberto Alesina, Arnaud Devleeschauwer, William Easterly, Sergio Kurlat, and Romain Wacziarg. 2003. "Fractionalization." *The Journal of Economic Growth.* 8:155–94.

41 Alfred Stepan and Graeme B. Robertson. 2003. "An 'Arab' more than a 'muslim' electoral gap." *Journal of Democracy.* 14: 30–44; Thad Dunning. 2008. *Crude Democracy: Natural Resource Wealth and Political Regimes.* New York: Cambridge University Press.

42 Samuel Huntington. 1993. *The Clash of Civilizations and the Remaking of World Order.* New York: Simon & Schuster.

43 Pippa Norris and Ronald Inglehart. 2011. *Sacred and Secular.* 2nd ed. New York: Cambridge University Press.

44 Alfred Stepan and Graeme B. Robertson. 2003. "An 'Arab' more than a 'muslim' electoral gap." *Journal of Democracy.* 14: 30–44.

45 Daron Acemoglu, Simon Johnson, and James A. Robinson. 2001. "The colonial origins of comparative development: An empirical investigation." *The American Economic Review.* 91 (5):1369–401; Daron Acemoglu and James A. Robinson. 2006. *Economic Origins of Dictatorship and Democracy.* New York: Cambridge University Press.

46 Christopher Clague, Suzanne Gleason, and Stephen Knack. 2001. "Determinants of lasting democracy in poor countries: Culture, development and institutions." *Annals of the American Academy of Social Sciences.* 573: 16–41.

47 Seymour Martin Lipset and Jason M. Lakin. 2004. *The Democratic Century.* Oklahoma: The University of Oklahoma Press. Chapter 11. See also similar findings in Axel Hadenius. 1994. "The duration of democracy." In David Beetham. 1994. *Defining and Measuring Democracy.* London: Sage.

48 The expansion in peacekeeping activities and the settlement of civil wars has attracted a substantial literature. See, for example, Roland Paris, 2004. *At War's End: Building Peace after Civil Conflict.* Cambridge: Cambridge University Press; Ho-Won Jeong. 2005. *Peace-building in Post-conflict Societies.* Boulder, Co: Lynne Rienner; Paul Collier and Nicholas Sambanis, eds. 2005. *Understanding Civil War.* Washington DC: The World Bank; James Dobbins et al. 2005. *The UN's Role in Nation-building: From the Congo to Iraq.* Santa Monica: Rand Corporation; Michael W. Doyle and Nicholas Sambanis. 2006. *Making War and Building Peace.* Princeton: Princeton University Press; Anna K. Jarsad and Timothy D. Sisk, eds. 2008. *From War to Democracy.* New York: Cambridge University Press; Lise Morjé Howard. 2009. *UN Peacekeeping in Civil Wars.* New York: Cambridge University Press; Monica Toft. 2010. *Securing the Peace: The Durable Settlement of Civil Wars.* Princeton: Princeton University Press.

49 Krishna Kumar, ed., 1998. *Post-conflict Elections, Democratization and International Assistance.* Boulder, CO: Lynne Rienner; Michael McFaul. 2010. *Advancing Democracy Abroad.* New York: Rowman and Littlefield; Christoph

Zurcher, et al. 2013. *Costly Democracy: Peacebuilding and Democratization after War*. Stanford, CA: Stanford University Press.

50   Michael W. Doyle and Nicholas Sambanis. 2006. *Making War and Building Peace*. Princeton: Princeton University Press.

51   Monty G. Marshall, and Benjamin R. Cole. 2014. *Global Report 2014*. Maryland: Center for Systemic Peace, University of Maryland. See also Virginia Page Fortna, and Lise Morjé Howard. 2008. "Pitfalls and prospects in the peacekeeping future." *Annual Review of Political Science*. 11: 283–301; V.P. Fortna. 2004. "Does peacekeeping keep peace? International intervention and the duration of peace after civil war." *International Studies Quarterly*. 48(2):269–92.

52   These three states scored highest on the State Fragility Index 2013; see Monty G. Marshall and Benjamin R. Cole. *State Fragility Index and Matrix 2013*. University of Maryland: Center for Systemic Peace. http://systemicpeace.org/inscr/SFImatrix2013c.pdf

53   Jack Snyder. 2000. *From Voting to Violence: Democratization and Nationalist Conflict*. New York: Norton; Edward D. Mansfield and Jack Snyder. 2007. *Electing to Fight: Why Emerging Democracies Go to War*. Cambridge, MA: MIT Press.

54   Dawn Brancati and Jack L. Snyder. 2011. "Rushing to the polls: The causes of premature post-conflict elections." *Journal of Conflict Resolution*. 55(3): 469–92.

55   This is discussed in detail in Pippa Norris. 2008. *Driving Democracy: Do Power-Sharing Institutions Work?* New York: Cambridge University Press.

4. International Forces

1   Joshua Muravchik. 1992. *Exporting Democracy*. Washington DC: AEI Press; Michael Cox, G. John Ikenberry, and Takashi Inoguchi, eds. 2000. *American Democracy Promotion: Impulses, Strategies, and Impacts*. New York: Oxford University Press.

2   See for example, https://www.ndi.org/kenya.

3   European Union. 2013. *Election Observation Mission to Kenya: Final Report*. Brussels: EU. http://eeas.europa.eu/eueom/missions/2013/kenya/pdf/eu-eom-kenya-2013-final-report_en.pdf

4   USAID. Feb 2014. "USAID support for Kenya's 2013 elections: Rapid assessment review." http://www.usaid.gov/sites/default/files/documents/1866/Kenya%2527s%25202013%2520Elections.pdf

5   Morton Halperin, Joseph T. Siegle, and Michael M. Weinstein. 2010. *The Democracy Advantage: How Democracies Promote Prosperity and Peace*. 2nd ed. New York: Routledge; Michael McFaul. 2010. *Advancing Democracy Abroad*. New York: Rowman and Littlefield.

6   David L. Cingranelli and Thomas E. Pasquarello. 1985. "Human rights practices and the distribution of U.S. foreign aid to Latin America." *American Journal of Political Science*. 29 (3): 539–63; James M. McCormick and Neil Mitchell. 1988. "Is U.S. aid really linked to human rights in Latin America?." *American Journal of Political Science*. 32 (1): 231–9; Graham T. Allison and R. P. Beschel. 1992. "Can the United States promote democracy?" *Political Science Quarterly*. 107 (1): 8198; Zoltan Barany and Robert G. Moser, 2009. *Is Democracy Exportable?* New York: Cambridge University Press.

7 Thad Dunning. 2004. "Conditioning the effects of aid: Cold war politics, donor credibility, and democracy in Africa." *International Organization*. 58: 409–23; A. A. Goldsmith. 2001. "Foreign aid and statehood in Africa." *International Organization*. 55(1):123–48; Steve E. Finkel, A. Pérez-Liñán, and Mitchell A. Seligson.2007. "The effects of U.S. foreign assistance on democracy building, 1990–2003." *World Politics*. 59: 404–39; Sarah Blodgett Berme. 2011. "Foreign aid and regime change: A role for donor intent." *World Development*. 39(11): 2021–31.

8 Gordon Crawford. 1997. "Foreign aid and political conditionality: Issues of effectiveness and consistency." *Democratization*. 4(3): 69–108; David Dollar and Lant Pritchett. 1998 *Assessing Aid: What Works, What Doesn't, and Why*. New York: Oxford University Press; Deborah Brautigam. 2000. *Aid Dependence and Governance*. Stockholm: Almqvist and Wiksell International.

9 Stephen Knack. 2004. "Does foreign aid promote democracy?" *International Studies Quarterly*. 48(1): 251–266.

10 See, for example, Susan D. Hyde. 2011. *The Pseudo-Democrat's Dilemma*. Ithaca: Cornell University Press; Sarah Birch. 2012. *Electoral Malpractice*. Oxford: Oxford University Press; Judith Kelley. 2012. *Monitoring Democracy: When International Election Observation Works and Why It Often Fails*. Princeton, NJ: Princeton University Press; Daniella Donno. 2013. *Defending Democratic Norms*. New York: Oxford University Press; Nahomi Ichino and Matthias Schuendeln. 2012. "Deterring or displacing electoral irregularities? Spillover effects of observers in a randomized field experiment in Ghana." *Journal of Politics*. 74(1): 292–307.

11 For balanced overviews of the debate about globalization, see David Held, Anthony McGrew, David Goldblatt, and Jonathan Perraton. 1999. *Global transformations: Politics, Economics, and Culture*. Stanford, CA: Stanford University Press. Chapter 7; Anthony McGrew and David Held, eds. 2007. *Globalization Theory: Approaches and Controversies*. Cambridge: Polity.

12 David Held and Anthony McGrew. 2007. *Globalization/Anti-Globalization: Beyond the Great Divide*. Cambridge: Polity; Jens Bartelson. 2000. "Three concepts of globalization." *International Sociology*. 15(2): 180–96.

13 Valerie Bunch and Sharon l. Wolchik. 2006. "International diffusion and post-communist electoral revolutions." *Communist and Post-Communist Studies*. 39(3): 283–304; Joshua Tucker. 2007. "Enough! Electoral fraud, collective action problems, and post-communist colored revolutions." *Perspectives on Politics*. 5(3): 535–51.

14 UNDP. 2004. *Arab Human Development Report 2004*. New York: UNDP/Oxford University Press.

15 Robert Holton. 2000. "Globalization's cultural consequences." *Annals of the American Academy of Political and Social Sciences*. 570:140–52; Frank Webster. 2006. *Theories of the Information Society*, 3rd ed. London: Routledge.

16 For the origins of the debate about this concept and the original advocates, see, Johan Galtung and Mari Holmboe Ruge. 1965. "The structure of foreign news." *Journal of Peace Research*. 2(1): 64–91; Johan Galtung. 1971. "A structural theory of imperialism." *Journal of Peace Research*. 8: 81–118; Johan Galtung. 1980. *The True Worlds*. New York: The Free Press; Herbert J. Schiller. 1971. *Mass Communication and American Empire*. Boston: Beacon; Herbert J. Schiller. 1973.

Communication and Cultural Domination. White Plains, NY: International Arts and Sciences Press; M. Masmoudi. 1981. "The new world information order." In *Crisis in International News: Policies and Prospects*, ed. J. Richstad and M.A. Anderson. New York: Columbia University Press. For a critical account, see J. Tomlinson. 1991. *Cultural Imperialism.* Baltimore: Johns Hopkins University Press.

17 For the idea of cosmopolitanism, see Ulf Hannerz. 1990. "Cosmopolitans and locals in world culture." In *Global Culture: Nationalism, Globalization and Modernity*, ed. Mike Featherstone. London: Sage; John Tomlinson. *Globalization and Culture.* Chicago: University of Chicago Press; Steven Vertovec and Robin Cohen, eds. 2002. *Conceiving Cosmopolitanism: Theory, Context and Practice.* Oxford: Oxford University Press.

18 Pippa Norris and Ronald Inglehart. *Cosmopolitan Communications.* New York: Cambridge University Press.

19 Pippa Norris and Ronald Inglehart. *Cosmopolitan Communications.* New York: Cambridge University Press. Chapter 2.

20 Axel Dreher, Noel Gaston, Noel, and Pim Martens. 2008. *Measuring Globalisation: Gauging Its Consequences.* Springer. http://globalization.kof .ethz.ch/

21 Jon C. Pevehouse. 2004. *Democracy from Above: Regional Organizations and Democratization.* New York: Cambridge University Press; Harvey Starr and Christina Lindborg. 2003. "Democratic dominoes: Diffusion approaches to the spread of democracy in the international system." *Journal of Conflict Resolution.* 35 (2): 356–81; Barbara Wejnart. 2005. "Diffusion, development and democracy, 1800–1999." *American Sociological Review.* 70 (1): 53–81.

22 The African Union. http://www.africaunion.org/root/au/Documents/Treaties/text/ Charter%20on%20Democracy.pdf

23 Karen Elizabeth Smith. 2003. *European Union Foreign Policy in a Changing World.* Oxford: Polity Press; Richard Youngs. 2002. *The European Union and the Promotion of Democracy.* Oxford: Oxford University Press.

24 Ted Piccone and Richard Youngs, eds. 2006. *Strategies for Democratic Change: Assessing the Global Response.* Washington DC: Democracy Coalition Project.

25 Edward Neuman and Roland Rich, eds. 2004. *The UN Role in Promoting Democracy: Between Ideals and Reality.* UN University Press; Richard D. Caplan. 2005. *International Governance of War-torn Territories: Rule and Reconstruction.* Oxford/New York: Oxford University Press; Thomas G. Weiss, David P. Forsythe, and Roger A. Coate. 2004. *United Nations and Changing World Politics.* Boulder, CO: Westview Press; Craig N. Murphy. 2006. *The United Nations Development Programme: A Better Way?* Cambridge: Cambridge University Press; Peter Burnell. 2011. *Promoting Democracy Abroad: Policy and Performance.* New Brunswick, NJ: Transaction Publishers.

26 Karen Elizabeth Smith. 2003. *European Union Foreign Policy in a Changing World.* Oxford: Polity Press.

27 DFID. 2006. *Governance, Development and Democratic Politics: DFID's Work in Building More Effective States.* London: DFID.

28 S.E. Finkel, A. Pérez-Liñán, and M.A. Seligson, 2007. "The effects of U.S. foreign assistance on democracy building, 1990–2003." *World Politics.* 59: 404–39.

29 Daniel Calingaert, Arch Puddington, and Sarah Repucci. 2014. "The democracy support deficit: Despite progress, major countries fall short.'" In *Supporting Democracy Abroad: An Assessment of Leading Powers*. Washington DC: Freedom House.

30 For a review of some of these initiatives, see Jean Grugel. 1999. *Democracy without Borders: Transnationalisation and Conditionality in New Democracies*. London: Routledge; Peter Burnell, ed. 2000. *Democracy Assistance: International Co-Operation for Democratization*. London: Frank Cass; Jon C. Pevehouse. 2002. "With a little help from my friends? Regional organizations and the consolidation of democracy." *American Journal of Political Science*. 46 (3): 611–26; Jon C. Pevehouse. 2002. "Democracy from the outside-in? International organizations and democratization." *International Organization*. 56 (3): 515+; Jon C. Pevehouse. 2004. *Democracy from Above: Regional Organizations and Democratization*. New York: Cambridge University Press; Thomas Carothers. 2005. *Critical Mission: Essays on Democracy Promotion*. Washington DC: Carnegie Endowment for International Peace; Andrew F. Cooper and Thomas Legler. 2007. *Intervention Without Intervening? The OAS Defense and Promotion of Democracy in the Americas*. New York: Palgrave Macmillan.

31 See, for example, http://www.gndem.org/; http://www.arabew.org/english/

32 See, for example, the ACE Project http://aceproject.org/; The Bridge training program http://www.bridge-project.org/

33 Antonio Spinelli. 2011. *Strategic Planning for Effective Electoral Management: A Practical Guide for Electoral Management Bodies to Conduct a Strategic Planning Exercise*. Washington DC: IFES

34 UNDP/IFES. 2005. *Getting to the CORE. A Global Survey on the Cost of Registration and Elections*. New York: UNDP.

35 UNDP Evaluation Office. 2012. *Evaluation of UNDP Contribution to Strengthening Electoral Systems and Processes*. New York: UNDP.

36 *UNDP Annual Report 2011/12*. New York: UNDP. http://www.undp.org/content/dam/undp/library/corporate/UNDP-in-action/2012/English/UNDP-AnnualReport_ENGLISH.pdf. It should be noted that this level of spending on democratic governance has been shrinking in recent years, from around $1.4bn in 2009 down to $US1bn (24% of the overall UNDP budget) in 2013.

37 Thomas Carothers. 1999. *Aiding Democracy Abroad*. Washington DC: Carnegie Endowment for International Peace; James Manor. 2007. *Aid That Works: Successful Development in Fragile States*. Washington DC: The World Bank; Nicolas Guilhot. 2005. *The Democracy Makers: Human Rights and International Order*. New York: Colombia University Press.

38 Susan D. Hyde. 2011. *The Pseudo-Democrat's Dilemma*. Ithaca: Cornell University Press; Judith Kelley. 2012. *Monitoring Democracy: When International Election Observation Works and Why it Often Fails*. Princeton, NJ: Princeton University Press.

39 UNDP Evaluation Office. 2012. *Evaluation of UNDP Contribution to Strengthening Electoral Systems and Processes*. New York: UNDP.

40 UNDP Evaluation Office. 2012. *Evaluation of UNDP Contribution to Strengthening Electoral Systems and Processes*. New York: UNDP.

41 AIDData 3.0 for CRS Code 15151 "elections" and 15150 "democratic participation and civil society" by recipient country are analyzed for these estimate.

For more details, see Michael J. Tierney, Daniel L. Nielson, Darren G. Hawkins, J. Timmons Roberts, Michael G. Findley, Ryan M. Powers, Bradley Parks, Sven E. Wilson, and Robert L. Hicks. 2011. "More dollars than sense: Refining our knowledge of development finance using AidData." *World Development.* 39 (11): 1891–906.

42 Susan D. Hyde. 2011. *The Pseudo-Democrat's Dilemma.* Ithaca, NY: Cornell University Press; Sarah Birch. 2012. *Electoral Malpractice.* Oxford: Oxford University Press; Judith Kelley. 2012. *Monitoring Democracy: When International Election Observation Works and Why It Often Fails.* Princeton, NJ: Princeton University Press.

43 Susan B. Hyde. 2011. *The Pseudo-Democrat's Dilemma.* Ithaca, NY: Cornell University Press; Judith Kelley. 2012. *Monitoring Democracy: When International Election Observation Works and Why It Often Fails.* Princeton, NJ: Princeton University Press.

44 Susan B. Hyde. 2011. *The Pseudo-Democrat's Dilemma.* IthacY: Cornell University Press.

45 Judith Kelley. 2008. "Assessing the complex evolution of norms: The rise of international election monitoring." *International Organization.* 62(2): 221–55; Judith Kelley. 2009. "D-Minus Elections: The politics and norms of international election observation." *International Organization.* 63 (4): 765–87; Judith Kelley. 2009. "The more the merrier? The effects of having multiple international election monitoring organizations." *Perspectives on Politics.* 7: 59–64; Judith Kelley. 2010. "Election observers and their biases." *Journal of Democracy.* 21: 158–172; Judith Kelley. 2012. "The international influences on elections in transition states." *Annual Review of Political Science.* 15; Judith Kelley. 2012. *Monitoring Democracy: When International Election Observation Works and Why It Often Fails.* Princeton, NJ: Princeton University Press; Susan. D. Hyde. 2007. "Experimenting in democracy promotion: International observers and the 2004 presidential elections in Indonesia." *Perspectives on Politics* 8(2): 511–27; Susan. D. Hyde. 2007. "The observer effect in international politics: Evidence from a natural experiment." *World Politics.* 60(1): 37–63; Susan. D. Hyde. 2011. *The Pseudo-Democrat's Dilemma.* Ithaca, NY: Cornell University Press.

46 Susan D. Hyde. 2011. *The Pseudo-Democrat's Dilemma.* Ithaca, NY: Cornell University Press.

47 Susan. D. Hyde, 2007. "Experimenting in democracy promotion: International observers and the 2004 presidential elections in Indonesia." *Perspectives on Politics.* 8(2): 511–27.

48 Judith Kelley. 2012. *Monitoring Democracy: When International Election Observation Works and Why It Often Fails.* Princeton, NJ: Princeton University Press.

49 Daniella Donno. 2013. *Defending Democratic Norms.* New York: Oxford University Press.

50 Daniella Donno. 2013. *Defending Democratic Norms.* New York: Oxford University Press.

51 Susan D. Hyde. 2011. *The Pseudo-Democrat's Dilemma.* Ithaca: Cornell University Press; Judith Kelley. 2012. *Monitoring Democracy: When International Election Observation Works and Why it Often Fails.* Princeton, NJ: Princeton University

Press; Daniella Donno. 2013. *Defending Democratic Norms.* New York: Oxford University Press; Steven Levitsky and Lucan Way. 2010. *Competitive Authoritarianism: Hybrid Regimes after the Cold War,* New York: Cambridge University Press.

52 Daniella Donno. 2013. *Defending Democratic Norms.* New York: Oxford University Press; Nahomi Ichino and Matthias Schuendeln. 2012. '"Deterring or displacing electoral irregularities? Spillover effects of observers in a randomized field experiment in Ghana.'" *Journal of Politics.* 74(1): 292–307.

53 Judith Kelley. 2012. *The Good, the Bad, and the Ugly: Rethinking Election Monitoring.* Stockholm: International IDEA.

54 Judith Kelley. 2012. *Monitoring Democracy: When International Election Observation Works and Why It Often Fails.* Princeton, NJ: Princeton University Press.

55 See, for example, James Manor. 2007. *Aid That Works: Successful Development in Fragile States.* Washington DC: The World Bank; Ted Piccone and Richard Youngs, eds. 2006. *Strategies for Democratic Change: Assessing the Global Response.* Washington DC: Democracy Coalition Project; Thomas Carothers. 1999. *Aiding Democracy Abroad.* Washington DC: Carnegie Endowment for International Peace; Jean Grugel. 1999. *Democracy without Borders: Transnationalisation and Conditionality in New Democracies.* London: Routledge; Peter Burnell, ed. 2000. *Democracy Assistance: International Co-Operation for Democratization.* London: Frank Cass.

56 James N. Druckman, Donald P. Green, James H. Kuklinski, and Arthur Lupia, eds. 2011. *Cambridge Handbook of Experimental Political Science.* NY: Cambridge University Press; Thad Dunning. 2012. *Natural Experiments in the Social Sciences.* NY: Cambridge University Press; Rebecca B. Morton and Kenneth C. Williams. 2010. *Experimental Political Science and the Study of Causality: From Nature to the Lab.* NY: Cambridge University Press; Rachel Glennerster and Kudzai Takavarasha. 2013. *Running Randomized Evaluations: A Practical Guide.* Princeton, NJ: Princeton University Press.

57 Devra C. Moehler. 2010. "Democracy, governance, and randomized development assistance." *Annals of the American Academy of Political and Social Science.* 628: 30–46.

58 See, for example, Nahomi Ichino and Matthias Schuendeln. 2012. "Deterring or displacing electoral irregularities? Spillover effects of observers in a randomized field experiment in Ghana." *Journal of Politics.* 74(1): 292–307; Susan D. Hyde. 2007. "Experimenting in democracy promotion: International observers and the 2004 presidential elections in Indonesia." *Perspectives on Politics.* 8(2): 511–27; Susan D. Hyde. 2007. "The observer effect in international politics: Evidence from a natural experiment." *World Politics.* 60(1): 37–63; Sjoberg, Fredrik. 2012. "Making voters count: Evidence from field experiments about the efficacy of domestic election observation." *Harriman Institute Working Paper 1.*.

59 Jasjeet S. Sekhon and Rocio, Titiunik. 2012. "When natural experiments are neither natural nor experiments." *American Political Science Review.* 106(1): 35–57.

60 See, for example, Stephen Knack. 2004. "Does foreign aid promote democracy?" *International Studies Quarterly.* 48 (1): 251–66; Steven E. Finkel, Anibal Perez-Linan, and Mitchell A. Seligson with Dinorah Azpuru. 2005. *Effects of U.S. Foreign*

Assistance on Democracy Building: Results from a Cross-National Quantitative Study. Washington DC: USAID; James Manor. 2007. *Aid That Works: Successful Development in Fragile States.* Washington DC: The World Bank.

61 Steven E. Finkel, Anibal Perez-Linan, and Mitchell A. Seligson with Dinorah Azpuru. 2005. *Effects of U.S. Foreign Assistance on Democracy Building: Results from a Cross-National Quantitative Study.* Washington DC: USAID.

62 Sarah Birch. 2011. *Electoral Malpractice.* Oxford: Oxford University Press. Pp. 64–67.

63 For a discussion, see Thomas Carothers. 1999. *Aiding Democracy Abroad.* Washington DC: Carnegie Endowment for International Peace.

64 Axel Dreher, Noel Gaston, Noel, and Pim Martens. 2008. *Measuring Globalisation: Gauging Its Consequences.* Springer. http://globalization.kof.ethz.ch/

65 Pippa Norris and Ronald Inglehart. *Cosmopolitan Communications.* New York: Cambridge University Press.

66 UNDP/IFES. 2005. *Getting to the CORE. A Global Survey on the Cost of Registration and Elections.* New York: UNDP.

67 AidData 3.0 *User Guidelines.* http://aiddata.org/

68 Further scrutiny revealed similar results when tested using lags of ten years and one year.

69 https://data.undp.org/dataset/Table-2-Human-Development-Index-trends/efc4-gjvq

70 Robert Edgerton. 2002. *The Troubled Heart of Africa: A History of the Congo.* St. Martin's Press.

71 Denis M. Tull. 2009. "Peacekeeping in the Democratic Republic of Congo: Waging peace and fighting war." *International Peacekeeping.* 16(2): 215–30; Catherine Gegout. 2009. "The West, realism and intervention in the Democratic Republic of Congo (1996–2006)." *International Peacekeeping.* 16(2): 231–44.

72 Meike Froitzheim, Fredrik Soderbaum, and Ian Taylor. 2011. "The limits of the EU as a peace and security actor in the Democratic Republic of the Congo." *Africa Spectrum.* 46(3): 45–70.

73 AIDData 3.0 for CRS Code 15151 "'elections'" is analyzed for this estimate. For more details, see Michael J. Tierney, Daniel L. Nielson, Darren G. Hawkins, J. Timmons Roberts, Michael G. Findley, Ryan M. Powers, Bradley Parks, Sven E. Wilson, and Robert L. Hicks. 2011. "More dollars than sense: Refining our knowledge of development finance using AidData." *World Development.* 39 (11): 1891–906.

74 David Fuamba, Yonekawa, Masako, and Seegers, Annette. 2013. "Managing spoilers in a hybrid war: The Democratic Republic of Congo (1996–2010)." *Politikon.* 40(2): 319–38.

75 http://www.cartercenter.org/resources/pdfs/news/peace_publications/election_reports/drc-2006-final-rpt.pdf

76 https://www.gov.uk/government/uploads/system/uploads/attachment_data/file/67652/elections-cd-2006.pdf

77 http://www.bbc.com/news/world-africa-13286306

78 The Carter Center. *Final Report: Presidential and Legislative Elections in the Democratic Republic of the Congo, Nov. 28, 2011.* http://www.cartercenter.org/resources/pdfs/news/peace_publications/election_reports/drc-112811-elections-final-rpt.pdf

79   UNDP. 2013. *The Role of UNDP in Supporting Democratic Elections in Africa.* UNDP: Ethiopia.
80   Fund for Peace. 2014. *The Fragile States Index 2014.* http://ffp.statesindex.org/rankings-2014
81   Human Rights Watch. http://www.hrw.org/drc

5. Institutional Checks

1   Jonathan Hartlyn, Jennifer McCoy, and Thomas Mustillo. 2008. "Electoral governance matters: Explaining the quality of elections in contemporary Latin America." *Comparative Political Studies.* 41: 73–98.
2   See Jon M. Carey. "Parchment, equilibria, and institutions." *Comparative Political Studies.* 33 (6–7): 735–61.
3   See, for example, International IDEA. 2006. *Electoral Management Design: The International IDEA Handbook.* Sweden: International IDEA.
4   See, for example, International IDEA. 2006. *Electoral Management Design: The International IDEA Handbook.* Sweden: International IDEA.
5   Sarah Birch. 2007. "Electoral systems and electoral misconduct." *Comparative Political Studies.* 40(12): 1533–56.
6   M. Steven Fish. 2006. "Stronger legislatures, stronger democracies." *Journal of Democracy.* 17(1): 5–20.
7   See Chad Vickery, ed. 2011. *Guidelines for Understanding, Adjudicating, and Resolving Disputes in Elections.* Washington DC: IFES.
8   See reports and data on these matters in US elections compiled by The Brennan Center for Justice. http://www.brennancenter.org/ and The National Conference of State Legislatures http://www.ncsl.org/ and The National Conference of State Legislatures http://www.ncsl.org/
9   Jonathan Salant. May 2013. "Will the Federal Election Commission Ever Work Again?" *Bloomberg BusinessWeek.* http://www.businessweek.com/articles/2013-05-02/will-the-federal-election-commission-ever-work-again
10   http://www.eac.gov/about_the_eac/help_america_vote_act.aspx
11   See, for example, The National Conference of State Legislatures http://www.ncsl.org.
12   See, for example, the Office for Democratic Institutions and Human Rights. 2012. *Needs Assessment Mission Report: France Presidential Election 22 April and 6 May 2012.* Warsaw: OSCE/ODIHR. http://www.osce.org/odihr/elections/89000?download=true.
13   Robert A. Pastor, 1999. "A brief history of electoral commissions." In Andreas Schedler, Larry Diamond, and Marc F. Plattner, eds. *The self-restraining state: Power and accountability in new democracies.* Boulder, CO: Lynne Rienner, pp. 75–82; Shaheen Mozaffar. 2002. "Patterns of electoral governance in Africa's emerging democracies." *International Political Science Review.* 23(1):85–101.
14   See, for example, the Office for Democratic Institutions and Human Rights. 2012. *Needs Assessment Mission Report: France Presidential Election 22 April and 6 May 2012.* Warsaw: OSCE/ODIHR. http://www.osce.org/odihr/elections/89000?download=true.
15   Sarah Birch. 2011. *Electoral Malpractice.* Oxford: Oxford University Press.
16   Arend Lijphart. 2012. *Patterns of Democracy.* New Haven: Yale University Press 2nd edition; George Tsebelis. *Veto Players: How Political Institutions Work.*

Princeton, NJ: Princeton University Press; Pippa Norris. 2008. *Driving Democracy*. New York: Cambridge University Press.

17 Silvio Waisbord. 2000. *Watchdog Journalism in South America: News, Accountability, and Democracy*. New York: Columbia University Press; Wolfgang Donsbach. 1995. "Lapdogs, Watchdogs and Junkyard Dogs." *Media Studies Journal*. 9 (4): 17–30; Pippa Norris, ed. 2010. *Public Sentinel: News Media and the Governance Agenda*. Washington DC: The World Bank.

18 Sarah Birch. 2011. *Electoral Malpractice*. Oxford: Oxford University Press.

19 Gabriel Almond and Sidney Verba. 1963. *The Civic Culture*.

20 See, for example, Christopher J. Anderson, Andre Blais, Shaun Bowler, Todd Donovan, and Ola Listhaug. 2005. *Losers' Consent: Elections and Democratic Legitimacy*. New York: Oxford University Press.

21 Pippa Norris. 2014. *Why Electoral Integrity Matters*. New York: Cambridge University Press.

22 This is similar to the notion of "self-enforcing democracy"; see Susan Alberts, Chris Warshaw, and Barry R. Weingast. 2011. "Democratization and counter-majoritarian institutions." In Tom Ginsburg, ed. *Comparative Constitutional Design*. NY: Cambridge University Press.

23 Sarah Birch. 2007. "Electoral systems and electoral misconduct." *Comparative Political Studies*. 40(12): 1533–56.

24 Fabrice Edouard Lehoucq and Iván Molina Jiménez. 2002. *Stuffing the Ballot Box: Fraud, Electoral Reform, and Democratization in Costa Rica*. New York: Cambridge University Press.

25 J. Kunicova and Susan Rose-Ackerman. 2005. "Electoral rules and constitutional structures as constraints on corruption." *British Journal of Political Science*. 35 (4): 573–606. See also Torsten Persson, Guido Tabellini, and Francesco Trebbi. 2003. "Electoral rules and corruption." *Journal of the European Economic Association*. 1(4): 22–34.

26 Sarah Birch. 2007. "Electoral systems and electoral misconduct." *Comparative Political Studies*. 40(12): 1533–56.

27 Lisa Handley and Bernie Grofman, eds. 2008. *Redistricting in comparative perspective*. New York: Oxford University Press.

28 Netina Tan. 2013. "Electoral engineering and hegemonic party resilience in Singapore." *Electoral Studies*. 32(4): 632–43.

29 Ericka A. Albaugh, 2011. "An autocrat's toolkit: adaptation and manipulation in 'democratic' Cameroon." *Democratization*. 18(2): 388–414.

30 AceProject.org http://aceproject.org/epic-en/CDTable?question=BD001

31 Sarah Birch. 2007. "Electoral systems and electoral misconduct." *Comparative Political Studies*. 40(12): 1533–56.

32 Donald L. Horowitz. 1985. *Ethnic Groups in Conflict*. Berkeley: University of California Press; Donald L. Horowitz. 1991. *A Democratic South Africa? Constitutional Engineering in a Divided Society* Berkeley: University of California Press; Donald L. Horowitz. 2002. *The Deadly Ethnic Riot*. Berkeley: University of California Press.

33 Antonio Spinelli. 2011. *Strategic Planning for Effective Electoral Management: A Practical Guide for Electoral Management Bodies to Conduct a Strategic Planning Exercise*. Washington DC: IFES

34 See, for example, state contrasts in the Pew Electoral Performance Index http://www.pewtrusts.org/en/multimedia/data-visualizations/2014/elections-performance-index. See also the discussion in Barry C. Burden and Charles Stewart III, eds. 2014. *The Measure of American Elections.* New York, NY: Cambridge University Press.

35 See Michael Pal. 2014. "Canadian Election Administration on Trial: The 'Robocalls' case and the Opitz decision." Paper presented at EIP/MEDW workshop prior to the IPSA World Congress, Montreal 18 July 2014; UK Electoral Commission. 2013. *Electoral fraud in the UK: Evidence and issues paper.* London: UK Electoral Commission. http://www.electoralcommission.org.uk

36 Robert A. Pastor. 1999. "The role of electoral administration in democratic transitions." *Democratization.* 6(4):1–27.

37 Charles R. Wise. 2001. "Electoral administration in crisis: An early look at lessons from Bush versus Gore." *Public Administration Review* 61(2): 131–9; Robert S. Montjoy. 2008. "The public administration of elections." *Public Administration Review.* 68 (5): 788–99.

38 For the older literature, see, for example, Arnold J. Heidenheimer, ed. 1970. *Comparative Political Finance: The Financing of Party Organizations and Election Campaigns.* Lexington, MA: D.C. Heath; Herbert Alexander. 1979. *Political Finance.* Beverly Hills, CA: Sage Electoral Studies Yearbook; Herbert Alexander, and Rei Shiratori, eds. 1994. *Comparative Political Finance among the Democracies.* Boulder, CO: Westview Press; Keith D. Ewing. 1992. *Money, Politics and Law.* Oxford, UK: Clarendon; Arthur Gunlicks. 1993. *Campaign and Party Finance in North America and Western Europe.* Boulder, CO: Westview. For more recent regional studies, see Kevin Casas-Zamora. 2005. *Paying for Democracy: Political Finance and State Funding for Parties.* Essex: ECPR; C. Malamud and E. Posada Carbo. 2005. *The Financing of Politics: Latin American and European Perspectives.* London: Inst. Stud. Americas; Daniel Smilov and Jurij Toplak. 2008. *Political Finance and Corruption in Eastern Europe the Transition Period.* Aldershot: Ashgate; Michael Koss. 2010. *The Politics of Party Funding: State Funding to Political Parties and Party Competition in Western Europe.* Oxford: Oxford University Press; K. Nassmacher. 2009. *The Funding of Party Competition: Political Finance in 25 Democracies.* Baden-Baden: Nomos Verlag.

39 Reginald Austin and Maja Tjernstrom. 2003. *Funding of Political Parties and Election Campaigns.* Stockholm: International IDEA; Magnus Ohman. 2012. *Political Finance Regulations around the World: An Overview of the IDEA database.* Stockholm: IDEA Publications Office; Magnus Ohman and H. Zainulbhai. 2013. *Political Finance Regulation: The Global Experience.* Washington, DC: International Foundation for Electoral Systems.

40 M. Steven Fish and Matthew Kroenig. 2009. *The Handbook of National Legislatures: A Global Survey.* New York: Cambridge University Press.

41 M. Steven Fish. 2006. "Stronger legislatures, stronger democracies." *Journal of Democracy.* 17(1): 5–20.

42 Julio Rios-Figueroa and Jeffrey K. Staton. 2013. "An evaluation of cross-national measures of judicial independence." *Journal of Law, Economics and Organization.* 31

43 Wittold Henisz's (2000) http://mgmt5.wharton.upenn.edu/henisz/POLCON/
    ContactInfo.html The coding is derived from information in Polity's Executive
    Constraints, p_xconst) and the ICRG's index of Law & Order.

44 Freedom House. *Freedom of the Press*. Washington DC: Freedom House. See
    http://www.freedomhouse.org/report/freedom-press/freedom-press-2014#
    .VE6LVPnF-So

45 Pippa Norris and Sina Odugbemi. 2010. "Evaluating media performance." In *Public
    Sentinel: News Media and the Governance Agenda*, ed. Pippa Norris. Washington
    DC: The World Bank.

46 Chappell Lawson. 2003. *Building the Fourth Estate: Democratization and the
    Rise of a Free Press in Mexico*. Berkeley: University of California Press; Ellen
    Mickiewicz. 1997. *Changing Channels: Television and the Struggle for Power in
    Russia*. New York: Oxford University Press; Ellen Mickiewicz. 2008. *Television,
    Power, and the Public in Russia*. New York: Cambridge University Press; Pippa
    Norris, ed. 2010. *Public Sentinel: News Media and the Governance Agenda*.
    Washington DC: The World Bank.

47 Organization for Security and Cooperation in Europe (OSCE/ODIHR).
    2012. *Handbook on Media Monitoring for Election Observation Missions*.
    Warsaw: OSCE/ODIHR.

48 M. Steven Fish. 2006. "Stronger legislatures, stronger democracies." *Journal of
    Democracy*. 17(1): 5–20.

6. Electoral Management

1 R. Michael Alvarez, Lonna Rae Atkeson, and Thad Hall. 2012. *Evaluating Elections:
   A Handbook of Methods and Standards*. New York: Cambridge University Press.

2 Martha Kropf and David C. Kimball. 2011. *Helping America Vote: The Limits of
   Election Reform*. New York: Routledge; R. Michael Alvarez, Thad Hall, and Susan
   Hyde, eds. 2008. *Election Fraud*. Washington DC: Brookings Institution Press.

3 Michael Douglas. 2014. "Ballot bungles: Lessons from the Australian Senate."
   Election Law Journal. 13(4): 559–69.

4 Rajeev Syal. 2014. '"Police asked to investigate more than 50 allegations of
   electoral fraud.'" *The Guardian*. 2 May 2014. http://www.theguardian.com/
   politics/2014/may/23/police-open-inquiries-allegations-electoral-fraud-uk. See also
   the UK Electoral Commission. 2014. *Electoral Fraud in the UK: Final Report and
   Recommendations*. London: UK Electoral Commission; Michael Pinto-Duschinsky.
   2014. *Electoral Omission*. London: Policy Exchange.

5 Michael Pal. 2014. "*Canadian Election Administration on Trial: The 'Robocalls'
   case and the Opitz decision*." Paper presented at EIP/MEDW workshop prior to the
   IPSA World Congress, Montreal 18 July 2014.

6 Lucas Leemanna and Daniel Bochsler. 2014. "A systematic approach to study electoral fraud." *Electoral Studies*. 35(3): 33–47.

7 Daniel Ziblatt. 2009. "Shaping democratic practice and the causes of electoral
   fraud: The case of nineteenth-century Germany." *American Political Science
   Review*. 103(1): 1–21.

8 R. Michael Alvarez and Thad E. Hall. 2006. "Controlling democracy: The principal
   agent problems in election administration." *Policy Studies Journal*. 34(4): 491–510;

R. Michael Alvarez and Thad E. Hall. 2008. "Building secure and transparent elections through standard operating procedures." *Public Administration Review*. 68(5): 828–38; R. Michael Alvarez, Thad E. Hall, and Llewellyn Morgan. 2008. "Who should run elections in the United States?" *Policy Studies Journal*. 36(3): 325–46; Richard L. Hasen. 2012. *The Voting Wars: From Florida 2000 to the Next Election Meltdown*. New Haven: Yale University Press; Barry C. Burden and Charles Stewart III, eds. 2014. *The Measure of American Elections*. New York: Cambridge University Press.

9 Robert F. Bauer, Benjamin L. Ginsberg, et al. 2014. *The American Voting Experience: Report and Recommendations of the Presidential Commission on Election Administration*. Washington DC. For more details, see www.supportthevoter .gov.

10 The Pew Charitable Trust. *Election Performance index*. http://www.pewtrusts.org/ en/multimedia/data-visualizations/2014/elections-performance-index#intro

11 http://www.pewtrusts.org/en/about/news-room/news/2014/11/06/where-did-voters-look-to-find-their-polling-places

12 *The Washington Post*. 4 Nov 2014. "Voting machine problems in Newport News, Va. Beach." http://www.washingtonpost.com/local/virginians-deciding-senate-congressional-races/2014/11/04/33164a92-63f9-11e4-ab86-46000e1d0035_story .html

13 *Bloomberg Politics*. 4 Nov 2014. "Your guide to 2014 midterm election voting problems." http://www.bloomberg.com/politics/articles/2014-11-04/your-guide -to-2014-midterm-election-voting-problems.

14 *The New York Times*. 4 Nov 2014. "As new rules take effect, voters report problems in some states." http://www.nytimes.com/2014/11/05/us/election-tests-new-rules-on -voting.html

15 For a similar distinction between structure, function and culture, see K. Lalenis, M. de Jong, and V. Mamadouh, eds. 2002. *The Theory and Practice of Institutional Transplantation*. Dordrecht: Kluwer; Christopher Pollitt and Gerrt Bouckaart. 2004. *Public Management Reform: A Comparative Analysis*. Oxford: Oxford University Press.

16 See, The Quality of Government Institute Cross-National and Time-Series Data Sets. http://www.qog.pol.gu.se/

17 Alan Wall et al. 2006. *Electoral Management Design: The International IDEA Handbook*. Sweden: International IDEA.

18 Rafael López-Pintor. 2000. *Electoral Management Bodies as Institutions of Governance*. New York: United Nations Development Programme; Alan Wall et al. 2006. *Electoral Management Design: The International IDEA Handbook*. Sweden: International IDEA.

19 Alan Wall et al. 2006. *Electoral Management Design: The International IDEA Handbook*. Sweden: International IDEA. See also Joel Baxter. 1997. "Techniques for effective election management." In *Elections: Perspectives on Establishing Democratic Practices*. New York: UN Department for Development Support and Management Services.

20 Antonio Spinelli. 2011. *Strategic Planning for Effective Electoral Management: A Practical Guide for Election Management Bodies to Conduct a Strategic Planning Exercise*. Washington, DC: IFES.

21 The Venice Commission. 2002. *Code of Good Practice in Electoral Matters.* Strasbourg: Council of Europe. http://www.venice.coe.int/

22 See, for example, Alan Wall et al. 2006. *Electoral Management Design: The International IDEA Handbook.* Stockholm: International IDEA, p. 22; Paul Thomas and Lorne R. Gibson. 2014. *Comparative Assessment of Central Electoral Agencies.* Elections Canada, p. 9; The Venice Commission. 2002. *Code of Good Practice in Electoral Matters.* Strasbourg: Council of Europe. http://www.venice.coe.int/

23 Alan Wall et al. 2006. *Electoral Management Design: The International IDEA Handbook.* Stockholm: International IDEA; The ACE Electoral Knowledge Network. http://aceproject.org/

24 See, for example, Badala Tachilisa Balule. 2008. "Election management bodies in the SADC region: An appraisal of the independence of Botswana's independent electoral commission." *South African Journal on Human Rights.* 24: 104–22; Emmanuel Debrah. 2011. "Measuring governance institutions' success in Ghana: The Case of the Electoral Commission, 1993–2008." *African Studies* 70(1): 25–45; Alexander B. Makulilo. 2009. "Independent Electoral Commission in Tanzania: A false debate?" *Representation.* 45(4): 435–53.

25 UNDP. 2012. *Evaluation of UNDP Contribution to Strengthening Electoral Systems and Processes.* New York: UNDP; Paul Thomas and Lorne R. Gibson. 2014. *Comparative Assessment of Central Electoral Agencies.* Ottowa: Elections Canada.

26 Robert A. Pastor. 1999. "A brief history of electoral commissions." In Andreas Schedler, Larry Diamond, and Marc F. Plattner, eds. *The Self-restraining State: Power and Accountability in New Democracies.* Boulder, CO: Lynne Rienner, pp. 75–82.

27 Shaheen Mozaffar and Andreas Schedler. 2002. "The comparative study of electoral governance: Introduction." *International Political Science Review.* 23(1): 5–27.

28 Rafael López-Pintor. 2000. *Electoral Management Bodies as Institutions of Governance.* New York: United Nations Development Programme.

29 Shaheen Mozaffar. 2002. "Patterns of electoral governance in Africa's emerging democracies." *International Political Science Review.* 23(1): 85–101.

30 Alan Wall, Andrew Ellis, Ayman Ayoub, Carl W. Dundas, Joram Rukambe, and Sara Staino. 2006. *Electoral Management Design: The International IDEA Handbook.* Sweden: International IDEA.

31 Alan Wall et al. 2006. *Electoral Management Design: The International IDEA Handbook.* Sweden: International IDEA.

32 Louis Massicotte, Andre Blais, and Antoine Yoshinaka. 2004. *Establishing the Rules of the Game.* Toronto: University of Toronto Press.

33 Michael R. Alvarez, Hall, Thad E. Hall, and Llewellyn Morgan. 2008. "Who should run elections in the United States?" *Policy Studies Journal.* 36(3): 325–46.

34 Christopher Pollitt and Gerrt Bouckaart. 2004. *Public Management Reform: A Comparative Analysis.* Oxford: Oxford University Press.

35 Christopher Pollitt and Gerrt Bouckaart. 2004. *Public Management Reform: A Comparative Analysis.* Oxford: Oxford University Press.

36 Chris Hanretty and Christel Koop. 2013. "Shall the law set them free? The formal and actual independence of regulatory agencies." *Regulation & Governance.* 7:195–214.

37 Alan Wall, et al. 2006. *Electoral Management Design: The International IDEA Handbook.* Sweden: International IDEA.

38 Alan Wall, et al. 2006. *Electoral Management Design: The International IDEA Handbook*. Sweden: International IDEA, pp. 7–16.

39 Popova, Marina. 2006. "Watchdogs or attack dogs? The role of the Russian Courts and the Central Election Commission in the resolution of electoral disputes." *Europe-Asia Studies*. 58(3): 391–414.

40 Alan Wall et al. 2006. *Electoral Management Design: The International IDEA Handbook*. Sweden: International IDEA.

41 http://www.infoelectoral.mir.es/web/guest/la-gestion-del-proceso-electoral

42 See, for example, Louis Massicotte, Andre Blais, and Antoine Yoshinaka. 2004. *Establishing the Rules of the Game*. Toronto: University of Toronto Press, chapter 4.

43 International IDEA. 2006. *International Election Standards*. Stockholm: International IDEA, p. 42.

44 Mark Thatcher. 2002. "Delegation to independent regulatory agencies: Pressures, functions and contextual mediation." *West European Politics*. 25(1): 125–47.

45 Alan Wall et al. 2006. *Electoral Management Design: The International IDEA Handbook*. Sweden: International IDEA.

46 Robert F. Bauer, Benjamin L. Ginsberg, et al., 2014. *The American Voting Experience: Report and Recommendations of the Presidential Commission on Election Administration*. Washington DC. For more details, see www.supportthevoter.gov.

47 Jonathan Fisher. 2013. "The limits – and limiters – of external influence: donors, the Ugandan Electoral Commission and the 2011 elections." *Journal of Eastern African Studies*. 7(3): 471–91.

48 OSCE/ODIHR. 2011. *Republic of Belarus Presidential Election 19 December 2011. Election Observer Mission Final Report*. Warsaw: OSCE/ODIHR.

49 Jonathan Hartlyn, Jennifer McCoy, and Thomas Mustillo. 2008. "Electoral governance matters: Explaining the quality of elections in contemporary Latin America." *Comparative Political Studies*. 41: 73–98; Guillermo Rosas. 2010. "Trust in elections and the institutional design of electoral authorities: Evidence from Latin America." *Electoral Studies* 29: 74–90.

50 Shaheen Mozaffar and Andreas Schedler. 2002. "The comparative study of electoral governance: Introduction." *International Political Science Review*. 23(1): 5–27; Ismaila M. Fall, Mathias Hounkpe, Adele L. Jinadu, and Pascal Kambale, eds. 2011. *Election Management Bodies in West Africa: A Comparative Study of the Contribution of Electoral Commissions to the Strengthening of Democracy*. Johannesburg: Open Society Initiative for West Africa; Mamoudou Gazibo. 2006. "The forging of institutional autonomy: A comparative study of Electoral Management Commissions in Africa." *Canadian Journal of Political Science*. 39(3): 611–33; Nicholas Kerr. "Popular perceptions of free and fair elections in Sub-Saharan Africa." In *Advancing Electoral Integrity*, eds. Pippa Norris, Richard W. Frank, and Ferran Martinez i Coma. Oxford: Oxford University Press.

51 Sarah Birch. 2008. "Electoral institutions and popular confidence in electoral processes." *Electoral Studies*. 27: 305–320.

52 Anne van Aaken, 2009. "Independent election management bodies and international election observer missions: Any impact on the observed levels of democracy? A conceptual framework." *Constitutional Political Economy*. 20(3–4): 296–322.

53 Jonathan Hartlyn, Jennifer McCoy, and Thomas Mustillo. 2008. "Electoral governance matters: Explaining the quality of elections in contemporary Latin America."

Comparative Political Studies. 41: 73–98; Sarah Birch. 2011. *Electoral Malpractice.* Oxford: Oxford University Press.

54 Pippa Norris. 2012. *Making Democratic Governance Work.* New York: Cambridge University Press.

55 Samuel P. Huntington. 1968. *Political Order in Changing Societies.* New Haven: Yale University Press; Francis Fukuyama. 2014. *Political Order and Political Decay: From the Industrial Revolution to the Globalisation of Democracy.* New York: Farrar, Straus and Giroux.

56 OECD. 2009. *Donor Approaches to Governance Assessments: 2009 Sourcebook.* Paris: OECD;

57 Joel D. Barkan. 2013. '"Technology Is Not Democracy.'" *Journal of Democracy.* 24(3): 156–165.

58 UNDP, 2011. *Comparative Experience in Electoral Administration and the Arab World,* April 2011. New York: UNDP.

59 International IDEA. 2006. *Electoral Management Design: The International IDEA Handbook.* Sweden: International IDEA.

60 Rafael Lopez-Pintor. 2006. *Getting to the Core: A Global Survey on the Costs of Registration and Elections.* New York: UNDP.

61 Geert Hofstede. 2001. *Culture's Consequences: Comparing Values, Behaviors, Institutions and Organizations Across Nations.* London: Sage.

62 The Venice Commission. 2002. *Code of Good Practice in Electoral Matters.* Strasbourg: Council of Europe. Clause 3a.bb. http://www.venice.coe.int/.

63 Susan Rose-Ackerman. 1999. *Corruption and Government: Causes, Consequences and Reform.* New York: Cambridge University Press; Susan C. Stokes, Thad Dunning, Marcelo Nazareno, and Valeria Brusco. 2013. *Brokers, Voters and Clientalism.* New York: Cambridge University Press.

64 Bo Rothstein. 2011. *The Quality of Government.* Chicago: University of Chicago Press.

65 Pippa Norris. 2012. *Making Democratic Governance Work.* New York: Cambridge University Press.

66 Peter Evans and J.E. Rauch. 1999. "Bureaucracy and growth: A cross-national analysis of the effects of 'Weberian' state structures on economic growth." *American Sociological Review.* 64(5): 748–65.

67 Jan Teorell, Carl Dahlström, and Stefan Dahlberg. 2011. *The QoG Expert Survey Dataset.* University of Gothenburg: The Quality of Government Institute. http://www.qog.pol.gu.se. See also Bo Rothstein and Jan Teorell. 2008. "What is quality of government? A theory of impartial government institutions." *Governance* 21(2): 165–90; Carl Dahlström, Victor Lapuente, and Jan Teorell. 2012. "Public administration around the world." In Sören Holmberg and Bo Rothstein, eds., *Good Governance. The Relevance of Political Science.* Cheltenham: Edward Elgar

68 Bo Rothstein and Jan Teorell. 2008. "What is quality of government? A theory of impartial government institutions." *Governance* 21(2): 165–90, p. 170.

69 Details about the Political Risk Service's Group (PRSG's) International Country Risk Guide are available from http://www.prsgroup.com/. It should be noted that the concept of political risk drives this measure of bureaucratic quality, which therefore emphasizes *continuity* of public policies rather than responsiveness. '"Bureaucratic quality'" is described by PRSG as follows: "High points are given

to countries where the bureaucracy has the strength and expertise to govern without drastic changes in policy or interruptions in government services. In these low-risk countries, the bureaucracy tends to be somewhat autonomous from political pressure and to have an established mechanism for recruitment and training. Countries that lack the cushioning effect of a strong bureaucracy receive low points because a change in government tends to be traumatic in terms of policy formulation and day-to-day administrative functions." http://www.prsgroup.com/ICRG_Methodology.aspx#PolRiskRating

70 Nicholas Charron and Victor Lapuente. 2010. "Does democracy produce quality of governance?" *European Journal of Political Research*. 49: 443–70.

71 Stephen Knack and Philip Keefer. 1995. "Institutions and economic performance: Cross-Country tests using alternative institutional measures." *Economics and Politics*. 7(3): 207–27; Gili S. Droro, Yong Suk Jang, and John W. Meyer. 2006. "Sources of rationalized governance: Cross-national longitudinal analysis, 1985–2002." *Administrative Science Quarterly*. 51(2): 205–29.

72 Daniel Kaufmann, Aart Kraay, and Massimo Mastruzzi. 2007. *Governance Matters VI: Aggregate and Individual Governance Indicators, 1996–2006*. Washington DC: The World Bank, Policy Research Working Paper; Daniel Kaufmann, Aart Kraay, and Massimo Mastruzzi. 2010. *The Worldwide Governance Indicators: Methodology and Analytical Issues*. Washington, DC: The Brookings Institute. www.govindicators.org.

73 http://info.worldbank.org/governance/wgi/index.aspx#home

74 http://info.worldbank.org/governance/wgi/index.aspx#home

75 Sarah Birch. 2011. *Electoral Malpractice*. Oxford: Oxford University Press; Jonathan Hartlyn, Jennifer McCoy, and Thomas Mustillo. 2008. "Electoral governance matters: Explaining the quality of elections in contemporary Latin America." *Comparative Political Studies*. 41: 73–98.

76 Pippa Norris. 2012. *Making Democratic Governance Work*. New York: Cambridge University Press; Sören Holmberg and Bo Rothstein, eds. 2013. *Good Governance. The Relevance of Political Science*. Cheltenham: Edward Elgar.

77 See Pippa Norris. 2014. *Why Electoral Integrity Matters*. New York: Cambridge University Press.

7. Conclusions: Lessons for Strengthening Electoral Integrity

1 Pippa Norris. 2014. *Why Electoral Integrity Matters*. NY: Cambridge University Press.

2 Pippa Norris. 2014. *Why Electoral Integrity Matters*. NY: Cambridge University Press.

3 Michael L. Ross. 2013. *The Oil Curse: How Petroleum Wealth Shapes the Development of Nations*. Princeton, NJ: Princeton University Press.

4 Pippa Norris and Ronald Inglehart. 2009. *Cosmopolitan Communications: Cultural Diversity in a Globalized World*. New York: Cambridge University Press.

5 Pippa Norris and Ronald Inglehart. 2009. *Cosmopolitan Communications: Cultural Diversity in a Globalized World*. New York: Cambridge University Press; Jon C. Pevehouse. 2004. *Democracy from Above: Regional Organizations and Democratization*. New York: Cambridge University Press.

6 R. Michael Alvarez, Lonna Rae Atkeson, and Thad Hall. 2012. *Evaluating Elections: A Handbook of Methods and Standards.* New York: Cambridge University Press; Toby S. James. 2012. *Elite Statecraft and Election Administration: Bending the Rules of the Game.* Basingstoke: Palgrave.

7 David Parmenter. 2007. *Key Performance Indicators.* John Wiley and Sons Inc.

8 UNDP. 2006. *Getting to the CORE – A Global Survey on the Cost of Registration and Elections.* New York: United Nations Development Programme. It should be noted that an updated version of this report is in the process of being produced.

9 International Monetary Fund. *Government Finance Statistics.* Table 7: Outlays by Function: General and Central Government. http://www2.imfstatistics.org/GFS/

10 UNDP. 2006. *Getting to the CORE – A Global Survey on the Cost of Registration and Elections.* New York: United Nations Development Programme.

11 See, for example, the ACE Electoral Knowledge Network http://aceproject.org/; Alvarez, R. Michael, and Thad E. Hall. 2008. '"Building secure and transparent elections through standard operating procedures.'" *Public Administration Review.* 68 (5): 828–38.

12 UNDP. 2012. *Evaluation of UNDP Contribution to Strengthening Electoral Systems and Processes.* New York: UNDP.

13 UNDP Global Programme for Electoral Cycle Support. http://web.undp.org/eu/UNDP_Global_Programme_for_Electoral_Cycle_Support%20.shtml

14 UNDP. 2012. *Evaluation of UNDP Contribution to Strengthening Electoral Systems and Processes.* New York: UNDP.

15 James N. Druckman, Donald P. Green, James H. Kuklinski, and Arthur Lupia, eds., 2011. *Cambridge Handbook of Experimental Political Science.* NY: Cambridge University Press; Thad Dunning. 2012. *Natural Experiments in the Social Sciences.* NY: Cambridge University Press; Rebecca B. Morton and Kenneth C. Williams. 2010. *Experimental Political Science and the Study of Causality: From Nature to the Lab.* NY: Cambridge University Press; Rachel Glennerster and Kudzai Takavarasha. 2013. *Running Randomized Evaluations: A Practical Guide.* Princeton, NJ: Princeton University Press.

16 Devra C. Moehler, 2010. "Democracy, governance, and randomized development assistance." *Annals of the American Academy of Political and Social Science.* 628: 30–46.

17 International IDEA. 2002. *International Electoral Standards: Guidelines for Reviewing the Legal Framework for Elections.* Stockholm: International IDEA.

18 Michael R. Alvarez and Thad E. Hall. 2006. "Controlling democracy: The principal agent problems in election administration." *Policy Studies Journal.* 34(4): 491–510; Michael R. Alvarez, Hall, Thad E. Hall, and Llewellyn Morgan. 2008. "Who should run elections in the United States?" *Policy Studies Journal.* 36(3): 325–46; Michael R. Alvarez and Thad E. Hall. 2008. "Building secure and transparent elections through standard operating procedures." *Public Administration Review.* 68 (5): 828–38; Lonna Rae Atkeson, Lisa Ann Bryant, and Thad E. Hall. 2010. "A new barrier to participation: Heterogeneous application of voter identification policies." *Electoral Studies.* 29(1): 66–73; Robert S. Montjoy, 2008. "The public administration of elections." *Public Administration Review.* 68 (5): 788–99; Robert S. Montjoy. 2010. "The changing nature ... and costs ... of election administration." *Public Administration*

Review. 70(6): 867–75; Michael R. Alvarez, Lonna Rae Atkeson, and Thad Hall. 2012. *Evaluating Elections: A Handbook of Methods and Standards.* New York: Cambridge University Press.

19 Paul Gronke, Eva Galanes-Rosenbaum, Peter A. Miller, and Daniel Toffey. 2008. "Convenience voting." *Annual Review of Political Science.* 11:437–55; Shaun Bowler and Todd Donovan. 2013. *The Limits of Electoral Reform.* New York: Oxford University Press.

20 Global Commission on Elections, Democracy and Security. 2012. *Deepening Democracy: A Strategy for improving the Integrity of Elections Worldwide.* Sweden: IDEA.

21 http://www.un.org/wcm/content/site/undpa/main/issues/elections/resolutions

22 United Nations. 1948. *Universal Declaration of Human Rights* http://www.un.org/en/documents/udhr/

23 http://www.un.org/wcm/content/site/undpa/main/issues/elections/resolutions

24 http://www.un.org/wcm/content/site/undpa/main/issues/elections/resolutions

25 See Pippa Norris and Andrea Abel van Es. 2016. *Checkbook Elections? Political Finance in Comparative Perspective.*

Technical Appendix

1 With the exception of elections in Libya, Luxembourg, Senegal, and Timor-Leste, however, which were excluded during the pilot start-up.

2 Pippa Norris. 2013. "Does the world agree about standards of electoral integrity? Evidence for the diffusion of global norms." Special issue of *Electoral Studies* 32(4): 576–88; Pippa Norris, Ferran MartíLightnez i Coma, and Richard W. Frank. 2013. "Assessing the quality of elections." *Journal of Democracy.* 24(4): 124–35.

Select Bibliography

Aaken, Anne van. 2009. "Independent Election Management Bodies and international election observer missions: Any impact on the observed levels of democracy? A Conceptual Framework." *Constitutional Political Economy* 20(3–4): 296–322.

Abbink, Jon. 2000. "Introduction: Rethinking democratization and election observation." In Jon Abbink and G. Hesseling. (Eds.) *Election Observation and Democratization in Africa*. New York: St. Martin"s Press, pp.1–17.

Acemoglu, Daron and James A. Robinson. 2005. *Economic Origins of Dictatorship or Democracy*. New York: Cambridge University Press.

Ākhatāra, Muhāmmada Iyāhaiyā. 2001. *Electoral Corruption in Bangladesh*. Burlington, VT: Ashgate.

Albaugh, Ericka A. 2011. "An autocrat's toolkit: Adaptation and manipulation in 'democratic' Cameroon." *Democratization* 18(2): 388–414.

Alesina, Alberto and Enrico Spolaore. 2003. *The Size of Nations*. Cambridge, MA: MIT Press.

Allen, H.W. and K.W. Allen. 1981. "Voting fraud and data validity." In J.M. Clubb, W.H. Flanigan, and H. Zingale, eds. *Analyzing Electoral History*. Beverley Hills, CA: Sage, pp. 153–93.

Alston, L. J. and A. A. Gallo. "Electoral fraud, the rise of Peron and demise of checks and balances in Argentina." *Explorations in Economic History* 47(2): 179–97.

Alvarez, R. Michael and Bernard Grofman. 2014. *Election Administration in the United States*. NY: Cambridge University Press.

Alvarez, R. Michael and Thad E. Hall. 2006. "Controlling democracy: The principal agent problems in election administration." *Policy Studies Journal* 34(4): 491–510.

2008. "Building secure and transparent elections through standard operating procedures." *Public Administration Review* 68 (5): 828–38.

2008a. "Who should run elections in the United States?" *Policy Studies Journal* 36(3): 325–46.

2008b. "Are Americans confident their ballots are counted?" *Journal of Politics* 70 (3): 754–66.

Alvarez, R. Michael, José Antonio Cheibub, Fernando Limongi, and Adam Przeworski. 1996. "Classifying political regimes." *Studies in International Comparative Development* 31: 3–36.

Alvarez, R. Michael, Lonna Rae Atkeson, and Thad E. Hall. 2012. (Eds). *Confirming Elections: Creating Confidence and Integrity through Election Auditing.* New York: Palgrave Macmillan.

Alvarez, R. Michael, Lonna Rae Atkeson, Thad E. Hall, and Andrew J. Lotempio. 2002. "Winning, losing and political trust in America." *British Journal of Political Science* 32(2): 335–51.

Alvarez, R. Michael, Lonna Rae Atkeson, and Thad E. Hall. 2012. *Evaluating Elections: A Handbook of Methods and Standards.* New York: Cambridge University Press.

Alvarez, R. Michael, Thad E. Hall, and Susan Hyde. 2008. (Eds.) *Election Fraud.* Washington DC: Brookings Institution Press.

Anderson, Christopher J. 1995. "Blaming the government: Citizens and the economy in five European countries." *Comparative Political Studies* 28 (3): 350–83.

Anderson, Christopher J. and Yuliya V. Tverdova. 2001. "Winners, losers, and attitudes about government in contemporary democracies." *International Political Science Review* 22: 321–38.

2003. "Corruption, political allegiances, and attitudes toward government in contemporary democracies." *American Journal of Political Science* 47(1): 91–109.

Anderson, Christopher J. and Christine A. Guillory. 1997. "Political institutions and satisfaction with democracy." *American Political Science Review* 91(1):66–81.

Anderson, Christopher J., Andre Blais, Shaun Bowler, Todd Donovan, and Ola Listhaug. 2005. *Losers' Consent: Elections and Democratic Legitimacy.* New York: Oxford University Press.

Anderson, Christopher J. and Silvia Mendes. 2006. "Learning to lose: Election outcomes, democratic experience and political protest potential." *British Journal of Political Science* 36(1): 91–111.

Anglin, Douglas G. 1995. "International monitoring of the transition to democracy in South Africa, 1992–1994." *African Affairs* 9(377): 519–43.

1998. "International election monitoring: The African experience." *African Affairs* 97: 471–95.

Ansolabehere, Stephen. 2009. "Effects of identification requirements on voting: Evidence from the experiences of voters on election day." *PS: Political Science & Politics* 42:127–30.

Ansolabehere, Stephen, Eitan Hersh, and Kenneth Shepsle. 2012. "Movers, stayers, and registration: Why age is correlated with registration in the U.S." *Quarterly Journal of Political Science* 7 (4):333–63.

Arrington, Theodore S. 2010. "Redistricting in the US: A review of scholarship and plan for future research." *Forum: A Journal of Applied Research in Contemporary Politics* 8(2).

Arriola, Leonardo R. 2012. *Multi-Ethnic Coalitions in Africa: Business Financing of Opposition Election Campaigns.* New York: Cambridge University Press.

Atkeson, Lonna Rae, and K.L. Saunders. 2007. "The effect of election administration on voter confidence: A local matter?" *PS: Political Science & Politics* 40: 655–60.

Atkeson, Lonna Rae, Lisa Ann Bryant, and Thad E.Hall, 2010. "A new barrier to participation: Heterogeneous application of voter identification policies." *Electoral Studies* 29(1): 66–73.

Atwood, Richard. 2012. *How the EU can support peaceful post-election transitions of power: lessons from Africa.* Directorate-General for External Policies of the Union, Directorate B Policy Department, European Parliament, Brussels.

Austin, Reginold and Maja Tjernstrom. 2003. (Eds). *Funding of Political Parties and Election Campaigns.* Stockholm: International IDEA.

Baker, B. 2002. "When to call black white: Zimbabwe's electoral reports." *Third World Quarterly* 23 (6): 1145–58.

Balule, Badala Tachilisa. 2008. "Election management bodies in the SADC region: An appraisal of the independence of Botswana's independent electoral commission." *South African Journal on Human Rights* 24: 104–22.

Banducci, Susan A., and Jeffrey A. Karp. 1999. "Perceptions of fairness and support for proportional representation." *Political Behavior* 21(3): 217–38.

Bardall, Gabrielle. "Election violence monitoring and the use of new communication technologies." *Democracy & Society.* 7(2).

Barkan, Joel D. 1993. "Kenya: Lessons from a flawed election." *Journal of Democracy* 4(3): 85–99.

2013. "Technology is not democracy." *Journal of Democracy* 24(3): 156–65.

Barro, Robert.1999. "Determinants of democracy." *Journal of Political Economy* 107(6): 158–93.

Basedau, Matthais, Gero Erdman, and Andreas Mehler. 2007. *Votes, Money and Violence: Political Parties in Sub-Saharan Africa.* Sweden: Nordiska Afrikainstitutet. http://urn.kb.se/resolve?urn=urn:nbn:se:nai:diva-492

Bauer, Robert F. and Benjamin L. Ginsberg, et al, 2014. *The American Voting Experience: Report and Recommendations of the Presidential Commission on Election Administration.* Washington DC.

Beaulieu, Emily. 2013. "Political parties and perceptions of election fraud in the U.S." Paper presented at the Workshop on Challenges of Electoral Integrity, Harvard University 2–3 June 2013.

Beaulieu, Emily. 2014a. *Electoral Protests and Democracy in the Developing World.* NY: Cambridge University Press.

2014b. "From voter ID to party ID: How political parties affect perceptions of election fraud in the U.S." *Electoral Studies* 35: 24–32.

Beaulieu, Emily and Susan D. Hyde. 2009. "In the shadow of democracy promotion: strategic manipulation, international observers, and election boycotts." *Comparative Political Studies* 42(3): 392–415.

Beber, Bernd and Alexandra Scacco. 2012. "What the numbers say: A digit-based test for election fraud." *Political Analysis* 20(2): 211–34.

Bekoe, Dorina. Ed. 2012. *Voting in Fear: Electoral Violence in Sub-Saharan Africa.* United States Institute of Peace, Washington, DC.

Benson, J.F. 2009. "Voter fraud or voter defrauded? Highlighting an inconsistent consideration of election fraud." *Harvard Civil Rights-Civil Liberties Law Review* 44 (1): 1–42.

Berinsky, Adam J. 2004. "The perverse consequences of electoral reform in the United States." *American Politics Research* 33(4): 471–91.

Berinsky, Adam J., Nancy Burns, and Michael W. Traugott. 2001. "Who votes by mail? A dynamic model of the individual-level consequences of voting-by-mail systems." *Public Opinion Quarterly* 65(2): 178–97.

Bermeo, Nancy. "Interests, inequality, and illusion in the choice for fair elections." *Comparative Political Studies* 43(8–9): 1119–47.

Bermeo, Sarah Blodgett. 2011. "Foreign aid and regime change: A Role for Donor Intent." *World Development* 39(11): 2021–31.

Bhasin, Tavishi and Jennifer Gandhi. 2013. "State repression in authoritarian elections." *Electoral Studies* 32(4): 620–31.

Birch, Sarah. 2007. "Electoral systems and electoral misconduct." *Comparative Political Studies* 40(12): 1533–56.

2008. "Electoral institutions and popular confidence in electoral processes: a cross-national analysis." *Electoral Studies* 27 (2): 305–20.

2010. "Perceptions of electoral fairness and voter turnout." *Comparative Political Studies* 43 (12): 1601–22.

2011. *Electoral Malpractice*. Oxford: Oxford University Press.

2012. *Electoral Malpractice*. http://www.essex.ac.uk/government/electoralmal practice/index.htm;

Bishop, Sylvia and Anke Hoeffler. 2014. "Free and fair elections: A new database." Oxford: Center for the Study of African Economies (CSAE) Working Paper WPS/2014-14.

Bjornlund, Eric C. 2004. *Beyond Free and Fair: Monitoring Elections and Building Democracy*. Washington DC: Woodrow Wilson Center Press.

Bjornskov, C. "How does social trust lead to better governance? An attempt to separate electoral and bureaucratic mechanisms." *Public Choice* 144, no. 1–2: 323–46.

Bland, Gary, Andrew Green, and Toby Moore. 2012. "Measuring the quality of election administration." *Democratization* 20 (2): 1–20

Blaydes, Lisa. 2011. *Elections and Distributive Politics in Mubarak's Egypt*. New York: Cambridge University Press.

Boatright, Robert G. Ed. 2011. *Campaign Finance: The Problems and Consequences of Reform*. New York: IDebate Press.

Bochsler, Daniel. 2012. "A quasi-proportional electoral system 'only for honest men'? The hidden potential for manipulating mixed compensatory electoral systems." *International Political Science Review* 33(4): 401–20.

Boda, M.D. 2005. "Reconsidering the 'free and fair' question." *Representation* 41(3): 155–160.

Bogaards, Matthijs, Matthias Basedau, and Christof Hartmann, 2010. "Ethnic party bans in Africa: an introduction." *Democratization* 17(4):599–617.

Bogaards, Matthijs. 2013. "Reexamining African Elections." *Journal of Democracy* 24(4):151–60.

Boix, Carles, Michael K. Miller, and Sebastian Rosato. 2013. "A complete dataset of political regimes, 1800–2007." *Comparative Political Studies* 46(12): 1523–54.

Boniface, Makulilo Alexander. 2011. "'Watching the watcher': An evaluation of local election observers in Tanzania." *Journal of Modern African Studies* 49(2): 241–62.

Boone, Catherine. 2011. "Politically allocated land rights and the geography of electoral violence: The case of Kenya in the 1990s." *Comparative Political Studies* 44(10): 1311–42.

Bowler, Shaun and Todd Donovan. 2011. "The limited effects of election reforms on efficacy and engagement." *Australian Journal of Political Science* 47(1): 55–70.

2013. *The Limits of Electoral Reform.* New York: Oxford University Press.

Brancati, Dawn and Snyder, Jack L. 2011. "Rushing to the polls: The causes of premature post-conflict elections." *Journal of Conflict Resolution* 55(3): 469–92.

Bratton, Michael and Nicholas van de Walle. 1997. *Democratic Experiments in Africa: Regime Transitions in Comparative Perspective.* New York: Cambridge University Press.

Bratton, Michael, Robert Mattes, and E. Gyimah-Boadi. 2005. *Public Opinion, Democracy and Market Reform in Africa.* Cambridge: Cambridge University Press.

Bratton, Michael. 2008. "Vote buying and violence in Nigerian election campaigns." *Electoral Studies* 27(4): 621–32.

Ed. 2013. *Voting and Democratic Citizenship in Africa.* Boulder, CO: Lynne Rienner Publishers.

Breunig, Christian and Achim Goerres. 2011. "Searching for electoral irregularities in an established democracy: Applying Benford's Law tests to Bundestag elections in unified Germany." *Electoral Studies* 30(3): 534–45.

Brown, Nathan J. Ed. 2011. *The Dynamics of Democratization: Dictatorship, Development and Diffusion.* Baltimore: The Johns Hopkins University Press.

Brownlee, Jason, 2011. "Executive elections in the Arab world: When and how do they matter?" *Comparative Political Studies* 44(7): 807–28

Brownlee, Jason. 2007. *Authoritarianism in an Age of Democratization.* New York: Cambridge University Press.

2008. "Bound to rule: Party institutions and regime trajectories in Malaysia and the Philippines." *Journal of East Asian Studies* 8(1): 89–118.

2009. "Portents of pluralism: How hybrid regimes affect democratic transitions." *American Journal of Political Science* 53(3): 515–32.

Brusco, V., M. Nazareno, and Susan C. Stokes. 2004. "Vote buying in Argentina." *Latin American Research Review* 39(2): 66–88.

Buckley, Sam. 2011. *Banana Republic UK? Vote Rigging, Fraud and Error in British Elections since 2001.* London: Open Rights Group.

Bunce, Valerie J. and Sharon L. Wolchik. 2006. "Favorable conditions and electoral revolutions." *Journal of Democracy* 17: 5–18.

2011. *Defeating Authoritarian Leaders in Post-Communist Countries.* New York: Cambridge University Press.

2010. "Defeating dictators: Electoral change and stability in competitive authoritarian regimes." *World Politics* 62(1): 43–86.

Burden, Barry C. and Charles Stewart III. 2014. (Eds). *The Measure of American Elections.* New York, NY: Cambridge University Press.

Burden, Barry C. and Jacob R. Neiheisel. 2013. "Election administration and the pure effect of voter registration on turnout." *Political Research Quarterly* 66:77–90.

Burden, Barry C., David T. Canon, Kenneth R. Mayer, and Donald P. Moynihan. 2011. "Election laws, mobilization, and turnout: The unanticipated consequences of election reform." *American Journal of Political Science* 58: 95–109.

2011. "Early voting and election day registration in the trenches: Local officials' perceptions of election reform." *Election Law Journal* 10:89–102.

Burnell, Peter. 2011. *Promoting Democracy Abroad: Policy and Performance*. New Brunswick, NJ: Transaction Publishers.

Butler, David and Bruce E. Cain. 1992. *Congressional Redistricting: Comparative and Theoretical Perspectives*. New York: Macmillan.

Cain, Bruce E. 2014. *Democracy More or Less*. New York: Cambridge University Press.

Cain, Bruce E., Donovan, Todd, and Tolbert, C.J. 2008. *Democracy in the States: Experimentation in Election Reform*. Washington DC: Brookings Institution Press.

Calimbahin, Cleo. 2011. "Exceeding (low) expectations: Autonomy, bureaucratic integrity, and capacity in the 2010 elections." *Philippine Political Science Journal* 32(55): 103–26.

Calingaert, Daniel, Arch Puddington, and Sarah Repucci. 2014. "The democracy support deficit: Despite progress, major countries fall short." In Freedom House. *Supporting Democracy Abroad: An Assessment of Leading Powers*. Washington DC: Freedom House.

Calingaert, Daniel. 2006. "Election rigging and how to fight it." *Journal of Democracy* 17(3): 138–51.

Callahan, W.A. 2000. *Poll Watching, Elections and Civil Society in South-East Asia*. Burlington, VT: Ashgate.

  2005. "The discourse of vote buying and political reform in Thailand." *Pacific Affairs* 78 (1): 95–102.

Campbell, Tracy. 2006. *Deliver the Vote: A History of Election Fraud, an American Political Tradition 1742–2004*. New York: Basic Books.

Carey, Sabine. 2007. "Violent dissent and rebellion in Africa." *Journal of Peace Research* 44(1): 1–39.

Carman, Christopher, Mitchell, James, and Johns, Robert. 2008. "The unfortunate natural experiment in ballot design: The Scottish Parliamentary elections of 2007." *Electoral Studies* 27(3): 442–59.

Carothers, Thomas. 1997. "The observers observed." *Journal of Democracy*. 8 (3): 17–31.

  1999. *Aiding Democracy Abroad*. Washington DC: The Brookings Institution.

  2002. "The end of the transition paradigm." *Journal of Democracy* 13: 5–21.

Carriquiry, Alicia L. 2011. "Election forensics and the 2004 Venezuelan presidential recall referendum as a case study." *Statistical Science* 26(4): 471–78.

Carroll, David J. and Avery Davis-Roberts. 2013. "The Carter Center and election observation: An obligations-based approach for assessing elections." *Election Law Journal* 12(1): 87–93.

Carter Center, The. 2014. *Elections Obligations and Standards Database: A Carter Center Manual*. Atlanta, Georgia: The Carter Center.

Carter Center, The. *Database of Obligations for Democratic Elections*. Carter Center: Atlanta. http://www.cartercenter.org/des-search/des/Introduction.aspx

Casas-Zamora, Kevin. 2004. *Paying for Democracy*. Essex: ECPR Press.

Case, William. 2011. "Electoral authoritarianism and backlash: Hardening Malaysia, oscillating Thailand." *International Political Science Review* 32(4): 438–57.

Castaneda, Gonzalo and I. Ibarra. "Detection of fraud with agent–based models: The 2006 Mexican election." *Perfiles Latinoamericanos* 18(36): 43–69.

Castaneda, Gonzalo. 2011. "Benford' s law and its applicability in the forensic analysis of electoral results." *Politica Y Gobierno* 18(2): 297–329.

Catterberg, Gabriella and Alejandro Moreno. 2006. "The individual bases of political trust: Trends in new and established democracies." *International Journal of Public Opinion Research* 18(1): 31–48.

Cederman, Lars-Erik, Kristian S. Gleditsch, and Simon Hug. 2012. "Elections and civil war." *Comparative Political Studies* 46(3).

Celestino, Mauricio Rivera, and Kristian Skrede Gleditsch. 2013. "Fresh carnations or all thorn, no rose? Nonviolent campaigns and transitions in autocracies." *Journal of Peace Research* 50 (3): 385–400.

Chaisty, Paul and Steven Whitefield. 2013. "Forward to democracy or back to authoritarianism? The attitudinal bases of mass support for the Russian election protests of 2011–2012." *Post-Soviet Affairs.*

Chand, Vikram. 1997. "Democratisation from the outside in: NGO and international efforts to promote open elections." *Third World Quarterly,* 18(3): 543–61.

Chang, Eric C.C. 2005. "Electoral incentives for political corruption under open-list proportional representation." *The Journal of Politics* 67(3): 716–30

Chaturvedi, Ashish. 2005. "Rigged elections with violence." *Public Choice* 125(1/2): 189–202.

Cheibub, José Antonio, Jennifer Gandhi, and James Raymond Vreeland. 2010. "Democracy and dictatorship revisited." *Public Choice* 143(1–2): 67–101.

Cingranelli, David L., David L. Richards, and K. Chad Clay. 2013. *The Cingranelli-Richards (CIRI) Human Rights Dataset.* http://www.humanrightsdata.org

Clark, Alistair. 2014. "Funding capacity in electoral democracy: Insights from electoral administration." PSA Annual Conference, Manchester, April 2014.

Coburn, Noah and Anna Larson.2013. *Derailing Democracy in Afghanistan: Elections in an Unstable Political Landscape.* New York: Columbia University Press.

Collier Paul, Anke Hoeffler, and Mans Soderbom. 2008. "Post-conflict risks." *Journal of Peace Research* 45 (4): 461–78

Collier, Paul and Anke Hoeffler. 1998. "On economic causes of civil war." *Oxford Economic Papers-New Series* 50(4): 563–73.

2002. "On the incidence of civil war in Africa." *Journal of Conflict Resolution* 46(1): 13–28.

2004. "Greed and grievance in civil war." *Oxford Economic Papers-New Series* 56(4): 563–95.

Collier, Paul and Pedro Vicente. 2011. "Violence, bribery and fraud: The political economy of elections in Sub-Saharan Africa." *Public Choice.* 153(1): 1–31.

Collier, Paul, Anke Hoeffler, and Dominic Rohner. 2009. "Beyond greed and grievance: Feasibility and civil war." *Oxford Economic Papers-New Series* 61(1): 1–27.

Collier, Paul, Anke Hoeffler, and Nicholas Sambanis. 2005. "The Collier-Hoeffler model of civil war onset and the case study project research design." Ch 1 in *Understanding Civil War.* (Eds). Paul Collier and Nicolas Sambanis. Washington DC: The World Bank.

Collier, Paul. 2009. *Wars, Guns and Votes: Democracy in Dangerous Places.* New York: HarperCollins.

Coppedge, Michael. 2012. *Democratization and Research Methods.* New York: Cambridge University Press.

Craig, Stephen C., Michael D. Martinez, and Jason Gainous 2006. "Winners, losers, and election context: Voter responses to the 2000 presidential election." *Political Research Quarterly* 59(4): 579–92.

Cruz, R. C. 2001. "Voting for the unexpected: Electoral fraud and political struggle in Costa Rica (1901–1948)." *Journal of Latin American Studies* 33: 893–4.

Curtice, John. 2013. "Politicians, voters and democracy: The 2011 UK referendum on the alternative vote." *Electoral Studies* 32 (2): 215–23.

Dahl, Robert A. 1971. *Polyarchy: Participation and Opposition*. New Haven: Yale University Press.

D"Anieri, Paul. Ed. 2010. *Orange Revolution and Aftermath: Mobilization, Apathy, and the State in Ukraine*. Baltimore: Johns Hopkins University Press.

Darnolf, Staffan. 2011. *Assessing Electoral Fraud in New Democracies: A New Strategic Approach*. Washington, DC: International Foundation for Electoral Systems: White Paper Series Electoral Fraud.

Davenport, Christian. 1997. "From ballots to bullets: An empirical assessment of how national elections influence state uses of political repression." *Electoral Studies* 6(4): 517–40.

2007. "State repression and political order." *Annual Review of Political Science* 10: 1–23.

2007. *State Repression and the Domestic Democratic Peace*. New York: Cambridge University Press.

Davenport, Christian and Molly Inman. 2012. "The state of state repression research since the 1990s." *Terrorism and Political Violence* 24(4): 619–34.

Davis-Roberts, Avery and David J. Carroll. 2010. "Using international law to assess elections." *Democratization* 17(3): 416–41.

Daxecker, Ursula E. 2012. "The cost of exposing cheating: International election monitoring, fraud, and post-election violence in Africa." *Journal of Peace Research* 49(4): 503–16.

Daxecker, Ursula E. and Gerald Schneider. 2014. "Electoral monitoring." In Pippa Norris, Richard W. Frank, and Ferran Martinez i Coma. (Eds.) *Advancing Electoral Integrity*. New York: Oxford University Press.

de Sousa, Luis and Marcelo Moriconi. 2014. "Why voters do not throw the rascals out? A conceptual framework for analysing electoral punishment of corruption." *Crime Law and Social Change* 60(5): 471–502.

Debrah, Emmanuel. 2011. "Measuring governance institutions' success in Ghana: The case of the Electoral Commission, 1993–2008." *African Studies* 70(1): 25–45.

Deckert, Joseph, Mikhail Myagkov, and Peter C. Ordeshook. 2011. "Benford's Law and the detection of election fraud." *Political Analysis* 19: 245–68.

Denver, David, R. Johns, and C. Carman. 2009. "Rejected ballot papers in the 2007 Scottish parliament election: The voters' perspective." *British Politics* 4, (1): 3–21.

Dercon, Stefan and Roxana Gutierrez-Romero. 2012. "Triggers and characteristics of the 2007 Kenyan electoral violence." *World Development* 40(4): 731–44.

Diamond, Larry. 2002. "Thinking about hybrid regimes." *Journal of Democracy* 13(2): 21–35.

Diamond, Larry and Leonardo Morlino. 2004. "Quality of democracy: An overview." *Journal of Democracy* 15(4): 20–31.

Doherty, David and Jennifer Wolak. 2012. "When do the ends justify the means? Evaluating procedural fairness." *Political Behavior* 34(2): 301–23.

Donno, Daniella. 2010. "Who is punished? Regional intergovernmental organizations and the enforcement of democratic norms." *International Organization* 64(4): 593–625.

2013. "Elections and democratization in authoritarian regimes." *American Journal of Political Science* 57(3): 703–16.

2013. *Defending Democratic Norms.* New York: Oxford University Press.

Donno, Daniella and Alberto Simpser. 2012. "Can international election monitoring harm governance?" *Journal of Politics.* 74(2):501–13.

Donno, Daniella and Nasos Roussias. 2012. "Does cheating pay? The effect of electoral misconduct on party systems." *Comparative Political Studies.* 45 (5):575–605.

Donsanto, C.C. 2008. "Corruption in the electoral process under U.S. federal law." In R. Michael Alvarez, Thad E. Hall, and Susan Hyde. (Eds). *Election fraud: detecting and deterring electoral manipulation.* Washington, DC: Brookings Institute.

Douglas, Michael. 2014. "Ballot bungles: Lessons from the Australian senate." *Election Law Journal* 13(4): 559–69.

Downs, Anthony. 1957. *An Economic Theory of Democracy.* New York: Harper and Row.

Doyle, Michael W and Nicolas Sambanis. 2000. "International peace-building: A theoretical and quantitative analysis." *American Political Science Review* 94(4): 779–801.

Drometer, Marcus and Rincke Johannes. 2009. "The impact of ballot access restrictions on electoral competition: evidence from a natural experiment." *Public Choice* 138(3–4): 461–74.

Dunning, Thad E. 2011. "Fighting and voting: Violent conflict and electoral politics." *Journal of Conflict Resolution* 55(3): 327–39.

2012. *Natural Experiments in the Social Sciences.* New York: Cambridge University Press.

Eisenstadt, T.A. 2004. "Catching the state off guard: Electoral courts, campaign finance, and Mexico's separation of state and ruling party." *Party Politics* 10(6): 723–45.

2004. *Courting Democracy in Mexico: Party Strategies and Electoral Institutions.* New York: Cambridge University Press.

Ekman, Joakim. 2009. "Political participation and regime stability: a framework for analyzing hybrid regimes." *International Political Science Review* 30(1): 7–31.

Elklit, Jørgen. 1999. "Electoral institutional change and democratization: You can lead a horse to water, but you can't make it drink." *Democratization* 6 (4): 28–51.

Elklit, Jørgen and Andrew Reynolds. 2002. "The impact of election administration on the legitimacy of emerging democracies: A new comparative politics research agenda." *Commonwealth & Comparative Politics* 40(2): 86–119.

2005. "A framework for the systematic study of election quality." *Democratization* 12 (2): 147–62.

Elklit, Jørgen and Palle Svensson. 1997. "What makes elections free and fair?" *Journal of Democracy* 8(3): 32–46.

Elklit, Jørgen, and Svend-Erik Skaaning. *Coding Manual: Assessing Election and Election Management Quality,* 2011. http://www.democracy-assessment.dk/start/page.asp?page=22

Estevez, Federico, Eric Magar, and Guillermo Rosas. 2008. "Partisanship in non-partisan electoral agencies and democratic compliance: Evidence from Mexico's Federal Electoral Institute." *Electoral Studies* 27(2): 257–71.

European Commission. 2007. *Compendium of International Standards for Elections.* 2nd ed. Brussels: European Commission, Brussels: EC/NEEDS.

Evrensel, Astrid. Ed. 2010. *Voter Registration in Africa: A Comparative Analysis.* Johannesburg: EISA.

Ewing, Keith. 2009. *The Funding of Political Parties in Britain*. Cambridge: Cambridge University Press.

Fall, Ismaila Madior, Mathias Hounkpe, Adele L. Jinadu, and Pascal Kambale. 2011. *Election Management Bodies in West Africa: A Comparative Study of the Contribution of Electoral Commissions to the Strengthening of Democracy*. Johannesberg: Open Society Institute.

Fawn, Rick. 2006. "Battle over the box: International election observation missions, political competition and retrenchment in the post-Soviet space." *International Affairs* 82(6): 1133+

Fell, Dafydd. 2005. *Party Politics in Taiwan: Party Change and the Democratic Evolution of Taiwan, 1991–2004*. London: Routledge.

Fife, Brian L. 2010. *Reforming the Electoral Process in America*. Santa Barbara, CA: Praeger.

Finkel, Evgeny and Brudny, Yitzhak M. 2012. "No more colour! Authoritarian regimes and colour revolutions in Eurasia." *Democratization* 19(1): 1–14.

Finnemore, Martha and Kathryn Sikkink. 1998. "International norm dynamics and political change." *International Organization* 52(3): 887–917.

Fish, M. Steven. 2006. "Stronger legislatures, stronger democracies." *Journal of Democracy* 17(1): 5–20.

Fish, M. Steven and Matthew Kroenig. 2009. *The Handbook of National Legislatures: A Global Survey*. New York: Cambridge University Press.

Fisher, Jeff. 2002. *Electoral Conflict and Violence*. Washington DC: IFES

Fisher, Jonathan. 2013. "The limits – and limiters – of external influence: Donors, the Ugandan Electoral Commission and the 2011 elections." *Journal of Eastern African Studies* 7(3) 471–91.

Fishkin, Joseph. 2011. "Equal citizenship and the individual right to vote." *Indiana Law Journal* 86(4): 1289–360.

Fjelde, Hanne and Harvard Hegre. 2014. "Political corruption and institutional stability." *Studies in Comparative International Development* 49(3): 267–99.

Flores, Thomas Edward and Irfan Nooruddin. 2012. "The effect of elections on post-conflict peace and reconstruction." *Journal of Politics* 74(2): 558–70.

Forest, Benjamin. 2012. "Electoral redistricting and minority political representation in Canada and the United States." *Canadian Geographer* 56(3): 318–38.

Foweraker, Joseph and R. Krznaric. 2002. "The uneven performance of third wave democracies: Electoral politics and the imperfect rule of law in Latin America." *Latin American Politics and Society* 44(3): 29–60.

Franklin, Mark. 2004. *Voter Turnout and the Dynamics of Electoral Competition in Established Democracies since 1945*. New York: Cambridge University Press.

Franzese, R.J. 2002. "Electoral and partisan cycles in economic policies and outcomes." *Annual Review of Political Science* 5: 369–421.

Frazer, Jendayi E. and E. Gyimah-Boadi. 2011. (Eds). *Preventing Electoral Violence in Africa*. Carnegie Mellon University.

Fukumoto, Kentaro and Yusaku Horiuchi. 2011. "Making outsiders' votes count: Detecting electoral fraud through a natural experiment." *American Political Science Review* 105(3): 586–603.

Fund, John H. 2004. *Stealing Elections: How Voter Fraud Threatens Our Democracy*. San Francisco, CA: Ecounter Books.

Fung, Archon. 2011. "Popular election monitoring." In Heather Gerken, Guy-Uriel E. Charles, and Michael S. Kang. *Race, Reform and Regulation of the Electoral Process: Recurring Puzzles in American Democracy.* New York: Cambridge University Press.

Gandhi, Jennifer. 2008. *Political Institutions under Dictatorship.* New York: Cambridge University Press.

Gandhi, Jennifer, and Ellen Lust–Okar. 2009. "Elections under authoritarianism." *Annual Review of Political Science* 12: 403–22.

Gazibo, Mamoudou. 2006. "The forging of institutional autonomy: A comparative study of Electoral Management Commissions in Africa." *Canadian Journal of Political Science* 39(3): 611–33.

Geddes, Barbara. 1999. "What do we know about democratization after twenty years?" *Annual Review of Political Science* 2: 115–44.

Geisler, G. 1993. "Fair – what has fairness got to do with it? Vagaries of election observations and democratic standards." *Journal of Modern African Studies* 31(4): 613–37.

Gelman, Andrew and Gary King. 1994. "Enhancing democracy through legislative redistricting." *American Political Science Review* 88(3): 541–59.

Geys, Benny. 2006. "Explaining voter turnout: A review of aggregate-level research." *Electoral Studies* 25(4): 637–63.

Gilbert, Leah and Mohseni Payam. 2011. "Beyond authoritarianism: The conceptualization of hybrid regimes." *Studies in Comparative International Development* 46(3): 270–97.

Gingerich, D.W. 2009. "Ballot structure, political corruption, and the performance of proportional representation." *Journal of Theoretical Politics* 21(4): 509–41.

Global Commission on Elections, Democracy and Security. 2012. *Deepening Democracy: A Strategy for Improving the Integrity of Elections Worldwide.* Sweden: IDEA.

Gomez, Edmund Terence. 2012. "Monetizing politics: Financing parties and Elections in Malaysia." *Modern Asian Studies* 46: 1370–97.

Goodwin-Gill, Guy. S. 2006. *Free and Fair Elections.* 2nd Edition. Geneva: Inter-parliamentary Union.

Gosnell, Herbert F. 1968. *Machine Politics: Chicago Model,* 2nd ed., Chicago and London: University of Chicago Press.

Greenberg, Ari and Robert Mattes. 2013. "Does the quality of elections affect the consolidation of democracy?" In Michael Bratton. (Ed.) *Voting and Democratic Citizenship in Africa.* Boulder: Lynne Rienner Publishers.

Greene, Kenneth F. 2007. *Why Dominant Parties Lose: Mexico's Democratization in Comparative Perspective.* New York: Cambridge University Press.

Grömping, Max. 2012. "Many eyes of any kind? Comparing traditional and crowd-sourced monitoring and their contribution to democracy." Paper presented at the Second International Conference on International Relations and Development, July 2012 in Thailand.

Gronke, Paul. 2013. "Are we confident in voter confidence? Conceptual and methodological challenges in survey measures of electoral integrity." Paper presented at the Workshop on Challenges of Electoral Integrity, Harvard University 2–3 June 2013.

Gronke, Paul and Daniel Krantz Toffey. 2008. "The psychological and institutional determinants of early voting." *Journal of Social Issues* 64(3): 503–24.

Gronke, Paul, Eva Galanes-Rosenbaum, and Peter Miller. 2007. "Early voting and turnout." *PS: Political Science and Politics* 40(4): 639–45.

Gronke, Paul, Eva Galanes-Rosenbaum, Peter A. Miller, and Daniel Toffey. 2008. "Convenience voting." *Annual Review of Political Science* 11:437–55.

Gunlicks, Arthur B. Ed. 1993. *Campaign and Party Finance in North America and Western Europe*. Boulder: Westview Press.

Gustafson, Marc. 2010. "Elections and the probability of violence in Sudan." *Harvard International Law Journal* Online 51: 47–62.

Hadenius, Axel and Jan Teorell. 2007. "Pathways from authoritarianism." *Journal of Democracy* 18(1): 143–56.

HafnerBurton, Emilie M., Susan D. Hyde, and Ryan S. Jablonski. 2014. "When do governments resort to election violence?" *British Journal of Political Science* 44(1): 149–79.

Hale, Henry E. 2011. "Formal constitutions in informal politics: Institutions and democratization in post-Soviet Eurasia." *World Politics* 63(4): 581+.

Hall, Thad E. 2011. "Voter opinions about election reform: Do they support making voting more convenient?" *Election Law Journal* 10(2): 73–87.

Hall, Thad E., J. Quin Monson, and Kelly D. Patterson. 2009. "The human dimension of elections: How poll workers shape public confidence in elections." *Political Research Quarterly* 62(3):507–22.

Hamm, Keith E. and Hogan Robert E. 2008. "Campaign finance laws and decisions in state legislative candidacy elections." *Political Research Quarterly* 61(3): 458–67.

Handley, Lisa and Bernie Grofman. 2008. Eds. *Redistricting in comparative perspective*. New York: Oxford University Press.

Hanham, H.J. 1959. *Elections and Party Management: Politics in the Time of Disraeli and Gladstone*. London: Longmans.

Hanmer, Michael J. 2009. *Discount Voting: Voter Registration Reforms and Their Effects*. New York: Cambridge University Press.

Hanmer, Michael J. and Michael W. Traugott. 2004. "The impact of vote-by-mail on voter behavior." *American Politics Research* 32:375–405.

Hanretty, Chris and Christel Koop. 2012. "Shall the law set them free? The formal and actual independence of regulatory agencies." *Regulation & Governance* 7(2): 195–214.

Hartlyn, Jonathan, Jennifer McCoy, and Thomas Mustillo. 2008. "Electoral governance matters: Explaining the quality of elections in contemporary Latin America." *Comparative Political Studies* 41: 73–98.

Hasen, Richard L. 2012. *The Voting Wars: From Florida 2000 to the Next Election Meltdown*. New Haven: Yale University Press.

Hasseling, Gerti and Jon Abbink. 2000. (Eds). *Election Observation and Democratization in Africa*. New York: Palgrave Macmillan

Hausmann, Ricardo and Rigobon Roberto. 2011. "In search of the black swan: Analysis of the statistical evidence of electoral fraud in Venezuela." *Statistical Science* 26(4): 543–63.

Heidenheimer, Arnold J., Michael Johnston, and V.T. Levine. 1990. (Eds). *Political Corruption: A Handbook*, New Brunswick, NJ: Transaction Publishers.

Heinzelman, Jessica and Patrick Meier. 2012. "Crowdsourcing for human rights monitoring: Challenges and opportunities for verification." In John Lannon. (Ed.)

Human Rights and Information Communication Technologies: Trends and Consequences of Use, IGI Global.

Hermet, Guy, Richard Rose, and Alain Rouquié. 1978. (Eds). *Elections without Choice*. London: Macmillan.

Herrnson, Paul, Richard G. Niemi, and Michael J. Hanmer, 2012. "The impact of ballot type on voter errors." *American Journal of Political Science* 56: 716–30.

Herrnson, Paul S., Richard G. Niemi, Michael J. Hanmer, Benjamin B. Bederson, Frederick G. Conrad, and Michael W. Traugott. 2008. *Voting Technology: The Not-So-Simple Act of Casting a Ballot*. Washington: Brookings.

Herron, Erik S. 2009. *Elections and Democracy after Communism?* New York: Palgrave Macmillan.

2010. "The effect of passive observation methods on Azerbaijan"s 2008 presidential election and 2009 referendum." *Electoral Studies* 29(3): 417–24.

Hershey, Marjorie Randon. 2009. "What we know about voter ID Laws, registration, and turnout." *PS: Political Science & Politics*, 42:87–91.

Hicken, A. 2007. "Institutional incentives: Do candidate-centered electoral rules encourage vote buying?" In Schaffer, Frederic C. (Ed.) *Elections for Sale: The Causes and Consequences of Vote Buying*. Boulder, CO: Lynne Rienner Publishers.

Hillman, Ben. 2013. "Public administration reform in post-conflict societies: Lessons from Aceh, Indonesia." *Public Administration and Development* 33(1): 1–14

Hoglund, Kristine. 2009. "Electoral violence in conflict-ridden societies: Concepts, causes, and consequences." *Terrorism and Political Violence* 21 (3): 412–27.

Hoglund, Kristine and Jarstad, Anna K. 2011. "Toward electoral security: Experiences from KwaZulu-Natal." *Africa Spectrum* 46(1): 33–59.

Howard, Marc Morjé and Philip G. Roessler. 2006. "Liberalizing electoral outcomes in competitive authoritarian regimes." *American Journal of Political Science* 50(2):365–81.

Howell, Patrick and Florian Justwan. 2013. "Nail-biters and no-contests: The effect of electoral margins on satisfaction with democracy in winners and losers." *Electoral Studies* 32(2): 334–43.

Hubbard, Glenn and Tim Kane. 2013. "In defense of Citizens United: Why campaign finance reform threatens American democracy." *Foreign Affairs* 92(4): 126–33.

Hyde, Susan D. 2007. "Experimenting in democracy promotion: International observers and the 2004 presidential elections in Indonesia." *Perspectives on Politics* 8(2): 511–27.

2007. "The observer effect in international politics: Evidence from a natural experiment." *World Politics* 60(1): 37–63.

2011. *The Pseudo-Democrat's Dilemma*. Ithaca: Cornell University Press.

Hyde, Susan D. and Nikolay Marinov. 2012. *Codebook for National Elections across Democracy and Autocracy (NELDA) 1945–2010*. Version 3. http://hyde.research.yale.edu/nelda/

2012. "Which elections can be lost?" *Political Analysis* 20(2): 191–210.

2014. "Information and self-enforcing democracy: The role of international election observation." *International Organization* 68(2): 329–59.

Ichino, Nahomi and Matthias Schuendeln. 2012. "Deterring or displacing electoral irregularities? Spillover effects of observers in a randomized field experiment in Ghana." *Journal of Politics* 74(1): 292–307.

International IDEA. 2002. *International Electoral Standards: Guidelines for Reviewing the Legal Framework for Elections*. Stockholm: International IDEA.

2004. *Handbook on the Funding of Political Parties and Election Campaigns*. Stockholm: International IDEA.

Jablonski, Ryan. 2013. "How aid targets votes: The impact of electoral incentives on foreign aid distribution." *World Politics* 66(02): 293–330. https://ncgg.princeton .edu/IPES/2013/papers/S215_rm1.pdf

Jacobs, Kristof and Leyenaar, Monique. 2011. "A conceptual framework for major, minor, and technical electoral reform." *West European Politics* 34(3): 495–513.

James, Toby S. 2010. "Electoral administration and voter turnout: Towards an international public policy continuum." *Representation* 45(4): 369–89.

2010. "Electoral modernisation or elite statecraft? Electoral administration in the U.K. 1997–2007," *British Politics* 5(2): 179–201.

2012. *Elite Statecraft and Election Administration: Bending the Rules of the Game*. Basingstoke: Palgrave.

Jimenez, Raul and Manuel Hidalgo. 2014. "Forensic Analysis of Venezuelan Elections during the Chavez Presidency." *Plos One*. 9(6): 20–29.

Jockers, Heinz, Dirk Kohnert, and Paul Nugent. 2010. "The successful Ghana election of 2008: A convenient myth?" *Journal of Modern African Studies* 48(1): 95–115.

Johnson, Michael. 2013. "More than necessary, less than sufficient: Democratization and the control of corruption." *Social Research* 80(4).

2014. *Corruption, Contention, and Reform: The Power of Deep Democratization*. Cambridge and New York: Cambridge University Press.

Jones, Douglas W. and Barbara Simons. 2012. *Broken Ballots: Will Your Vote Count?* Chicago: University of Chicago Press.

Joshi, Madhav. 2013. "Inclusive institutions and stability of transition toward democracy in post-civil war states." *Democratization* 20(4): 743–70.

Kairys, David. 2013. "The contradictory messages of Rehnquist-Roberts era speech law: Liberty and justice for some." *University of Illinois Law Review* 1: 195–220.

Kalandadze, Katya and Orenstein, Mitchell A. 2009. "Electoral protests and democratization beyond the color revolutions." *Comparative Political Studies* 42(11): 1403–25.

Kang, M.S. 2005. "The hydraulics and politics of party regulation." *Iowa Law Review* 91(1): 131–87.

Katz, Richard S. 2005. "Democratic principles and judging 'free and fair.'" *Representation* 41(3):161–79.

Kaya, Ruchan and Bernhard, Michael. 2013. "Are elections mechanisms of authoritarian stability or democratization? Evidence from post-communist Eurasia." *Perspectives on Politics* 11(3): 734–52.

Keefer, Philip and R. Vlaicu. 2008. "Democracy, credibility, and clientelism." *Journal of Law Economics & Organization* 24(2): 371–406.

Kelley, Judith. 2008. "Assessing the complex evolution of norms: The rise of international election monitoring." *International Organization* 62(2): 221–55.

2009. "D-minus elections: The politics and norms of international election observation." *International Organization* 63 (4): 765–87.

2009. "The more the merrier? The effects of having multiple international election monitoring organizations." *Perspectives on Politics* 7: 59–64.

2010. "Election observers and their biases." *Journal of Democracy* 21: 158–72.

2010. *Quality of Elections Data Codebook.* http://sites.duke.edu/kelley/data/;

2011. "Do international election monitors increase or decrease opposition boycotts?" *Comparative Political Studies* 44(11): 1527–56.

2012. "The international influences on elections in transition states." *Annual Review of Political Science* 15.

2012. *Monitoring Democracy: When International Election Observation Works and Why it Often Fails.* Princeton, NJ: Princeton University Press.

Project on International Election Monitoring http://sites.duke.edu/kelley/data/

Kendall-Taylor, Andrea. 2012. "Purchasing power: Oil, elections and regime durability in Azerbaijan and Kazakhstan." *Europe-Asia Studies* 64(4): 737–60.

Kerr, Nicholas. 2014. "Public perceptions of election quality in Africa: A cross-national analysis." In Pippa Norris, Richard Frank, and Ferran Martinez i Coma. (Eds.) *Advancing Electoral Integrity.* New York: Oxford University Press.

Keyssar, Alexander. 2009. *The Right to Vote: The Contested History of Democracy in the United States.* New York: Basic Books. Revised edition.

King, Gary. 1990. "Electoral responsiveness and partisan bias in multiparty democracies." *Legislative Studies Quarterly* 15(2).

Kitschelt, Herbert and Steven L. Wilkinson. 2007. (Eds). *Patrons, Clients and Policies.* New York: Cambridge University Press.

Klassen, Andrew James. 2014. *Perceptions of Electoral Fairness.* Unpublished PhD thesis. Canberra, Australian National University.

Klein, A. "The puzzle of ineffective election campaigning in Japan." *Japanese Journal of Political Science* 12: 57–74.

Klein, Richard L. and Patrick Merloe. 2001. *Building Confidence in the Voter Registration Process: An Washington DC: An NDI Monitoring Guide.* National Democratic Institute for International Affairs (NDI).

Koehler, Kevin. 2008. "Authoritarian elections in Egypt: Formal institutions and informal mechanisms of rule." *Democratization* 15(5): 974–90.

Kornblith, Miriam. 2013. "Chavism after Chavez?" *Journal of Democracy* 24(4): 136–50.

Koss, Michael. 2008. "The convergence of party funding regimes in Western Europe: Towards an analytical framework." *Osterreichische Zeitschrift Fur Politikwissenschaft* 37(1): 63+.

2011. *The Politics of Party Funding.* Oxford: Oxford University Press.

Krook, Mona Lena. 2009. *Quotas for Women in Politics: Gender and Candidate Selection Reform Worldwide.* New York: Oxford University Press.

Kropf, Martha and David C. Kimball. 2011. *Helping America Vote: The Limits of Election Reform.* New York: Routledge.

Kumar, Krishna. 1998. *Post-conflict Elections, Democratization, and International Assistance.* Boulder, CO: Lynne Reinner.

Kunicova, J. and Susan Rose-Ackerman. 2005. "Electoral rules and constitutional structures as constraints on corruption." *British Journal of Political Science* 35(4): 573–606.

Kuntz, Philipp and Mark R. Thompson 2009. "More than just the final straw stolen elections as revolutionary triggers." *Comparative Politics* 41(3): 253+.

Landman, Todd and Edzia Carvalho. 2010. *Measuring Human Rights.* London: Routledge.

Lanning, K. 2008. "Democracy, voting, and disenfranchisement in the United States: A social psychological perspective." *Journal of Social Issues* 64(3): 431–46.

Lasthuizen, Karin, Leo Huberts, and Leonie Heres. 2011. "How to measure integrity violations." *Public Management Review* 13(3): 383–408.

Lawson, Chappell. 2003. *Building the Fourth Estate: Democratization and the Rise of a Free Press in Mexico*. Berkeley: University of California Press.

Laycock, Samantha, Alan Renwick, Daniel Stevens, and Jack Vowles. 2013. "The UK's electoral reform referendum of May 2011." *Electoral Studies* 32(2): 211–14.

Lean, S.F. 2007. "Democracy assistance to domestic election monitoring organizations: Conditions for success." *Democratization* 14(2): 289–312

Leduc, Lawrence, Richard Niemi, and Pippa Norris. 2010. Eds. *Comparing Democracies 3: Elections and Voting in the 21st Century*. London: Sage.

Leemanna, Lucas and Daniel Bochsler. 2014. "A systematic approach to study electoral fraud." *Electoral Studies* 35(3): 33–47.

Lehoucq, Fabrice Edouard and Iván Molina Jiménez. 2002. *Stuffing the Ballot Box: Fraud, Electoral Reform, and Democratization in Costa Rica*. New York: Cambridge University Press.

Lehoucq, Fabrice Edouard. 2002. "Can parties police themselves? Electoral governance and democratization." *International Political Science Review* 23(1): 29–46.

2003. "Electoral fraud: Causes, types, and consequences." *Annual Review of Political Science* 6: 233–56.

Lessig, Lawrence. 2011. *Republic, Lost*. New York: Twelve.

Levitsky, Steven and Lucan A. Way. 2010a. "Why democracy needs a level playing field." *Journal of Democracy* 21(1): 57–68.

2010b. *Competitive Authoritarianism: Hybrid Regimes after the Cold War*, New York: Cambridge University Press.

Leyenaar, Monique and Reuven Y. Hazan. 2011. "Reconceptualising electoral reform." *West European Politics* 34(3): 437–55.

Lijphart, Arend. 1994. *Electoral Systems and Party Systems: A Study of Twenty-Seven Democracies, 1945–1990*. New York: Oxford University Press.

Lindberg, Staffan I. 2005. "Consequences of electoral systems in Africa: A preliminary inquiry." *Electoral Studies* 24 (1): 41–64.

2006a. *Democracy and Elections in Africa*. Baltimore, MD: The Johns Hopkins University Press.

2006b. "The surprising significance of African elections." *Journal of Democracy* 17 (1): 139–51.

Ed. 2009. *Democratization by Elections: A New Mode of Transition*. Baltimore, MD: The Johns Hopkins University Press.

2013. "Confusing categories, shifting targets." *Journal of Democracy* 24(4): 161–7.

Liow, Joseph Chinyong. 2012. "March 2008 general election: Understanding the new media factor." *Pacific Review* 25(3): 293–315.

Little, Andrew T. 2012. "Elections, fraud, and election monitoring in the shadow of revolution. *Quarterly Journal of Political Science* 7(3): 249–83.

Lo, B.B. 2003. "Russian elections: Uncivil state." *World Today* 59 (11): 22–4.

López-Pintor, Rafael. 2000. *Electoral Management Bodies as Institutions of Governance*, New York: United Nations Development Programme.

2006. *Getting to the CORE: On the Cost of Registration and Elections*. New York: UNDP

2010. *Assessing Electoral Fraud in New Democracies: A Basic Conceptual Framework.* Washington DC: The International Foundation for Electoral Systems, IFES.

Lukinova, Evgeniya, Mikhail Myagkov, and Peter C. Ordeshook. 2011. "Ukraine 2010: Were Tymoshenko's cries of fraud anything more than smoke?" *Post-Soviet Affairs* 27(1): 37–63.

Lust-Okar, Ellen and Jamal Amaney. 2002. "Rulers and rules: Reassessing the influence of regime type on electoral law formation." *Comparative Political Studies* 35(3): 337–66.

Lust-Okar, Ellen. 2000. "Legislative politics in the Arab world: The resurgence of democratic institutions." *International Journal of Middle East Studies* 32(3): 420–2.

2004. "Divided they rule: The management and manipulation of political opposition." *Comparative Politics* 36(2): 159+.

Lynch, G. and G. Crawford. "Democratization in Africa 1990–2010: An assessment." *Democratization* 18(2): 275–310.

Lynch, Gabrielle and Gordon Crawford. 2011. "Democratization in Africa 1990–2010: an assessment." *Democratization* 18(2): 275–310.

Magaloni, Beatriz. 2006. *Voting for Autocracy: Hegemonic Party Survival and Its Demise in Mexico.* Cambridge: Cambridge University Press.

2008. "Credible power-sharing and the longevity of authoritarian rule." *Comparative Political Studies* 41(4–5): 715–41.

2010. "The game of electoral fraud and the ousting of authoritarian rule." *American Journal of Political Science* 54(3): 751–65.

Mainwaring, Scott and Aníbal Pérez-Liñán. 2014. *Democracies and Dictatorships in Latin America: Emergence, Survival, and Fall.* New York: Cambridge University Press.

Makulilo, Alexander Boniface. 2011. "'Watching the watcher': An evaluation of local election observers in Tanzania." *Journal of Modern African Studies* 49(2): 241–62.

Mansfield, Edward D. and Jack Snyder. 2007. *Electing to Fight: Why Emerging Democracies Go to War.* Cambridge, MA: MIT Press

Marshall, Monty G., Ted Robert Gurr and Keith Jaggers. 2014. *Polity IV Project: Political Regime Characteristics and Transitions, 1800–2013. Dataset Users' Manual.* University of Maryland, Center for Systemic Peace. http://www.systemicpeace.org/inscr/p4manualv2013.pdf

Martinez i Coma, Ferran and Richard W. Frank. 2014. "Expert judgments." In Pippa Norris, Richard W. Frank, and Ferran Martinez i Coma. (Eds.) *Advancing Electoral Integrity.* New York: Oxford University Press, Chapter 4.

Massicotte, Louis, Andre Blais, and Antoine Yoshinaka. 2004. *Establishing the Rules of the Game.* Toronto: University of Toronto Press.

McAllister, Ian. 2014. "Corruption and confidence in Australian political institutions." *Australian Journal of Political Science* 49(2): 174–85.

McAllister, Ian and Stephen White. 2011. "Public perceptions of electoral fairness in Russia." *Europe-Asia Studies* 25(1): 78–96.

2014. "Electoral integrity and support for democracy in Belarus, Russia, and Ukraine." *Journal of Elections, Public Opinion and Parties* 63(4): 663–83.

McCann, J.A. and Jorge I. Dominguez. 1998. "Mexicans react to electoral fraud and political corruption: An assessment of public opinion and voting behavior." *Electoral Studies* 17(4): 483–503.

McDonald, Michael P. 2004. "A comparative analysis of redistricting institutions in the United States, 2001–02." *State Politics and Policy Quarterly* 4: 371–95.

McDonald, Michael P. and Samuel Popkin. 2001. "The myth of the vanishing voter." *American Political Science Review* 95(4): 963–74.

McFaul, Michael and N. Petrov. 2004. "What the elections tell us." *Journal of Democracy* 15(3): 20–31.

McGrath, Amy. 1997. *Corrupt Elections: Ballot Rigging in Australia*. Sydney, NSW: H.S.Chapman Society.

Mebane, Walter R. Jr. 2012. "Comment on 'Benford's Law' and the detection of election fraud." *Political Analysis* 19(3): 269–72.

Meyer, M. and J. Booker. 1991. *Eliciting and Analyzing Expert Judgment: A Practical Guide*. London: Academic Press.

Mickiewicz, Ellen. 1997. *Changing Channels: Television and the Struggle for Power in Russia*. New York: Oxford University Press.

2008. *Television, Power, and the Public in Russia*. New York: Cambridge University Press.

Minnite, Lorraine Carol. 2010. *The Myth of Voter Fraud*. Ithaca: Cornell University Press.

Moehler, D.C. 2009. "Critical citizens and submissive subjects: Elections losers and winners in Africa." *British Journal of Political Science* 39(2): 345–66.

Moehler, Devra C. and Staffan I. Lindberg. 2009. "Narrowing the legitimacy gap: Turnovers as a cause of democratic consolidation." *Journal of Politics* 71(4): 1448–66.

Molina, I. and Fabrice Edouard Lehoucq. 1999. "Political competition and electoral fraud: A Latin American case study." *Journal of Interdisciplinary History* 30(2): 199+.

Moller, Jorgen and Svend-Erik, Skaaning. 2010. "Post-communist regime types: Hierarchies across attributes and space." *Communist and Post-Communist Studies* 43(1): 51–71.

"Beyond the radial delusion: conceptualizing and measuring democracy and non-democracy." *International Political Science Review* 31(3): 261–83.

Montjoy, Robert S. 2008. "The public administration of elections." *Public Administration Review* 68(5): 788–99.

2010. "The changing nature ... and costs ... of election administration." *Public Administration Review* 70(6): 867–75.

Morse, Yonatan L. 2012. "The era of electoral authoritarianism." *World Politics* 64(1): 161–98.

Mozaffar, Shaheen. 2002. "Patterns of electoral governance in Africa's emerging democracies." *International Political Science Review* 23(1):85–101.

Mozaffar, Shaheen and Andreas Schedler. 2002. "The comparative study of electoral governance: Introduction." *International Political Science Review* 23(1): 5–27.

Munck, Geraldo L. 2009. *Measuring Democracy: A Bridge between Scholarship and Politics*. Baltimore: The Johns Hopkins Press.

Munck, Geraldo L. and Jay Verkuilen. 2002. "Conceptualizing and measuring democracy: Evaluating alternative indices." *Comparative Political Studies* 35(1): 5–34.

2002. "Generating better data: A response to discussants." *Comparative Political Studies* 35(1): 52–7.

Myagkov, Mikhail, and Peter C. Ordeshook. 2005. "The trail of votes in Ukraine's 1998, 1999, and 2002 elections." *Post-Soviet Affairs* 21(1): 56–71.

Myagkov, Mikhail and Peter C. Ordeshook, 2008. "Ukraine's 2007 parliamentary elections free and fair, or fraud once again?" *Problems of Post-Communism* 55(6): 33–41

Myagkov, Mikhail, Peter C. Ordeshook, and Dimitri Shakin. 2005. "Fraud or fairytales: Russia and Ukraine's electoral experience." *Post-Soviet Affairs* 21(2): 91–131.

2009. *The Forensics of Election Fraud: Russia and Ukraine.* New York: Cambridge University Press.

Nagle, J.C. 2004. "How not to count votes." *Columbia Law Review* 104 (6): 1732–63.

Nassmacher, Karl-Heinz. Ed. 2001. *Foundations for Democracy: Approaches to Comparative Political Finance.* Baden-Baden: Nomos.

2009. *The Funding of Party Competition: Political Finance in 25 Democracies.* Berlin: Nomos.

National Democratic Institute. 2005. *Money in Politics: A Study of Party Financing Practices in 22 Countries.* Washington DC: National Democratic Institute.

Nazzarine, S.R. 2003. "A faceless name in the crowd: Freedom of association, equal protection, and discriminatory ballot access laws." *University of Cincinnati Law Review* 72(1): 309–61.

Neiheisel, Jacob R and Barry C. Burden. 2012. "The impact of election day registration on voter turnout and election outcomes." *American Politics Research* 40:636–64

Newell, James. *The Politics of Italy: Governance in a Normal Country.* New York: Cambridge University Press.

Norris, Pippa. Ed. 1999. *Critical Citizens.* Oxford: Oxford University Press.

2003. *Democratic Phoenix.* New York: Cambridge University Press.

2004. *Electoral Engineering: Voting Rules and Political Behavior.* New York: Cambridge University Press.

2008. *Driving Democracy: Do Power-Sharing Institutions Work?* New York: Cambridge University Press.

Ed. 2010. *Public Sentinel: News Media and the Governance Agenda.* Washington DC: The World Bank.

2011. "Cultural explanations of electoral reform: A policy cycle model." *West European Politics* 34(1): 531–50.

2011. *Democratic Deficit: Critical Citizens Revisited.* New York: Cambridge University Press.

2012. *Making Democratic Governance Work: How Regimes shape Prosperity, Welfare and Peace.* New York: Cambridge University Press.

2013. "Does the world agree about standards of electoral integrity? Evidence for the diffusion of global norms." Special issue of *Electoral Studies* 32(4):576–88.

2013. "The new research agenda studying electoral integrity." Special issue of *Electoral Studies* 32(4): 563–75.

2014. "Electoral integrity and political legitimacy." In Lawrence LeDuc, Richard Niemi, and Pippa Norris (Eds.) *Comparing Democracies 4.* London: Sage.

2014. *Why Electoral Integrity Matters.* New York: Cambridge University Press.

Norris, Pippa and Andrea Abel van Es. 2016. *Checkbook Elections? Political Finance in Comparative Perspective.*

Norris, Pippa, Richard W. Frank, and Ferran Martinez i Coma. 2014. "Measuring electoral integrity: A new dataset." *PS Politics and Political Science* 47(4): 789–98.

Norris, Pippa, Richard W. Frank and Ferran Martinez i Coma. 2014. Eds. *Advancing Electoral Integrity.* New York: Oxford University Press.

Norris, Pippa, Richard W. Frank, and Ferran Martinez i Coma. 2015. Eds. *Contentious Elections: From Ballots to Barricades*. New York: Routledge.

Norris, Pippa and Ronald Inglehart. 2009. *Cosmopolitan Communications: Cultural Diversity in a Globalized World*. New York: Cambridge University Press.

Norris, Pippa, Ferran Martinez i Coma, and Richard W. Frank. *The Expert Survey of Perceptions of Electoral Integrity*. www.electoralintegrityproject.com

2013. "Assessing the quality of elections." *Journal of Democracy* 24(4): 124–35.

Nou, J. 2009. "Privatizing democracy: Promoting election integrity through procurement contracts." *Yale Law Journal* 118 (4): 744–93.

Nunnally, Shayla C. 2011. "(Dis)counting on democracy to work: Perceptions of electoral fairness in the 2008 presidential election." *Journal of Black Studies* 42(6): 923–42.

Nyblade, B. and S.R. Reed. "Who cheats? Who loots? Political competition and corruption in Japan, 1947–1993." *American Journal of Political Science* 52(4): 926–41.

Obi, Cyril. 2011. "Taking back our democracy? The trials and travails of Nigerian elections since 1999." *Democratization* 18(2): 366–87.

Öhman, Magnus and Hani Zainulbhai. 2011. *Political Finance Regulation: The Global Experience*. Washington, DC: IFES. http://www.ifes.org/files/Political_Finance_Regulation_The_Global_Experience.pdf

O'Leary, Cornelius. 1962. *The Elimination of Corrupt Practices in British Elections, 1968-1911*. Oxford: Oxford University Press.

Omotola, J.S. "Elections and democratic transition in Nigeria under the Fourth Republic." *African Affairs* 109(437): 535–53.

Opitz, Christian, Hanne Fjelde, and Kristine Hoglund. 2013. "Including peace: The influence of electoral management bodies on electoral violence." *Journal of Eastern African Studies* 7(4): 713–31.

Organisation of American States/ International IDEA. 2005. *Funding of Political Parties and Election Campaigns in the Americas*. OAS/International IDEA.

Organization for Security and Cooperation in Europe (OSCE/ODIHR). 2007. *Handbook for Long-Term Election Observers: Beyond Election Day Observation*. Warsaw: OSCE/ODIHR.

2010. *Election Observation Handbook*. Warsaw: OSCE/ODIHR. 6th Ed.

2012. *Handbook on Media Monitoring for Election Observation Missions*. Warsaw: OSCE/ODIHR.

Ottaway, Marina. 2003. *Democracy Challenged: The Rise of Semi-Authoritarianism*. Washington DC: Carnegie Endowment for International Peace.

Overton, Spencer. 2006. *Stealing Democracy: The New Politics of Voter Suppression*. New York: Norton.

Paris, Roland. 2004. *At War's End: Building Peace after Civil Conflict*. Cambridge: Cambridge University Press.

Pastor, Robert A. 1999. "A brief history of electoral commissions." In Andreas Schedler, Larry Diamond, and Marc F. Plattner. (Eds.) *The Self-restraining State: Power and Accountability in New Democracies*. Boulder, CO: Lynne Rienner, pp. 75–82.

1999. "The role of electoral administration in democratic transitions." *Democratization* 6(4): 1–27.

Pastor, Robert A., Robert Santos and Alison Prevost. 2011. "Voting and ID requirements: A survey of registered voters in three states." *American Review of Public Administration* 40(4): 461–81.

Paxton, Pamela, Kenneth A. Bollen, Deborah M. Lee, and HyoJuong Kim. 2003. "A half-century of suffrage: New data and a comparative analysis." *Studies in Comparative International Development* 38:93–122.

Pericchi, Luis and David Torres. 2011. "Quick anomaly detection by the Newcomb-Benford Law, with applications to electoral processes data from the USA, Puerto Rico and Venezuela." *Statistical Science* 26(4): 502–16.

Persily, N. 2001. "Candidates *v.* parties: The constitutional constraints on primary ballot access laws." *Georgetown Law Journal* 89(7): 2181–225.

Pinto-Duschinsky, Michael. 2005. "Financing politics: A global view." *Journal of Democracy* 13(4).

2014. *Electoral Omission*. London: Policy Exchange.

Piven, Frances Fox, L. Minnite and M. Groarke. 2009. *Keeping Down the Black Vote*. London: The New Press.

Popova, Marina. 2006. "Watchdogs or attack dogs? The role of the Russian courts and the Central Election Commission in the resolution of electoral disputes." *Europe-Asia Studies* 58(3): 391–414.

Post, Robert C. 2014. *Citizens Divided: Campaign Finance Reform and the Constitution*. Cambridge, MA: Harvard University Press.

Powell, G. Bingham. 2000. *Elections as Instruments of Democracy*. New Haven, CT: Yale University Press.

2004. "The chain of responsiveness." *Journal of Democracy* 15(4): 91–105.

2014. "Why elections matter." In Lawrence LeDuc, Richard Niemi, and Pippa Norris. (Eds.) *Comparing Democracies 4*. London: Sage.

Power, Timothy J. and Matthew MacLeod Taylor. *Corruption and Democracy in Brazil: The Struggle for Accountability*. Notre Dame, Ind.: University of Notre Dame Press.

Przeworski, Adam, Michael E. Alvarez, Jose Antonio Cheibub, and Fernando Limongi. 2000. *Democracy and Development: Political Institutions and Well-Being in the World, 1950–1990*. New York: Cambridge University Press.

Quimpo, N.G. 2009. "The Philippines: Predatory regime, growing authoritarian features." *Pacific Review* 22(3): 335–53.

Qvortup, M. 2005. "First past the postman: Voting by mail in comparative perspective." *Political Quarterly* 76(3):414–19.

Rahat, Gideon and Hazan, Reuven Y. 2011. "The barriers to electoral system reform: A synthesis of alternative approaches." *West European Politics* 34(3): 478–94.

Rallings, Colin, Michael Thrasher, and G. Borisyuk. "Much ado about not very much: The electoral consequences of postal voting at the 2005 British General Election." *British Journal of Politics & International Relations* 12(2): 223–38.

Regan, P.M., R.W. Frank, and D.H. Clark. 2009. "Political institutions and elections: New datasets." *Conflict Management and Peace Science* 26(3): 320–37.

Reilly, Benjamin. 2002. "Post-conflict elections: Constraints and dangers." *International Peacekeeping* 9(2): 118.

2004. "Elections in post-conflict societies." In Edward Newman and Roland Rich. (Eds.) *The UN Role in Promoting Democracy: Between Ideals and Reality*. Tokyo: United Nations University Press.

Reynolds, Andrew. 2011. *Designing Democracy in a Dangerous World*. New York: Oxford University Press.

Reynolds, Andrew and M. Steenbergen. 2006. "How the world votes: The political consequences of ballot design, innovation and manipulation." *Electoral Studies* 25(3): 570–98.

Romanelli, Raffaele. Ed. 1998. *How Did They Become Voters? The History of Franchise in Modern European Representation*. The Hague: Kluwer Law

Rosas, Guillermo. 2010. "Trust in elections and the institutional design of electoral authorities: Evidence from Latin America." *Electoral Studies* 29(1): 74–90.

Rose, Richard and William Mishler. 2009. "How do electors respond to an 'unfair' election? The experience of Russians." *Post-Soviet Affairs* 25(2): 118–36.

Rose, Richard, William Mishler, and Neil Monroe. 2011. *Popular Support for an Undemocratic Regime: The Changing Views of Russians*. New York: Cambridge University Press.

Ross, Michael L. 2013. *The Oil Curse: How Petroleum Wealth Shapes the Development of Nations*. Princeton, NJ: Princeton University Press.

Rothstein, Bo. 2009. "Creating political legitimacy: Electoral democracy versus quality of government." *American Behavioral Scientist* 53(3): 311–30.

Samples, John Curtis. 2006. *The Fallacy of Campaign Reform*. Chicago: University of Chicago Press.

Santa-Cruz, Arturo. 2005. "Constitutional structures, sovereignty, and the emergence of norms: The case of international election monitoring." *International Organization* 59(03): 663–93.

Santiso, C. and A. Loada. 2003. "Explaining the unexpected: Electoral reform and democratic governance in Burkina Faso." *Journal of Modern African Studies* 41(3): 395–419.

Scarrow, Susan. 2004. "Explaining political finance reforms: Competition and context." *Party Politics* 10: 653–75.

2007. "Political finance in comparative perspective." *Annual Review of Political Science* 10: 193–210.

Schaffer, Fredric Charles. 2002. "Might cleaning up elections keep people away from the polls? Historical and comparative perspectives." *International Political Science Review* 23(1):69–84.

Ed. 2007. *Elections for Sale: The Causes and Consequences of Vote Buying*. Boulder and London: Lynne Rienner.

2008. *The Hidden Costs of Clean Election Reform*. Cornell: Cornell University Press.

Schaffer, Frederic Charles and Tova Andrea Wang. 2009. "Is everyone else doing it? Indiana's voter identification law in international perspective." *Harvard Law & Policy Review* 3:397–413.

Schedler, Andreas. 1999. "Civil society and political elections: A culture of distrust?" *Annals of the American Academy of Political and Social Science* 565: 126–41.

2002. "The menu of manipulation." *Journal of Democracy* 13(2): 36–50.

Ed. 2006. *Electoral Authoritarianism: The Dynamics of Unfree Competition*. Boulder and London: Lynne Rienner.

2010. "Authoritarianism's last line of defense." *Journal of Democracy* 21(1): 69–80.

2012. "Judgment and measurement in political science." *Perspectives on Politics* 10(1): 21–36

2012. *The Politics of Uncertainty Sustaining and Subverting Electoral Authoritarianism*. CIDE: Mexico City.

Scher, Richard K. 2010. *The Politics of Disenfranchisement: Why Is It So Hard to Vote in America?* New York: M.E. Sharpe.

Schmeets, Hans. Ed. 2010. *International Election Observation and Assessment of Elections*. The Hague: Statistics Netherlands.

Schuler, Ian. 2008. "SMS as a tool in election observation." *Innovations* 3(2): 143–57.

Schumpeter, Joseph. 1942. *Capitalism, Socialism and Democracy*. London: George Allen & Unwin.

Sekhon, Jasjeet S. and Titiunik, Rocio. 2012. "When natural experiments are neither natural nor experiments." *American Political Science Review* 106(1): 35–57.

Selway, Joel and Kharis Templeman. 2012. "The myth of consociationalism? Conflict Reduction in Divided Societies." *Comparative Political Studies* 45(12): 1542–71.

Serritzlew, Soren, Kim Mannemar Sonderskov, and Gert Tinggaard Svendsen. 2014. "Do corruption and social trust affect economic growth? A review." *Journal of Comparative Policy Analysis* 16(2):121–39.

Seymour, Charles. 1970. *Electoral Reform in England and Wales: The Development and Operation of the Parliamentary Franchise 1832–1885*. UK: David and Charles reprint.

Sharafutdinova, Gulnaz. *Political Consequences of Crony Capitalism inside Russia* . Notre Dame, Ind.: University of Notre Dame Press.

Shock, David R. 2008. "Securing a line on the ballot: Measuring and explaining the restrictiveness of ballot access laws for non-major party candidates in the United States." *Social Science Journal* 45(1): 48–60.

Simmons, Beth A. 2009. *Mobilizing for Human Rights: International Law in Domestic Politics*. New York: Cambridge University Press.

Simpser, Alberto. 2012. "Does electoral manipulation discourage voter turnout? Evidence from Mexico." *Journal of Politics* 74(3): 782–95.

2013. *Why Parties and Governments Manipulate Elections: Theory, Practice and Implications*. New York: Cambridge University Press.

Sisk, Timothy and Andrew Reynolds. 1998. Eds. *Elections and Conflict Management in Africa*. Washington DC: US Institute of Peace Press.

Sjoberg, Fredrik. 2012. "Making voters count: Evidence from field experiments about the efficacy of domestic election observation." Harriman Institute Working Paper 1.

Slater, Dan. 2010. *Ordering Power: Contentious Politics and Authoritarian Leviathans in Southeast Asia*. New York: Cambridge University Press.

Smets, Kaat and Carolien van Ham. 2013. "The embarrassment of riches? A meta-analysis of individual-level research on voter turnout." *Electoral Studies* 32(2): 344–59.

Smith, Lahra. 2009. "Explaining violence after recent elections in Ethiopia and Kenya." *Democratization* 16(5): 867–897.

Snyder, Jack. 2000. *From Voting to Violence: Democratization and Nationalist Conflict*. New York: Norton.

Spinelli, Antonio. 2011. *Strategic Planning for Effective Electoral Management: A Practical Guide for Election Management Bodies to Conduct a Strategic Planning Exercise*. Washington, DC: IFES.

Steenbergen, Marco R. and Gary Marks. 2007. "Evaluating expert judgments." *European Journal of Political Research* 46: 347–66.

Stewart, J. 2006. "A banana republic? The investigation into electoral fraud by the Birmingham Election Court." *Parliamentary Affairs* 59(4): 654–67.

Stockemer, Daniel, Bernadette LaMontagne, and Lyle Scruggs. 2013. "Bribes and ballots: The impact of corruption on voter turnout in democracies." *International Political Science Review* 34(1): 74–90.

Stokes, Susan, Thad Dunning, Marcelo Nazareno, and Valeria Brusco. 2013. *Brokers, Voters, and Clientelism: The Puzzle of Distributive Politics*. New York: Cambridge University Press.

Straus, Scott. 2011. "It's sheer horror here: Patterns of violence during the first four months of Cote d'Ivoire's post-electoral crisis." *African Affairs* 110(440): 481–9.

2012. "Wars do end! Changing patterns of political violence in sub-Saharan Africa." *African Affairs* 111(443): 179–201.

Straus, Scott and Charles Taylor. 2012. "Democratization and electoral violence in Sub-Saharan Africa, 1990–2008." In Dorina Bekoe. (Ed.) *Voting in Fear: Electoral Violence in Sub-Saharan Africa.* Washington, DC: United States Institute of Peace.

Stroh, Alexander. 2010. "Electoral rules of the authoritarian game: undemocratic effects of proportional representation in Rwanda." *Journal of Eastern African Studies* 4(1): 1–19.

Struwig, Jare, Benjamin J. Roberts, and Elme Vivier. 2011. "A vote of confidence: election management and public perceptions." *Journal of Public Administration* 46(3): 1122–38.

Svolik, Milan W. 2012. *The Politics of Authoritarian Rule.* New York: Cambridge University Press.

Tan, Netina. 2013. "Electoral engineering and hegemonic party resilience in Singapore." *Electoral Studies* 32(4): 632–43.

Tancangco, Luzviminda G. 1992. *The Anatomy of Electoral Fraud: Concrete Bases for Electoral Reforms.* Manila: MJAGM: Distributor Matrix.

Tay, Louis, Mitchel N. Herian, and Ed Diener. 2014. "Detrimental effects of corruption and subjective well-being: Whether, how, and when." *Social Psychological and Personality Science* 5(7): 751–9.

Taylor, Charles, Jon Pevehouse, and Scott Straus. 2013. "Perils of pluralism: Electoral violence and competitive authoritarianism in Sub-Saharan Africa." Simons Papers in Security and Development 23, School for International Studies, Simon Fraser University

Taylor, Steven L. 2009. *Voting Amid Violence: Electoral Democracy in Colombia.* Northeastern University Press.

Teorell, Jan. 2010. *Determinants of Democratization.* New York: Cambridge University Press.

Thompson, Mark R. and Philipp Kuntz. 2004. "Stolen elections: The case of the Serbian October." *Journal of Democracy* 15(4): 159–72

2009. "More than just the final straw: Stolen elections as revolutionary triggers." *Comparative Politics* 41(3):253–72.

Tierney, Michael J., Daniel L. Nielson, Darren G. Hawkins, J. Timmons Roberts, Michael G. Findley, Ryan M. Powers, Bradley Parks, Sven E. Wilson, and Robert L. Hicks. 2011. "More dollars than sense: Refining our knowledge of development finance using aid data." *World Development* 39(11): 1891–906.

Trenschel, Alexander and Fernando Mendez. 2005. Eds. *The European Union and e-voting.* London: Routledge.

Tuccinardi, Domenico. Ed. 2014. *International Obligations for Elections: Guidelines for Legal Frameworks.* Stockholm: International IDEA.

Tucker, Joshua. 2007. "Enough! Electoral fraud, collective action problems, and post-communist colored revolutions." *Perspectives on Politics* 5(3): 535–51.

Tyler, Tom R. 1984. "The role of perceived injustice in defendants' evaluations of their courtroom experience." *Law & Society Review* 18(1): 51–74.

1990. *Why People Obey the Law*. New Haven: Yale University Press.

1994. "Governing amid diversity: The effect of fair decision-making procedures on the legitimacy of government." *Law & Society Review* 28(4): 809–31.

Tyler, Tom R., Jonathan D. Casper, and Bonnie Fisher. 1989. "Maintaining allegiance toward political authorities: The role of prior attitudes and the use of fair procedures." *American Journal of Political Science* 33(3): 629–52.

Tyler, Tom R., Kenneth A. Rasinski, and Kathleen M. McGraw. 1985. "The influence of perceived injustice on the endorsement of political leaders." *Journal of Applied Social Psychology* 15(8): 700–25.

Ugues, Jr, Antonio. 2010. "Citizens' views on electoral governance in Mexico." *Journal of Elections, Public Opinion & Parties* 20(4): 495–527.

2014. "Electoral management in Central America." In Pippa Norris, Richard W. Frank, and Ferran Martinez i Coma (Eds.) *Advancing Electoral Integrity*. New York: Oxford University Press.

UK Electoral Commission. 2014. *Electoral fraud in the UK: Final report and recommendations*. London: UK Electoral Commission.

UNDP/IFES. 2005. *Getting to the CORE. A Global Survey on the Cost of Registration and Elections*. New York: UNDP.

United Nations. 2005. *Declaration of Principles for International Election Observation and Code of Conduct for International Elections Observers*. New York: United Nations. http://www.cartercenter.com/documents/2231.pdf

United Nations Development Programme. 2011. *Understanding Electoral Violence in Asia*. UNDP Asia-Pacific Regional Center.

United Nations Development Programme. 2012. *Evaluation of UNDP Contribution to Strengthening Electoral Systems and Processes*. New York: UNDP.

United Nations General Assembly resolution 63/163 (April 12th, 2012) *"Strengthening the role of the United Nations in enhancing periodic and genuine elections and the promotion of democratization."*

van der Walle, Nicholas. 2003. "Presidentialism and clientelism in Africa's emerging party systems." *The Journal of Modern African Studies* 41(02):297–321 DOI: dx.doi.org/10.1017/S0022278X03004269

van Ham, Carolien. 2012. *Beyond Electoralism? Electoral fraud in third wave regimes 1974–2009*. PhD Thesis. Florence: European University Institute.

2013. "Getting elections right? Measuring electoral integrity." Paper presented at the 2013 Annual Workshop on Concepts and indicators of electoral integrity, Harvard University, 3–4 June 2013.

2014. "Getting elections right? Measuring electoral integrity." *Democratization*. (forthcoming).

Verba, Sidney and Norman Nie. 1972. *Participation in America: Political Democracy and Social Equality*. New York: Harper and Row.

Verba, Sidney, Norman Nie, and Jae-on Kim. 1978. *Participation and Political Equality: A Seven-Nation Comparison*. New York: Cambridge University Press.

Verba, Sidney, Kay Schlozman, and Henry E. Brady. 1995. *Voice and Equality: Civic Voluntarism in American Politics*. Cambridge, MA: Harvard University Press.

Vickery, Chad and Erica Shein. 2012. *"Assessing Electoral Fraud in New Democracies."* Washington DC: IFES. http://www.ifes.org/~/media/Files/Publications/White%20PaperReport/2012/Assessing_Electoral_Fraud_Series_Vickery_Shein.pdf

Volkov, Denis. 2012. "The protesters and the public." *Journal of Democracy* 23(3): 55–62.

Wahmn, Michael, Jan Teorell, and Axel Hadenius. 2013. "Authoritarian regime types revisited: Updated data in comparative perspective." *Contemporary Politics* 19(1):19–34.

Wall, Alan, Andrew Ellis, Ayman Ayoub, Carl W. Dundas, Joram Rukambe, and Sara Staino. 2006. International IDEA. 2006. *Electoral Management Design: The International IDEA Handbook*. Sweden: International IDEA.

Wand, J.N., K.W. Shotts, J.S. Sekhon, Walter Mebane, M.C. Herron, and Henry E. Brady. 2001. "The butterfly did it: The aberrant vote for Buchanan in Palm Beach County, Florida." *American Political Science Review* 95(4): 793–810.

Wand, Jonathan, Gary King, and Olivia Lau. 2011. "Anchors: Software for anchoring vignettes data." *Journal of Statistical Software* 42(3): 1–25. http://j.mp/m5tITE

Wang, Tova Andrea. 2012. *The Politics of Voter Suppression: Defending and Expanding Americans' Right to Vote*. Ithaca: Cornell University Press.

    2014. *Voter Identification Requirements and Public International Law: An Examination of Africa and Latin America*. Atlanta: The Carter Center.

Weghorst, Keith R. and Staffan I. Lindberg. 2011. "Effective opposition strategies: Collective goods or clientelism?" *Democratization* 18(5): 1193–214.

Weidmann, Nils B. and Michael Callen. 2013. "Violence and election fraud: Evidence from Afghanistan." *British Journal of Political Science* 43(1): 53–75

Welsh, Brigitte. 2013. "Malaysia's elections: A step backward." *Journal of Democracy* 24(4): 136–50.

White, Stephen. "Non-competitive elections and national politics: The USSR Supreme Soviet elections of 1984." *Electoral Studies* 4(3): 215–29.

    2011. "Elections Russian-style." *Europe-Asia Studies* 63(4): 531–56.

White, Stephen and Ian McAllister. 2014. "Did Russia (Nearly) have a Facebook revolution in 2011? Social media's challenge to authoritarianism." *Politics* 34(1): 72–84.

Wigell, M. 2008. "Mapping 'hybrid regimes': Regime types and concepts in comparative politics." *Democratization* 15(2): 230–50.

Wilking, Jennifer R. 2011. "The portability of electoral procedural fairness: Evidence from experimental studies in China and the United States." *Political Behavior* 33(1): 139–59.

Wilkinson, Steven. 2006. *Votes and Violence: Electoral Competition and Ethnic Riots in India*: New York: Cambridge University Press.

Willis, Justin and Atta el Battahani. 2010. "We changed the laws: Electoral practice and malpractice in Sudan since 1953." *African Affairs* 109(435): 191–212.

Wilson, Kenneth. 2012. "How Russians view electoral fairness: A qualitative analysis." *Europe-Asia Studies* 64(1): 145–68.

Wise, Charles R. 2001. "Electoral administration in crisis: An early look at lessons from Bush versus Gore." *Public Administration Review* 61(2): 131–39.

Wlezien, Christopher and Stuart Soroka. 2012. "Political institutions and the opinion–policy link." *West European Politics* 35(6): 1407–32.

Wong, Chin-Huat, Chin James, and Othman Norani. 2010. "Malaysia: Towards a topology of an electoral one-party state." *Democratization* 17(5): 920–49.

Young, John Hardin. 2009. *International Election Principles: Democracy and the Rule of Law*. Chicago: American Bar Association.

Ziblatt, Daniel. 2009. "Shaping democratic practice and the causes of electoral fraud: The case of nineteenth-century Germany." *American Political Science Review* 103(1): 1–21.

Index

CPSIA information can be obtained
at www.ICGtesting.com
Printed in the USA
LVHW021809090921
697458LV00015B/1640